T0367966

Knowledge Management
Through the Technology Glass

Series in Innovation and Knowledge Management

Series Editor: Suliman Hawamdeh *(University of Oklahoma)*

Series on Innovation and Knowledge Management – Vol. 2

Knowledge Management
Through the Technology Glass

Meliha Handzic

The University of New South Wales, Australia

 **World Scientific**

NEW JERSEY • LONDON • SINGAPORE • BEIJING • SHANGHAI • HONG KONG • TAIPEI • CHENNAI

Published by

World Scientific Publishing Co. Pte. Ltd.

5 Toh Tuck Link, Singapore 596224

USA office: 27 Warren Street, Suite 401-402, Hackensack, NJ 07601

UK office: 57 Shelton Street, Covent Garden, London WC2H 9HE

British Library Cataloguing-in-Publication Data
A catalogue record for this book is available from the British Library.

KNOWLEDGE MANAGEMENT: Through the Technology Glass
Series on Innovation and Knowledge Management — Vol. 2

ISBN-13 978-981-256-024-7
ISBN-10 981-256-024-6

Printed in Singapore

Preface

This book has been written to address a paradoxical situation surrounding the role of technology in knowledge management. At one extreme on the spectrum of views found in the literature are authors who see technology as a key to knowledge management. At the other end are authors who see technology as a peripheral issue compared to social and organisational ones.

This book adopts a dialectical perspective that sees knowledge management as a socio-technological phenomenon. Accordingly, it takes, as its starting point, a view that technology does have some role to play in knowledge management, but does not imply that it is the single most or least important aspect of it. Rather, the goal is to provide much needed empirical evidence regarding the "true" potential and limitations of technology for managing knowledge in organisations.

Many authors suggest that technology is attractive to organisations because the rapid pace of technological advance always promises something new and "leading edge" to be exploited. This book identifies and presents a number of novel and traditional technologies and situations in which these technologies can help to improve processes of creation, sharing, retention and discovery of knowledge, and thus performance.

The book is organised as a structured compilation of articles founded on the most recent research and experience in the field of knowledge management. It brings together diverse information and communication technologies and systems currently seen in knowledge management research and practice in a logical sequence incorporating the most important and representative examples into an integrated framework.

Part I of the book provides justification for knowledge management and sets the scene for the rest of the book. It begins with Chapter 1 that describes the rise of knowledge management and presents an underlying theoretical framework for the book. In Chapter 2, this framework is used to categorise ICT into technologies that support storing, finding, sharing and generating knowledge.

The four chapters in Part II examine a variety of "codification" orientated systems and technologies that support knowledge storing and finding. The first two articles are concerned with knowledge repositories. In Chapter 3 the focus is on the benefits of web based memory and unstructured knowledge records for societies, while Chapter 4 examines the effectiveness of structured data stores in enhancing organisational decision-making. The next two articles examine processes of finding and representing knowledge for human interpretation. Chapter 5 discusses the use of knowledge mapping as an effective tool for finding needed knowledge, while Chapter 6 addresses the question of discovering hidden association patterns embedded in codified data.

Part III of the book is devoted to "personalisation" orientated systems and technologies. The first two chapters examine the role of technology in stimulating new knowledge development. Chapter 7 focuses on innovative technology that supports creative idea generation, while Chapter 8 compares the effectiveness of guidance and feedback mentoring systems in learning. The next two articles are devoted to knowledge sharing support. In Chapter 9 the emphasis is on major facilitating/ inhibiting factors that influence user acceptance of knowledge sharing technology in an organisation. The last Chapter 10 examines the virtual reality models as visualisation tools for social network analysis.

While the previous three parts of the book address mainly individual systems and technologies, Part IV is devoted to integrated solutions. The next three chapters illustrate examples of complete knowledge management solutions based solely on technology. Chapter 11 evaluates a virtual knowledge/learning space from the student users' perspective; Chapter 12 highlights the characteristics and value of a simulation game approach to knowledge management research; and Chapter 13 describes a portal designed to support a global community of practice. In contrast, Chapter 14 examines people's perceptions of the importance and their satisfaction with technology in comparison with social aspects of the total knowledge management system.

The final, Part V of the book addresses major issues and challenges facing knowledge management. Chapter 15 deals with a practical method for implementing knowledge management in organisations. The last Chapter 16, as is appropriate, looks at the future of knowledge management. In this chapter the focus is on the emerging trends involving the use of intelligent systems and the merging of knowledge management with e-commerce.

This book represents a small but important step in helping individuals and organisations to get an objective picture of the role of technology in knowledge management based on formal and sound empirical research. More importantly, the book shows that the impact of various systems and technologies is highly contingent upon the context in which the knowledge is generated, transferred and used. This may help managers to choose more suitable technological solutions to enhance and exploit their organisational knowledge.

Contents

PART I

Introduction: Exploring the Role of
Technology in Knowledge Management

CHAPTER I

The Rise of Knowledge Management:

In Pursuit of Excellence

Necessity is the mother of all inventions
— Proverb

This chapter provides an overarching introduction to the field of knowledge management (KM). It examines the emerging context and rationale for KM, the implications and benefits of KM for organisations, and the current understanding of the KM concept itself. The aim is to provide a broad theoretical basis for exploring the role of technology in KM and to set the scene for the remaining chapters of the book.

1.1 Introduction

The growing interest in knowledge management has been fuelled by a number of development trends: globalisation with the increasing intensity of competition; virtualisation or digitalisation enabled by advances in information and communication technology; and the transformation to knowledge based economy together with changing organisational structures, new worker profiles, preferences and predispositions (Raich 2000; Hall, 2003). This new emerging world is variously referred to as third wave, information age, knowledge-based or knowledge economy or society. Regardless of the terminology, these names, and others, refer to the transition that is taking place in the business environment.

As organisations move towards becoming more knowledge-based, their business success will increasingly depend on how successful knowledge workers are at developing and applying knowledge productively and efficiently. The ability to identify and leverage key knowledge plays a critical role in organisational survival and advancement. Consequently, the companies are facing the need to improve the management of their knowledge.

The knowledge economy demands that organisations integrate their activities, processes and systems in order to exploit their resources more efficiently and subsequently gain economies of scope and access to and from new markets (Burnes, 2000). Those organisations that are unable to change or choose not to adapt in a timely manner are likely to become vulnerable and unable to compete in the future.

The basic assumption of KM is that organisations that manage organisational and individual knowledge better will deal more successfully with the challenges of the new business environment. More specifically, knowledge management is considered to be central to achieving process and product improvement, executive decision making and organisational adaptation and renewal (Earl, 2001). The central task of those concerned with knowledge management is to determine ways to better cultivate, nurture and exploit knowledge at different levels and in different contexts.

However, while there is a widespread agreement of the importance of knowledge with respect to the struggle for economic success, there are differences among researchers and practitioners alike in what constitutes useful knowledge and the ways in which it should be managed (Holsapple and Joshi, 1999). There are major disagreements as to whether it should be considered a technical issue, a human resources issue, a procedural issue or a part of strategic management (Handzic and Hasan, 2003). The variation between different schools of thoughts on knowledge management are an indication of the many problems faced. To gain a greater understanding of the KM phenomena, the following sections will examine major drivers, outcomes and models of KM, and introduce an integrated KM framework as a basis for understanding the role of technology in KM.

1.2 Drivers of KM

We are currently experiencing a period of major change in the world economy. This is characterised by increased complexity, uncertainty and surprises. Some analysts think of it as a period of living in the centre of the "Bermuda Triangle" (Raich, 2000) where individuals and organisations have to deal with the increasing turbulence and speed of change. This change is brought about by the mega-trends of globalisation, digitalisation (or virtualisation) and transformation to a knowledge-based economy.

Knowledge Economy

The transformation from the old economy to a new, knowledge-based economy, is driven largely by the recognition that knowledge rather than financial capital, land or labour is the major source of continued economic growth, value and improved standards of living. Figure 1.1 shows that while every economy relies on knowledge to some extent as its base, in the "knowledge economy" knowledge itself is for sale and ideas are the main output or product of the economic institutions.

Tiwana (2001) identifies major characteristics of the new economy in terms of knowledge centricity, increasing returns, network effects,

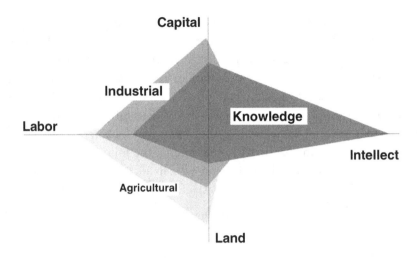

Figure 1.1 Shifting economy

accelerated clockspeed, transparency, customer loyalty, innovation, ad-hoc alliances, and products as experiences. He notes that knowledge centricity is typically demonstrated in the increasing dependence of services and non-physical as well as physical goods on knowledge for their production and distribution.

Tiwana further notes that knowledge-based offerings have increasing returns. Once the first unit is produced at a significant cost, additional units can be produced at a near-zero incremental cost (e.g., piece of software). Network effects are evidenced in the positive correlation between the market size and the value of the knowledge offering. Thus, companies trying to capture as much market as possible do so even at an initial loss (e.g., offering free software). Rapid and unpredictable changes dominate. To cope, business must have adequate organisational and technological mechanisms to support speedy adaptation and knowledge application. As businesses become increasingly networked with others (e.g., customers, partners) their knowledge becomes more transparent and potent. Firms are differentiated by differences in levels of assimilation and mobilisation of their knowledge.

Success in the new economy requires intimate knowledge of the company customer base. Such knowledge can help businesses provide tailored products and services and thus attract and retain their customer's loyalty. Success often requires inventing new business processes, new industries and new customers rather than re-arranging old ones. With the rapidity of knowledge obsolesce, new knowledge must be integrated fast. This can be done through the formation of temporary collaborations between partners and members on an as-needed basis. Finally, in the knowledge economy, products and services are increasingly perceived as experiences. Accordingly, organisations act as knowledge integrators, finding out and offering customers individualised experiences they want and need.

Knowledge Organisation

Economic progress throughout history has been driven by commerce and business organisations. These organisations have internal structures that mediate roles and relationships among people working towards some identifiable goal. Their existence is the result of a successful balance between the forces in their environment and their own creativity and adaptivity (Bennet and Bennet, 2003). Currently, at the forefront of organisational performance are the organisations which recognised that information, knowledge and their intelligent application are the essential factors of success in the new economy, and take advantage of information technology to achieve high level of efficiency and effectiveness. Various metaphors used to describe a knowledge organisation include: agile production system, living organism, complex adaptive system, self-organising system and virtual organisation.

The knowledge organisation can be best viewed as an intelligent complex adaptive system. It is complex because the system is composed of a large number of individual specialists called intelligent agents, who have multiple and complex relationships with the system and environment. It is adaptive because these intelligent agents direct and discipline their own performance through organised feedback from colleagues, customers and headquarters. It has been suggested in the literature (Bennet and Bennet, 2003) that a successful knowledge organisation exhibits the following characteristics: high performance, customer-driven, improvement-driven, high flexibility and adaptiveness, high levels of expertise and knowledge, high rates of learning and innovation, innovative IT-enabled, self-directed and managed, proactive and futurist, valuing expertise and sharing knowledge.

One of the ways to achieve effective knowledge creation, transfer and utilisation within an organisation is through communities of practice (Wenger, 1998). This approach to organisational structuring advocates the formation of centres of expertise for each knowledge domain, discipline or subject matter speciality. The alternative approach suggests organising around projects and related activities. Information and communication technology can be the catalyst to form and sustain heterogeneous communities. With the support of the intranet or internet, these communities can include diverse people from different space and time zones of the globe (Hasan and Crawford, 2003).

While information technology is not necessary to create a knowledge organisation, the use of advanced technologies can transform the way the whole business works. The concept of "cybercorp" has been heralded as the new business revolution (Martin, 1996). It is envisaged as a totally virtual organisation based on the capabilities of the modern communication, i.e., the internet and the mobile phone. Typically, a virtual organisation consists of three fundamental parts: knowledge professionals and workers who possess core competencies; relationships and networks of people including partners, suppliers and customers grouped around a common brand; and a culture based on co-operation and collaboration and sitting in the centre of global networks linked electronically (Raich, 2000).

A knowledge organisation must of necessity become a learning organisation, so that the entire firm will learn while it works and be able to adapt quickly to market changes and other environmental perturbations. It has been suggested that the building blocks of a learning organisation are systematic problem solving, experimentation, learning from past experience, learning from others and transferring knowledge (Garvin, 1998). The way to build it is to first foster the environment that is conducive to learning, then open up boundaries to stimulate the informal exchange of ideas and finally create formal learning forums and programmes with explicit learning goals tailored to business needs.

Learning organisations have also been described as places "where people continually expand their capacity to create the results they truly desire, where new and expansive patterns of thinking are nurtured, where collective aspiration is set free, and where people are continually learning how to learn together" (Senge, 1990). To achieve these ends these organisations use systems thinking, personal mastery, mental models, shared vision and team learning. Furthermore, knowledge creating companies are characterised as places where "inventing new knowledge is not a specialised activity, but the way of behaving, indeed a way of being, in which everyone is a knowledge worker". The way to achieve this is to use metaphors, encourage dialogue, and make tacit ideas explicit.

Knowledge Work and Workers

In knowledge based organisations, the largest part of their workforce is engaged in knowledge work (Schultze, 2003). The following paragraphs summarises different perspectives on this new phenomenon. The economic perspective emphasises how knowledge work differs from other types of work in the nature of knowledge possessed and produced by workers. Knowledge work assumes the possession of mostly abstract, theoretical and esoteric knowledge gained through formal education. It also suggests that workers have to produce new knowledge rather than just manipulate existing knowledge. The labour process perspective concerns itself with the formation and composition of a new class of white-collar workers between the proletariat and bourgeoisie who perform managerial, professional and clerical tasks. Their work is characterised by scientific base, formal education, autonomy, ethical rules, culture, client orientation, social sanction and authorisation.

The work practice perspective focuses on the work that workers do and classifies it into knowledge production and knowledge reproduction. Re-production includes transfer and application. Specific processes and practices that form part of knowledge work include generating new knowledge, interpreting and representing it, as well as expressing, monitoring, translating and networking. For example, software engineering qualifies as knowledge work based on the presence of creativity and problem-solving aspects of the work; co-location which allows work remote from the employing firm; and "gold collar" conditions of employment, including exceptional remuneration and benefits packages (Edwards, 2003).

Given that all work requires the application of knowledge, the emergence of knowledge work as a separate category of work has been criticised. However, it does offer a possibility of categorising groups of workers by highlighting their similarities and differences. Generally speaking, a knowledge worker is any worker who performs knowledge work (as described in the previous section) in every element of the economy. It covers various managerial, professional and clerical occupations. Examples of occupations that qualify as knowledge workers include executives, legislators, engineers, scientists, administrators and counselors. According to Australian statistics (ABS, 2003) there has been a significant increase in the percentage of knowledge workers in the country's labour force over the last couple of years, this being consistent with the country's transition to a knowledge economy.

Of particular interest for KM is a special category of knowledge workers, KM professionals, who make knowledge management in an organisation work. KM professionals are a new phenomenon and there is still no clear picture about what roles they should play in an organisation and what competencies and skills they need to have to play these roles. Currently there is a wide range of KM related job titles and roles found in organisations. Examples include titles such as Chief Knowledge Officer (CKO), Knowledge Asset Manager, Knowledge Officer, Web Master, etc.

From this variety three distinct categories can be recognised: *knowledge manager*, *knowledge engineer* and *knowledge scientist* (Weidner, 2003). The knowledge manager is expected to be primarily concerned with the knowledge needs of the enterprise. The knowledge engineers, with various specialisations, are perceived as advisors on what can be done given the current "state of the art". Knowledge scientists are seen as showing them what is possible if they were willing to try. A snapshot of actual CKOs portrays them as highly educated and experienced individuals, generally satisfied with their position, freedom and latitude it affords (McKeen and Staples, 2003). At present, their primary goal is to raise awareness of KM, and they have little direct authority and effect changes through persuasion, negotiation and communication.

1.3 Outcomes of KM

The importance of KM for organisational performance has been widely recognised and acknowledged in the management literature. In general, KM is assumed to create value for organisations from applying their accumulated knowledge to their products and services outputs. These ensure organisational survival or advancement. KM can impact organisational performance in a number of different ways, these can be grouped into three broad categories: *risk minimisation, efficiency improvement* and *innovation* (Von Krogh et al., 2000).

Risk Minimisation

Risk minimisation is closely linked to identifying and holding onto the core competencies that the company has. In most organisations, people have been recognised as key holders of valuable knowledge. KM can minimise the risk of losing valuable knowledge by identifying, locating and capturing what is known by individuals and groups of organisational employees that is of critical importance for organisational survival. Frank (2002) offers five tips to reduce knowledge loss: do not let people leave, mentor and coach, share best practices, share lessons learned and document. Indeed, documented project management knowledge, expertise and skills accumulated in the construction industry were found to benefit both employees and the public at large (Land et al., 2002). At another level, society's knowledge records are preserving the cultural capital of nations (Handzic, 2003).

KM can also impact people's learning, adaptability and job satisfaction (Becerra-Fernandez et al., 2004). For example, KM can facilitate employees' creativity and group effectiveness through informal and formal socialisation (Handzic and Chaimungkalanont, 2003). Socialisation forms a vital component of Nonaka's (1998) knowledge creation model. It enables tacit knowledge to be transferred between individuals through shared experience, space and time. Examples include spending time, working together or informal social meetings. More importantly, socialisation drives the creation and growth of personal tacit knowledge bases. By seeing other people's perspective and ideas, a new interpretation of what one knows is created.

Efficiency and Effectiveness Improvement

In today's complex economy, businesses are constantly confronted with the need to operate more efficiently in order to stay competitive and satisfy increasing market demands. Organisations are under increasing pressure from customers to deliver solutions and services faster and cheaper. KM can improve organisational efficiency by transferring experiences and best practices throughout the organisation in order to avoid unnecessary duplication and to reduce cost. Technology is often an important part of achieving efficiency improvements. For example, a best practice replication program at Ford (Rollo and Clarke, 2001) achieved process improvements in plants around the globe, and nine-figure cost savings from a simple intranet-based KM system for knowledge sharing.

KM can also help organisations become more effective by helping them select and perform the most appropriate processes and make the best possible decisions. KM can help organisations to avoid repeating past mistakes, foresee potential problems and reduce the need to modify plans (Becerra-Fernandez, 2004). For example, The Australian Government responded to increasing community expectations of better social services and access to empowering information sources by integrating historically separate health, housing and community services via a virtual corporate environment (Rollo and Clarke, 2001). The outcome is that various community and service providers have been given equitable and wide-spread access to expert knowledge and can directly contact the right people for service delivery.

Process and Product Innovation

There is a growing belief that knowledge can do more than improve efficiency and effectiveness. KM can impact process innovations, value-added products and knowledge-based products (Becerra-Fernandez, 2004). Innovation of products, processes and structures have been assessed as a critical component in the success of new-age firms. The new products and services resulting from the interaction of knowledge and technology bring profound changes in the way businesses operate and compete in the new economy.

Typically, innovative organisations focus on both new knowledge and on knowledge processes. They constantly engage and motivate people, creating the overall enabling context for knowledge creation. These organisations take a strategic view of knowledge, formulate knowledge visions, tear down knowledge barriers, develop new corporate values and trust, catalyse and coordinate knowledge creation, manage various contexts involved, develop conversational culture and globalise local knowledge (Nanaka and Nishiguchi, 2001).

The unifying thread among various theoretical views is the perception that innovation is the key driver of an organisation's long-term economic success. According to Von Krogh (2000) the greatest challenge for organisations is to move in knowledge-enabling direction by consciously and deliberately addressing knowledge management. Pfizer is one good example of such an organisation (Rollo and Clarke, 2001). This company uses KM primarily to beat the industry average. Its main approach to management of the research process involves the "mining" of scientific publications to make its researchers aware of the progress and projects of others. This approach has resulted in the discovery of the well-known Viagra drug.

1.4 KM Frameworks

There have been a number of recent efforts at developing KM frameworks to better understand KM phenomena. In order to make sense of the variety of existing KM frameworks, some form of categorisation or grouping is needed. One way to group them is into partial and integrated models or ontologies.

Partial KM Frameworks

Partial KM frameworks encompass a broad range of issues, methods and theories that differ in scope and focus. Some are knowledge oriented, like the intellectual capital models of McAdam and McCreedy (1999) and the economic school in Earl's (2001) taxonomy. The list of types and perspectives elaborated in Alavi and Leidner's (2001) review also fits this category. Knowledge-orientated models are well known in the business environment. The HR literature relies heavily on this grouping of KM models and frameworks, as does the Accounting discipline's work on intangible assets. From this perspective, KM focuses on hiring, retaining, training of personnel, i.e., "intellectual assets", and organisational knowledge is often defined as the sum of the knowledge of its personnel. However, in the broader view of KM this is just one aspect that would be included in an integrated approach.

Other models, like Nonaka's (1998) knowledge spiral and Earl's (2001) behavioural school are process orientated. Process orientated frameworks are perhaps the most frequently quoted and used category in the knowledge management literature. The knowledge creation spiral of Nonaka views organisational knowledge creation as a process involving a continual interplay between explicit and tacit dimensions of knowledge. Four levels of carriers of knowledge in the organisation area are assumed, namely individual, group, organisational and inter-organisational. The spiral model describes a dynamic process in which explicit and tacit knowledge are exchanged and transformed through four modes: socialisation, combination, externalisation and internalisation.

Several frameworks emphasise the dependence of knowledge on socio-technological influences. Nonaka and Konno's (1998) model of 'ba' suggests four types of ba (originating, interacting, cyber and exercising) that act as promoters of knowledge processes (socialising, externalising, combining, and internalising) respectively. Earl's (2001) technocratic school that supports and structures IS work in KM also belongs to this category. Much KM work within the field of Information Systems, makes the distinction between knowledge as an object that can be stored in a computerised system, and knowledge embedded in people. This group of models or frameworks address issues of complexity and change in areas of organisational culture and learning, change and risk management and the support of communities of practice. Frameworks in this KM grouping also emphasise the dependence of knowledge on context.

Integrated KM Frameworks

There have been a number of attempts to bring together this diversity of partial approaches and propose more comprehensive and integrated frameworks in order to provide holistic views and common ground for KM research, and improved methods for KM practice (for review see Handzic and Hasan, 2003). Among some of the most recent developments is Handzic's (2003) integrated KM framework. The KM framework presented in Figure 1.2 is an extended version of the original model. It illustrates various components involved in the conduct of knowledge management and their relationships. This framework is used as a basis

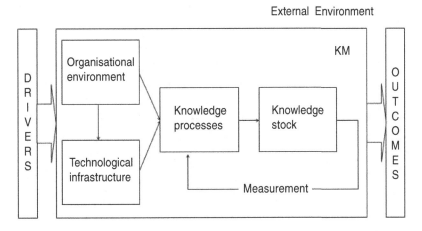

Figure 1.2 Extended framework of KM

for examining the role of technology in KM in the later chapters of this book.

The core KM model suggests two types of organisational factors: *organisational environment* (e.g., leadership, culture, structure, etc.) and *technological infrastructure* (e.g., information and telecommunication technologies) as major enablers that facilitate *knowledge processes* (e.g., creation, transfer, utilisation) and foster the development of *knowledge stocks* (e.g., explicit and tacit, know what and how). The model also suggests that organisational environment governs the choice and implementation of the technological infrastructure that supports knowledge processes. Finally, the core model incorporates a feedback loop to suggest the need for continuous knowledge *measurement* and potential adjustment of strategies over time. The extended KM model includes two additional components: KM *drivers* and *outcomes*. This model suggests that various KM *drivers* (e.g., changes in external environment) trigger KM initiatives (i.e., specific configurations of knowledge processes and enablers that act upon knowledge stocks) that, in turn, lead to various KM *outcomes* (e.g., improved performance, innovation).

In essence, the Handzic framework synthesises human and object perspectives of knowledge by adopting a two-dimensional model of organisational knowledge, with explicit and tacit know-what and know-how dimensions. This model adapts and extends the original work by Polanyi (1966) and Nonaka (1998). The integrated framework further considers knowledge management as a complex multidimensional concept that includes three essential and inter-related components: knowledge stocks, processes and enablers. In this way, it provides a missing link between different partial perspectives discussed earlier in the chapter. Furthermore, it recognises knowledge management as both a social and technological phenomenon, a view strongly emphasised in the opinions of KM academics and practitioners in a recent survey (Edwards et al., 2003). Finally, it suggests the evolutionary and context dependent nature of KM. This is consistent with the view that the main objective of KM is to help the organisation realise the best value from its knowledge assets (Bollinger and Smith, 2001).

1.5 Conclusions

This chapter examines the main drivers, outcomes and conceptualisations of KM in order to set the scene and provide theoretical foundation for exploring the role of technology in KM. The chapter recognises that KM is fuelled by the changing nature of the business environment. The emerging environment is identified as global, directly based on the production, distribution and use of knowledge in the development and distribution of products and services, and heavily reliant on information and communication technology.

This chapter also recognises that KM contributes to organisational performance in many ways. It impacts people, processes, products and structures in attempting to minimise risk, improve efficiency and effectiveness, and create innovative processes or products. In this way, KM provides sustainable competitive advantages that ensure the organisation's survival or advancement.

Finally, this chapter promotes the view of KM as a dynamic phenomenon with an emphasis on knowledge processes in expanding cycles of knowledge growth. KM is considered as a socio-technical undertaking enabled and facilitated by a variety of social, organisational and technical factors. which must be considered in any KM initiative. Finally, KM is recognised as being severely dependent on context so that there is no 'one size fits all' solution.

References

ABS (2003), "Science and Technology Statistics Update", *Australian Bureau of Statistics Bulletin*, No. 9, December.

Alavi, M. and Leidner, D.E. (2001), "Knowledge Management and Knowledge Management Systems: Conceptual Foundations and Research Issues", *MIS Quarterly*, 25(1), 107–136.

Becerra-Fernandez, I., Gonzales, A. and Sabherwal, R. (2004), *Knowledge Management: Challenges, Solutions, and Technologies*, Pearson Education, New Jersey.

Bennet, D. and Bennet, A. (2003), "The Rise of the Knowledge Organisation", chapter 1 in Holsapple, C.W. (ed.), *Handbook on Knowledge Management*, Vol 1, Springer, Berlin, pp. 5–20.

Burnes, B. (2000), *Managing Change — A Strategic Approach to Organisational Dynamics*, Pearson Education, Harlow.

Bollinger, A.S. and Smith, R.D. (2001), "Managing Organisational Knowledge as a Strategic Asset". *Journal of Knowledge Management* 5(1), 8–18.

Earl, M. (2001), "Knowledge Management Strategies: Toward a Taxonomy", *Journal of Management Information Systems*, 18(1), 215–233.

Edwards, J., Handzic, M., Carlsson, S. and Nissen, M. (2003), "Knowledge Management Research and Practice: Visions and Directions", *Knowledge Management Research & Practice*, 1(1), 49–60.

Edwards, J.S. (2003), "Managing Software Engineers and Their Knowledge", chapter 1 in Aurum et al. (eds.), *Managing Software Engineering Knowledge*, Springer, Berlin, pp. 5–27.

Frank, B. (2002), "Five Tips to Reduce Knowledge Loss", in *Thought & Practice, The Journal of the KM Professional Society (KMPro)*, December, pp. 1–3.

Garvin, D.A. (1998), "Building a Learning Organisation", *Harvard Business Review on Knowledge Management*, HBS Press, Boston, pp. 47–80.

Hall, R. (2003), *Knowledge Management in the New Business Environment*, Acirrt Report, University of Sydney.

Handzic, M. and Hasan, H. (2003), "The Search for an Integrated KM Framework", chapter 1 in Hasan H. and Handzic M. (eds.), *Australian Studies in Knowledge Management*, UOW Press, Wollongong, pp. 3–34.

Handzic, M. (2003), "An Integrated Framework of Knowledge Management", *Journal of Information and Knowledge Management*, 2(3), September.

Handzic, M. and Chaimungkalanont, M. (2003), "The Impact of Socialisation on Organisational Creativity", in *Proceedings of the European Conference on Knowledge Management (ECKM 2003)*, Oxford, September 18–19.

Hasan, H. and Crawford, K. (2003), "Distributed Communities of Learning and Practice", chapter 5 in Hasan H. and Handzic M. (eds.), *Australian Studies in Knowledge Management*, UOW Press, Wollongong.

Holsapple, C.W. and Joshi, K.D. (1999), "Description and Analysis of Existing Knowledge Management Frameworks", in *Proceedings of the 32nd Hawaii International Conference on System Sciences*, p. 11.

Land, L.P.W., Land, M. and Handzic, M. (2002), "Retaining Organisational Knowledge: A Case Study of an Australian Construction Company", *Journal of Information & Knowledge Management*, 1(2), 119–129.

Martin, J. (1996), *Cybercorp: The New Business Revolution*, AMACOM, Washington.

McAdam, R. and McCreedy, S. (1999), "A Critical Review of Knowledge Management Models", *The Learning Organisation*, 6(3), 91–100.

McKeen, J.D. and Staples, D.S. (2003), "Knowledge Managers: Who They Are and What They Do", in Holsapple, C.W, (ed.), Handbook on Knowledge Management, Vol 1, Springer, Berlin, pp. 21–41.

Nanaka, I. and Nishiguchi, T. (2001), *Knowledge Emergence*, Oxford University Press, New York.

Nonaka, I. (1998), "The Knowledge-Creating Company", *Harvard Business Review on Knowledge Management*, HBS Press, Boston, pp. 21–45.

Nonaka, I. and Konno, N. (1998), "The Concept of Ba: Building a Foundation for Knowledge Creation". *California Management Review*, 40(3), 40–54.

Polanyi, M. (1966), "The Logic of Tacit Inference", *Philosophy*, 41(1), 1–18.

Raich, M. (2000), *Managing in the Knowledge Based Economy*, Raich, Zurich.

Rollo, C. and Clarke, T. (2001), *International Best Practice: Case Studies in Knowledge Management*. Standards Australia International Limited.

Senge, P. (1990), *The Fifth Discipline, the Art and Practice of the Learning Organisation*, Century Business, London.

Shultze, U. (2003), "On Knowledge Work", chapter 3 in Holsapple, C.W. (ed.), *Handbook on Knowledge Management*, Vol. 1, Springer, Berlin, pp. 43–58.

Tiwana, A. (2001), *The Essential Guide to Knowledge Management*, Prentice Hall, New Jersey.

Von Krogh, G., Ichijo, K. and Nonaka, I. (2000), *Enabling Knowledge Creation*, Oxford University Press, New York.

Weidner, D. (2003), "The Education of the Knowledge Professions — Meeting the Challenge", in *Thought & Practice*, Vol. 1, December.

Wenger, E. (1998), *Communities of Practice*, Cambridge University Press, Cambridge.

CHAPTER 2

Managing Knowledge with Technology:

Mission Possible

It is not computers that make the difference,
but what people do with them.
— Paul Strassmann

This chapter attempts to provide an understanding of the role of technology in KM. It identifies some promising ways in which technology can be employed in organisational knowledge management. In general, technology is perceived as a tool in enabling and facilitating processes of knowledge development, transfer and utilisation. The focus of the chapter is on different categories of technologies and their roles in facilitating knowledge sharing, representation and transformation, as well as improving people's ability to acquire and create knowledge.

2.1 Introduction

The role of technology in KM is the source of major disagreement within the KM community (Holsapple, 2003; Edwards, 2004). At one extreme of the spectrum of views are those who consider that KM has nothing (or very little) to do with KM. The frequent quote heard in this camp is "a good KM solution is 10% technology and 90% culture" (Snowden, 2003). At the other extreme are those that see KM as being all (or mostly) about technology. The first view is largely driven by the interests of those wishing to privilege the role of people in organisations, the second by those wishing to sell KM tools and systems (Swan, 2003).

The proponents of the view that technology is incidental to KM argue that knowledge is a uniquely human concept. It exists only in the context of human interpretation and processing. What is represented and processed by computers is called data or information. From this perspective, computer-based technology has no key role in the KM field. Instead, it deals with data and information that become knowledge only upon human interpretation. The goal of KM is to create a connected environment for knowledge exchange. It allows knowledge seekers to identify and communicate with knowledge sources, i.e., experts (Handzic and Hasan, 2003).

In contrast, the proponents of the view that technology is a cornerstone of KM see knowledge as an object that can be separated from its source. It can be codified and then stored in a computer-based system to be made available on demand (Handzic and Hasan, 2003). From this perspective, computer-based technology serves as a means for representing and processing knowledge. The technology camp also predicts that breakthroughs in KM will be technological. These will continue to change the nature of knowledge creation, publication and sharing, and will have social and managerial implications (Holsapple, 2003). Thus, organisations that ignore or minimise technology in the conduct of KM may lose the chance of success.

More recently there have been attempts to bridge this artificial divide between technology and people orientated perspectives of KM. The argument is that human culture is at least in part formed by our capacity to create and use tools. Therefore ignoring technology would be foolish, as would be denying human complexity (Snowden, 2003). One consequence of the on-going polemic is the creation of an integrated view that considers KM as a socio-technological phenomenon with both technology and people playing an important role. Another consequence is the generation of a contingent view of KM that links the relative emphasis on either people or technology to the nature of business context. Essentially, the contingency view suggests that no one approach is best under all circumstances (Handzic and Hasan, 2003).

Taking the view that technology does have a role to play in KM, the objective of this chapter is to explore major opportunities and circumstances in which various information and communication technologies may help to support the KM effort in organisations. The focus is on those technologies suggested by the literature as potentially valuable and convenient (Alavi and Leidner, 2001).

2.2 Technology and Integrated KM

This book promotes an integrated view of KM presented in Chapter 1 which synthesises human and object perspectives of knowledge; considers knowledge management as a complex concept that includes three essential and inter-related components: knowledge stocks, processes and enablers; considers KM as both social and technological phenomenon; suggests the dynamic evolutionary nature of KM; and finally recognises its context dependent drivers and outcomes.

Within this integrated framework, technology is clearly placed among major influencing factors on knowledge processes. More specifically, technology is perceived as a catalyst that enables and facilitates the development, transfer and application of knowledge, and thus contributes to organisational learning, improvement and innovation. The framework also recognises that social influences (e.g., organisational leadership and culture) impact the choice and implementation of KM technologies.

Various knowledge processes can be supported by technology. According to Becerra-Fernandez et al. (2004), technology can facilitate sharing as well as growth of knowledge. For example, communication technology can allow the movement of information at a greater speed and efficiency than ever before. Furthermore, information technology can capture and quickly manipulate data from measurements of natural phenomena to improve our understanding of those phenomena. Thus, technology can increase the speed at which knowledge and ideas proliferate. It can also enable the measurement of increasingly complex processes at a lower cost.

A wide range of commercial software products and tools are available to address various aspects of knowledge management (Tsui, 2003). Such wide availability has been attributed to the dynamic progress in the field of ICT. A number of new technologies have been created, and some of the existing ones renamed as KM tools to support KM activities. It is argued that all types of information and communication technologies can be viewed to a greater or lesser extent as KM tools as they support processes through which knowledge is moved or modified.

According to Tsui (2003) the two most dominant approaches to deploying technology-based KM initiatives in organisations are codification and personalisation. The proponents of codification approach show a central preoccupation with explicit knowledge. They favour greater emphasis on the use of information technology, especially organisational databases, search engines and discovery tools. On the other hand, the proponents of personalisation seem to be more interested in tacit knowledge and sharing. They often focus more on people and cultural issues in the attempt to establish virtual groups or knowledge communities. Locating and connecting people of common interest is the prime goal here. Communication technology, such as e-mails and discussion forums are examples of technologies that can facilitate socialisation and knowledge exchange.

It is not unusual for organisations to adopt a combination of the two approaches in deploying KM initiatives. Some authors argue that such a holistic approach to KM is the only possible way to realise the full power of knowledge (Davenport and Prusak, 1998). Others, like Hansen et al. (1999) emphasise that trying to pursue the wrong approach or both at the same time can waste time and money and even undermine business success. They propose that the codification approach is more suited for situations where work tasks are similar and existing knowledge assets can be reused. In contrast, they suggest that the personalisation approach is more suited for situations where the tasks are fairly unique and knowledge largely tacit.

In order to better understand and appreciate the potential roles of various technologies in supporting knowledge processes, the discussion below has been arranged in four thematic categories: (i) building knowledge repositories, (ii) promoting virtual socialisation and collaboration, (iii) facilitating knowledge search and discovery and (iv) stimulating creativity and complex problem solving. Categories 1 and 3 support "codification", and categories 2 and 4 "personalisation" strategies.

2.3 Categorisation of Technology Roles

Building Knowledge Repositories

Knowledge has been widely recognised as a critical organisational resource for competitive advantage in the new economy. One of the important objectives of knowledge management is to capture, codify, organise and store relevant organisational knowledge for later use by organisational members (Hansen et al., 1999). A knowledge management framework (Hahn and Subramani, 2000) suggests that the availability of a KM system such as a codified knowledge repository should lead to increased organisational knowledge and result in improved performance. The Interim Australian KM standard (Standards Australia, 2003) proposes a number of technologies including databases, textbases, data warehouses and data marts as useful in building organisational knowledge repositories. It describes these technologies in the following terms:

> *Databases and Textbases.* Electronic data generated by daily transactions are usually recorded in business documents and notes or in transaction records. These are typically stored in structured database systems and constitute a part of the

organisational memory. In addition to data and text, multimedia systems organise and make available to users their knowledge assets in a variety of other representational forms, including images, audio and video formats.

Data Warehouses and Data Marts. Unlike organisational databases that typically store current data related to specific business functions, a data warehouse stores data that retains historical and cross-functional perspectives. Data is extracted daily from the business transaction systems and from any other systems deemed relevant. Compared to data warehouses which combine databases across an entire enterprise, data marts are usually smaller and focus on a particular subject or department.

Currently, there is ample evidence to show that organisations do implement these technologies as part of their best KM practices (AA, 1998). However, there is little empirical evidence regarding the impact of these knowledge repositories on organisational performance (Alavi and Leidner, 2001). Some researchers point out that our ability to accumulate and store knowledge artefacts has by far surpassed our ability to process them, and warn of the danger that vast institutional memories may easily become tombs rather than wellsprings of knowledge (Handzic and Bewsell, 2003). Thus, it is argued here that one of the most challenging roles for technology with respect to building effective organisational knowledge repositories is to make stored knowledge more visible and accessible. The next section addresses this issue in more detail.

Facilitating Knowledge Search and Discovery

Many enterprise systems acquire large volumes of knowledge artefacts from multiple and often remote sources. The complexity of interrelated knowledge artefacts stored in these repositories make it often difficult for people to locate relevant artefacts or comprehend and interpret their meaning. Locating relevant knowledge in corporate memories is one of the important objectives of developing and deploying knowledge management systems in organisations. Researchers in the areas of artificial intelligence and information retrieval have been particularly influential in directing the development and evolution of such systems. Search engines and intelligent agents are increasingly becoming evident in the market where they comprise a considerable proportion of the available commercial KM software (Tsui, 2003). The Interim KM Standard (Standards Australia, 2003) describes these technologies in the following way:

> *Search Engines.* Commercial search engines provide a standard interface for text searching and enable access to the unstructured information on the internet. In this way they allow organisations to gather external third-party information. Search engine utilities also perform a similar function and provide access to large knowledge repositories on intranets and extranets.

> *Intelligent Agents.* Intelligent agents are software programmes that act as personal or communication assistants to their users and carry out some sets of operations on their behalf with some degree of independence or autonomy. Intelligent agents that grew from expert systems and artificial intelligence research learn from data input during the course of their performance and modify their behaviour accordingly. Examples of the tasks that agents can do include: retrieving documents, conducting a user-initiated search activity, maintaining profile on behalf of their users, or learning and deducing from user specified profiles and assisting in the formalisation of a query or target search.

Although knowledge can be embedded in a computerised system using rules or heuristics, it is argued here that many knowledge-based systems, expert systems, case-based reasoning systems and software agents may not qualify as knowledge management systems. The position of this text is that knowledge management systems should not be viewed as automating expert tasks, but rather informing about such tasks. As cognitive overload increasingly chokes the effective utilisation of codified knowledge in organisations, scholars are pointing to some promising alternative knowledge technologies. Knowledge maps or K-maps are seen as a particularly feasible method of coordinating, simplifying, highlighting and navigating through complex silos of knowledge artefacts (Wexler, 2001). Knowledge maps point to knowledge but they do not contain it. They are guides, not repositories. Typically, they point to people, documents and repositories. The main purpose of knowledge maps is to direct people where to go when they need certain expertise. In addition to the guiding function, knowledge maps may also identify strengths to exploit and knowledge gaps to fill.

Considering that knowledge workers often must rely on enterprise systems for their work activities, it is critical that they understand better the knowledge available in these systems. The proposition made here is that an appropriate knowledge discovery tool may help organisational members to improve their task performance by enhancing their understanding of the patterns hidden in the stored knowledge artefacts. By definition, knowledge discovery involves uncovering previously unknown valid and useful patterns in data for description and prediction purposes (Fayyad et al., 1996). The uncovered patterns in the form of relationships, categories, clusters or trends are described and presented in a mode understandable by humans to help them better predict future behaviour of interest. The Interim KM Standard (Standards Australia, 2003) describes the following technologies as useful in knowledge discovery and representation:

> *Data Mining and Visualisation Tools:* Data mining and knowledge discovery are terms used to describe applications that look for hidden patterns in groups of data to discover previously unknown trends or relationships. These applications often use complex and sophisticated algorithms to discover knowledge. Visualisation tools are intended to assist people in analysing complex data sets by mapping physical properties to the data. Visualisation can map expertise, links between people across the organisation and

identify missing knowledge areas. Making organisational knowledge visible can support improvements and changes to the way knowledge is used, shared and transferred. Some of the characteristics often used to help visualise data include light effects, colour, direction and size of shadows, relative sizes and distances between objects, speed, curvature and transparency.

Promoting Virtual Socialisation and Collaboration

In the personalisation knowledge management approach knowledge is tied to the people who develop it and it is shared through person-to-person interaction (Hansen et al., 1999). The spiral model of knowledge creation (Nonaka and Takeuchi, 1995) recognises the crucial importance of socialisation in developing and transferring tacit knowledge in an organisation. The main aim of technology is seen in enabling and facilitating interaction among people for the purpose of knowledge sharing and collective learning (Handzic, 2001). The Interim Australian Standard (Standards Australia, 2003) recommends several types of technologies for consideration by organisations when developing KM solutions that support virtual socialisation. These are summarised as follows:

> *Communication and Collaboration Technologies:* Various applications have been developed that use ICT networks to facilitate peer-to-peer communication and knowledge sharing. Examples include e-mail, bulletin boards, chat-rooms, whiteboards, audio and video conferencing. They also include various specialised groupware applications. The term refers to a particular type of application focused on collaborative processes among people. Communication and collaboration technologies may be classified by the features offered to support group activities from facilitating communication, through to process and task structuring, to regulating interaction. Alternative approaches involve classification by technology application context, or by time

and place factors. Examples include computer supported meetings (same place and time), video conferencing (different place, same time), mailboxes (same place, different time) or bulletin boards (different place and time).

Portals, Intranets and Extranets: A portal is an interface that provides a single point of access to multiple sources of knowledge. Corporate portals usually point to numerous sources of internal and external knowledge in structured and searchable directories and databases, collaborative groupware tools and utilities to manage e-mail, discussion group materials, reports, memos and meeting minutes. They also improve work efficiency by providing single gateway to personalised content. Intranets and extranets provide connectivity that can support knowledge sharing inside and outside the organisation. An intranet is an internal corporate network that allows authorised personnel electronic access to documents, forms and web-applications. An extranet extends selected resources of the intranet to outside groups of customers, suppliers, business partners or employees in remote locations. Management of content is necessary to ensure its relevancy and currency. The extension of knowledge resources to external stakeholders means that authentication and privacy standards are critical factors.

A comprehensive survey of best KM practices (AA, 1998), reveals that most organisations implement some kind of technology to connect people and enable their interaction and collaboration. However, there are differences among researchers regarding the value of virtual (technology-mediated) interaction in comparison with real (face-to-face) interaction in knowledge management. Some researchers warn that technologies lack the emotional richness and depth of real, live, in-person interaction (Santosus, 2001), and are an unsuitable vehicle to fully develop relationships and to gain an understanding of complex situations (Bender and Fish, 2000). Others argue that communication mediated by technology is no less effective than face-to-face communication (Warkentin et al., 1997). More and more cyber-communities are also beginning to challenge traditional ideas about communities' needs for a physical presence.

Stimulating Creativity and Complex Problem Solving

There is a widespread recognition in the knowledge management literature of the importance of creativity and innovation for organisational success in a changing environment (Drucker, 1985). The evolutionary principle proposes that those who are innovative will survive, while those who are not will become extinct. An organisation's adaptive response may be a choice between development and decay. Recent surveys show that creativity and innovation are among the top priorities for senior executives in industry (BW, 1998).

It is argued that great innovations need creative thinking and ideas. While some theorists believe that creativity is reserved for the gifted, others (and us) see creativity as a skill that can be learned (Ford, 1996) and stimulated by technology (Aurum et al., 2001). Thus, organisations' needs for creativity and innovation require an appropriate response from various parties including the education sector and IT industry. An interesting observation is that the Interim Australian Standard (Standards Australia, 2003) does not include any creative software products in their list of useful KM technologies. However, other literature mentions a variety of technologies that can be used to stimulate creativity (Handzic and Cule, 2002).

> *Mind Games:* This group of technologies is focused on fostering creativity and innovative problem solving. Most systems are designed to stimulate creative thinking based on the principles of associations, memory retrieval and the use of analogy and metaphor. In multi-participant settings, it is also assumed that generation of creative ideas will be stimulated though participants' interaction where one idea leads to another and the process tends to build upon itself.

Virtual Reality: Virtual reality technology enables an individual to become actively immersed in a simulated environment. It can have a dramatic impact on a number of areas including manufacturing, education and training, medical interventions, military preparedness and entertainment. Virtual reality offers a tool that enables people to learn more easily through experiential exercise rather than through memorising rules.

A simulation game approach may also be helpful in solving complex problems. For example, in a conventional management game, one or more players have to make managerial decisions in a simulated world (Casimir, 1986). Typically in such a game, a number of players make decisions for organisations modelled after industrial companies in a competitive environment, or a single player tries to minimise/maximise certain results in a simulated world. The game is played in a discrete number of rounds or periods. Once the players enter their decisions the results are computed and reported back to them. Normally, the players can interfere with the simulated world at any time during a round or a period, and adjust their future strategies based on what they have learnt from past experience and feedback.

2.4 Issues and Challenges for Practice and Research

The preceding section illustrates several major classes of technologies and their related roles in supporting knowledge processes. These are summarised in Figure 2.1. Readers should note that these tools and roles are not mutually exclusive and organisations may adopt any combination of them to tackle their particular problems or support particular motives. If the prime reason for knowledge management is minimising the risk of losing valuable knowledge, the response may involve identifying and holding onto the core competencies that the company has. Thus, risk minimisation is closely related to knowledge initiatives and technologies specifically aimed at locating and capturing valuable company knowledge (Von Krogh et al., 2000).

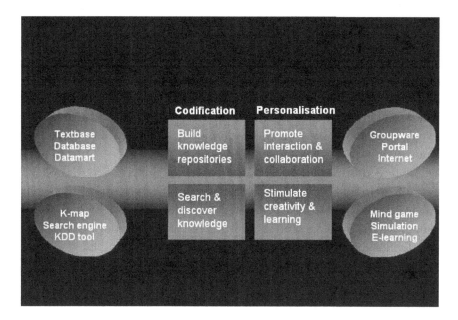

Figure 2.1 Types of KM technologies and roles

In today's complex economy, businesses are constantly confronted with the need to operate more efficiently in order to stay competitive and satisfy increasing market demands. Seeking efficiency usually relates to knowledge initiatives for transferring experiences and best practices throughout the organisation in order to avoid unnecessary duplication and to reduce cost. Technology is often an important part of achieving efficiency improvements (Von Krogh et al., 2000). Therefore, researchers and practitioners in the field of KM need to turn their attention to new approaches and tools for improving knowledge transfer, as a possible means for achieving enhanced efficiency and sustaining competitive advantage for knowledge intensive firms.

There is a growing belief that knowledge can do more than improve efficiency. The new products and services resulting from knowledge and technology may bring profound changes in the way businesses operate and compete in the new economy. The unifying thread among various theoretical views is the perception that innovation is the key driver of an organisation's long-term economic success. Innovation of products, processes and structures have been assessed as a critical component in the success of new-age firms. Typically, innovative organisations focus on new knowledge and creation processes (Nanaka and Nishiguchi, 2001). Technology may help in nurturing creative thought, enabling idea sharing and use, getting knowledge out of individual minds into social environment, and by turning individual creativity into collective innovativeness.

Despite the existing substantial theoretical support for the role of technology in KM, there is still a large gap in the body of knowledge in this area. The ultimate challenge for KM is to determine the best strategies to improve the development, transfer and use of organisational knowledge at individual and collective levels. Hahn and Subramani (2000) identify a number of issues and challenges related to the utilisation of ICT for knowledge management support in phases of deployment. In the planning of long term effects, the issue is balancing knowledge exploitation and exploration. In the setup phase, the issue is balancing information overload and potentially useful content. In the maintenance phase, the challenge is balancing additional workload and accurate content. Finally, in the development phase, the issues are high context dependence of knowledge, and the need for flexibility, evolutionary development and user acceptance of the knowledge system.

Alavi and Leidner (2001) propose five major research questions concerning the application of IT in KM initiatives. These include the questions about: (i) consequences of increasing the breath and depth of knowledge via information technology for organisational performance; (ii) ways of ensuring that knowledge captured via technology is effectively modified where necessary prior to application, (iii) ways of ensuring that ICT captures modifications to knowledge along with the original knowledge, (iv) development of trust in knowledge captured via technology, and (v) factors related to the quality and usefulness of IT systems applied to KM initiatives. These questions together with the ones discussed earlier in this chapter form a good basis for empirical research in this area.

In summary, the idea that modern KM is inseparable from a consideration of computer-based technology (Holsapple, 2003) provides justification for research that improves technologies of KM (e.g., enabling and facilitating knowledge flows, supporting manupulation activities); and provides better understanding of the technology use and users (e.g., what works and under what conditions) and the outcomes of that use (e.g., enhancing productivity, innovation, reputation, etc.). The following chapters report the results of a series of empirical studies undertaken to address some of these and other research opportunities of interest to the author.

2.5 Conclusions

The integrated KM framework from Chapter 1 provides a basis for understanding the role of technology in KM. It places technology among major influencing factors in KM that enable and facilitate knowledge processes and thus contribute to organisational learning, improvement and innovation. All types of technologies outlined in the current chapter can be viewed to a greater or lesser extent as KM tools that support organisational knowledge development by encouraging those processes through which knowledge is moved or modified. This chapter has mainly focused on categories of technologies that may play important roles in facilitating knowledge sharing, representation and transformation, as well as improving people's ability to acquire and create knowledge.

Among specific categories of technologies that may play important roles in building knowledge repositories are — databases, textbases, datawarehouses and datamarts; in promoting virtual socialisation and collaboration — groupware, portals, intranets, extranets and internets; in facilitating knowledge search and discovery — search engines, knowledge maps, and data mining tools; and in stimulating creativity and complex problem solving — electronic brainstorming, virtual reality and simulation games. The integrated view presented here may help make sense of the diverse field of KM and guide organisations in choosing technologies that best suit their knowledge needs and activities. It also provides an agenda for future research.

References

AA (1998), *Best Practices in Knowledge Management*, Arthur Andersen.

Alavi, M. and Leidner, D.E. (2001), "Knowledge Management and Knowledge Management Systems: Conceptual Foundations and Research Issues", *MIS Quarterly*, 25(1), 107–136.

Aurum, A., Handzic, M., Cross, J. and Van Toorn, C. (2001), "Software Support for Creative Problem Solving", in *Proceedings of the IEEE International Conference on Advanced Learning Technologies (ICALT'2001)*, 6–8 August, Madison, USA.

Becerra-Fernandez, I., Gonzales, A. and Sabherwal, R. (2004), *Knowledge Management: Challenges, Solutions, and Technologies*, Pearson Education, New Jersey.

Bender, S. and Fish, A. (2000), "The Transfer of Knowledge and the Retention of Expertise: The Continuing Need for Global Assignments", *Journal of Knowledge Management*, 4(2).

BW (1998), *Business Wire*, 14 December 1998.

Casimir, R.J. (1986), "DSS, Information Systems and Management Games", *Information and Management*, 11, 123–129.

Drucker, P. F., (1985), *Innovation and Entrepreneurship: Practices and Principles*, Harper & Row, New York, 1985.

Earl, M. (2001), "Knowledge Management Strategies: Toward a Taxonomy", *Journal of Management Information Systems*, 18(1), 215–233.

Edwards, J.S. (2004), "Supporting Knowledge Management with IT", (forthcoming).

Edwards, J.S., Handzic, M., Carlsson, S. and Nissen, M. (2003), "Knowledge Management Research and Practice: Visions and Directions", *Knowledge Management Research & Practice*, 1(1), 49–60.

Fayyad, U., Piatetsky-Shapiro, G. and Smyth, P. (1996), "Knowledge Discovery and Data Mining: Towards a Unifying Framework", in *Proceedings of the Second International Conference on Knowledge Discovery and Data Mining, KDD-96*, Oregon.

Ford, C.M. (1996), "Theory of Individual Creative Action in Multiple Social Domains", *Academy of Management Review*, 21(4), 1112–1142.

Hahn, J. and Subramani, M.R. (2000), "A Framework of Knowledge Management Systems: Issues and Challenges for Theory and Practice", in *Proceedings of the International Conference on Information Systems, ICIS'2000*, Brisbane, Australia, pp. 302–312.

Handzic, M. (2001), "Knowledge Management: A Research Framework", in *Proceedings of the 2nd European Conference on Knowledge Management (ECKM2001)*, November, Bled, Slovenia.

Handzic, M. and Cule, M. (2002), "Creative Decision Making: Review, Analysis and Recommendations", in *Proceedings of the Conference on Decision Making in Internet Age (DSIage 2002)*, Cork, July, pp. 443–452.

Handzic, M. and Bewsell, G. (2003), "Corporate Memories: Tombs or Wellsprings of Knowledge?", in *Proceedings of IRMA2003 Conference*, USA.

Handzic, M. and Hasan, H. (2003), "The Search for an Integrated Framework of KM", chapter 1 in Hasan, H. and Handzic, M. (eds.), *Australian Studies in Knowledge Management*, UOW Press, Wollongong, pp. 3–34.

Hansen, et al. (1999), "What's Your Strategy for Managing Knowledge?", *Harvard Business Review*, March–April, pp. 106–116.

Holsapple, C.W. (2003), "Knowledge and Its Attributes", in Holsapple, C.W. (ed.), *Handbook on Knowledge Management*, Springer, Berlin, Vol. 1, pp. 165–188.

McAdam, R. and McCreedy, S. (1999), "A Critical Review of Knowledge Management Models", *The Learning Organisation*, 6(3), 91–100.

Nanaka, I. and Nishiguchi, T. (2001), *Knowledge Emergence*, Oxford University Press, New York.

Nonaka, I. and Konno, N. (1998), "The Concept of Ba: Building a Foundation for Knowledge Creation", *California Management Review*, 40(3), 40–54.

Nonaka, I. and Takeuchi, H. (1995), *The Knowledge Creating Company: How Japanese Companies Create the Dynamics of Innovation*, Oxford University Press, New York.

Polanyi, M. (1966), "The Logic of Tacit Inference", *Philosophy*, 41(1), 1–18.

Raich, M. (2000), *Managing in the Knowledge Based Economy*, Raich, Zurich, Switzerland.

Santosus, M. (2001), *KM and Human Nature*, CIO.com *"In the Know"*, http://www.cio.com/knowledge/edit/k121801_nature.html. [accessed on 18/12/2001].

Snowden, D. (2003), "Innovation as an Objective of Knowledge Management. Part I: The Landscape of Management", *Knowledge Management Research & Practice*, 1(2), 113–119.

Standards Australia (2003), *Interim Australian Standard: Knowledge Management, AS5037 (int)*, Standards Australia International Limited, Sydney.

Stewart, T.A. (1997), *Intellectual Capital: The New Wealth of Organisations*, Doubleday, New York.

Swan, J. (2003), "Knowledge Management in Action", in Holsapple, C.W. (ed.), *Handbook on Knowledge Management*, Vol. 1, Springer, Berlin, pp. 271–296.

Tsui, E. (2003), "Tracking the Role and Evolution of Commercial Knowledge Management Software", in Holsapple, C.W. (ed.), *Handbook on Knowledge Management*, Vol. 2, Springer, Berlin, pp. 5–27.

Von Krogh, G., Ichijo, K. and Nonaka, I. (2000), *Enabling Knowledge Creation*, Oxford University Press, New York.

Warkentin, M.E., Sayeed, L. and Hightower, R. (1997), "Virtual Teams versus Face-to-Face Teams: An Exploratory Study of Web-based Conference System", *Decision Sciences*, 28(4).

Wexler, M.N. (2001), "The Who, What and Why of Knowledge Mapping", *Journal of Knowledge Management*, 5(3), 249–263.

PART II

Codification Technologies:

Supporting Knowledge Storage and Finding

CHAPTER 3

Web-based Knowledge Records:

Empowering Societies

The new source of power is not money in the hands of a few,
but information in the hands of many.
— John Naisbitt

In this chapter we explore the role of web technology in managing knowledge records. We present a view of knowledge records as society's tools for establishing evidence, protecting human rights, supporting the rule of law, preserving cultural capital and providing knowledge services. A sample of selected Australian web sites is analysed to demonstrate how the web is used to facilitate storage and access to knowledge that empowers justice and helps governments to achieve a wiser and fairer society. The chapter concludes with a set of guidelines for developing and implementing quality knowledge records systems.

3.1 Introduction

New knowledge is expanding at a pace that makes it an immense management task to keep up with. The Internet and the web technologies can help with this problem. Web technology provides virtually unlimited storage as part of huge server farms that may be located all around the world. With blinding speed, the Internet can link knowledge workers to mountains of digital records stored on the web all over the world, otherwise too expensive and too difficult to tap (Laudon and Laudon, 1998). It is therefore not surprising that individuals and collectives are increasingly using these technologies to store and gain easy access to their key knowledge resources.

The growing number of knowledge workers in the new economy requires easy access to all kinds of knowledge. For example, investors require lists of possible investments, stock prices and changes in stock prices to help them make better decisions. Scientists need to quickly obtain photographs taken by space-craft for research purposes. Internet library access is vital to students and teachers for locating relevant articles, papers, books and conference reports. Many hundreds of library catalogues are already on-line through the Internet. In addition, users can access many thousands of databases that have been opened to the public by corporations, governments and non-profit organisations (Laudon and Laudon, 1998). Individuals can gather knowledge on almost any conceivable topic and get empowered by the wealth of knowledge from these vast storehouses.

Various benefits for users deriving from the use of the Internet and the web technologies have been suggested in the literature. These range from reducing communication costs, to enhancing communication, accelerating the distribution of knowledge, and facilitating knowledge service delivery (Laudon and Laudon, 1998). Of particular interest to this chapter is the role of the Web in facilitating the storage of vast amounts of knowledge records. This chapter introduces the web as an important type of knowledge repository and examines its application in the public sector's knowledge records management. The emphasis is on benefits to a knowledge society in terms of wisdom and justice.

3.2 The World Wide Web

The world wide web ("the web") is at the heart of the explosion in the business and government uses of the Internet. It is a system with a universally accepted set of standards for storing, retrieving, formatting and displaying information in a networked environment (Laudon and Laudon, 1998). The web represents a giant knowledge depository linked by the Internet. It makes available to the requesting public, knowledge artifacts in the form of documents, files, photos, drawings, videos, sound and other various holders of knowledge (Becerra-Fernandez et al., 2004).

The invention of the Internet together with its web capability has been compared to Gutenberg's invention of the printing technology in the fifteenth century. The web handles all types of digital records and links knowledge resources that span multiple web servers. It accelerates the distribution of knowledge. It also facilitates document publishing and distribution, thus assisting the sharing of accumulated knowledge across individuals, organisations and societies.

Knowledge artifacts are stored and displayed on the web in the form of electronic pages. Web pages are hypermedia documents that often express the content in an artistic and dynamic fashion using stylish typography, colourful graphics, push-button interactivity, sound and video. These pages can be linked electronically to other pages regardless of where they are located and can be viewed by any type of computer. By clicking on highlighted words or buttons on a web page, one can link to related pages to find additional content of interest, or links to other points on the web (Laudon and Laudon, 1998, Becerra-Fernandez et al., 2004).

The web pages created by an individual, business organisation or a government agency are called a web site. For an entity to establish a presence on the web it must set up a web site of one or more pages. The default page for that website is a home page. A home page is a text and graphical screen display that usually welcomes the user and explains the entity that has established the page. The home page will lead the user to other static and dynamic web pages. Essentially, web technology supports the integrating school of thought on KM (Edwards, 2004) by placing focus on a single system (the web site) to provide all knowledge needs to the users.

Typically, web sites are created to widely disseminate product and service knowledge, broadcast advertising and messages to customers, to collect orders and customer data, and to co-ordinate organisations on a global scale. Appropriate, substantial and up-to-date knowledge records are considered crucial for the success of any web site (Lowe, 2003).

3.3 The Concept of Knowledge Record

The term "knowledge record" is a derivative of two terms: "knowledge" and "record". The term knowledge has different meanings for different people. From the cognitive perspective, for example, knowledge is perceived as externally justified beliefs, based on formal models, universal and explicit, that operate through cognitive processes. On the other hand, from the constructivist perspective, knowledge is viewed as acts of construction or creation, creative arts, not universal, beliefs that depend on personal sense making (Van Krogh, 1998). Often, knowledge is defined in terms of relationships between data and information. In theory, knowledge is described as deeper and richer information (Davenport and Prusak, 1998); information combined with experience, context, interpretation and reflection (Davenport et al., 1998); valuable information in action (Grayson and O'Dell, 1998); and information that has been internalised by a person to the degree that he or she can make use of it (Devlin, 1999). However, in practice, the terms data, information and knowledge are often used interchangeably (Huang et al., 1999).

Knowledge is usually classified as either explicit or tacit (Nonaka and Takeuchi, 1995, Nonaka, 1998). Explicit knowledge is described as formal, systematic knowledge that can be expressed or communicated without vagueness or ambiguity. It can be stored in books, manuals, databases and in other ways. Tacit knowledge, on the other hand, is considered as highly personal know-how that is derived from experience and beliefs and usually hard to articulate and communicate. Such knowledge exists in the individual minds of people (Polanyi, 1966).

Furthermore, some taxonomies make a distinction between declarative, procedural, inferential and motivational forms of knowledge (Quinn et al., 1996), as well as conditional, relational and pragmatic types (Alavi and Leidner, 2001). Other schemes recognise individual and artifact loci, varying degrees of knowledge structure, and individual and collective levels of knowledge (Hahn and Subramani, 2000). A pragmatic approach to classifying knowledge simply attempts to identify knowledge useful to organisations. In summary, knowledge is a complex and multi-faceted concept.

Knowledge resides in different locations or reservoirs, including people, artifacts and structures. Electronic knowledge repositories such as data warehouses and websites represent a way of storing knowledge in artifacts. This requires externalising knowledge into explicit forms such as words, concepts and visuals (Nonaka, 1998). We use the word "record" to denote any kind of explicit form that is created and kept as part of the knowledge externalisation process. Electronic records can be further grouped into structured fielded records such as those found in databases and data warehouses, and unstructured or semi-structured digital documents such as those found on the web containing text, graphics, animations, sound and video.

Digital records represent an increasingly important part of an entity's integrated knowledge base. With embedded multimedia objects, they have the potential to be highly expressive. However, they often make knowledge search and discovery difficult. Mechanisms such as the web are playing an increasingly important role in facilitating storage and distribution of these knowledge records. The main objective of the following case study is to examine a sample of the Australian government websites and their role in publishing and disseminating useful and timely knowledge to their public. The text presented here is derived from two recent papers (Handzic, 2003, 2004).

3.4 Case Study: Exploring Australian Web Sites

The wealth of a society is linked to its knowledge capital. Many nations, including Australia, are transforming themselves into knowledge economies and societies (Edvinsson, 2003). Knowledge management plays a major role in this transformation. However, our current understanding of the level of penetration and impact of KM in societies is very limited. Preliminary empirical evidence from Australia reveals a relatively high level of awareness, combined with a low level of implementation of knowledge management in academia (Handzic and VanToorn, 2002); some KM activities in major public sector agencies (Stephens, 2001); and some efforts focused on delivering better e-government services to the public (NOIE, 2002).

There is also widespread recognition that different societies treat their knowledge in different ways. Eastern cultures seem to value more "tacit" knowledge that is kept in people's heads and transferred through socialisation. Western cultures, on the other hand, appear to focus more on "explicit" knowledge, captured and preserved in collective and codified repositories (Nonaka and Takeuchi, 1995). Based on this distinction, a widely adopted broad classification of knowledge management strategies comprises two classes: personalisation and codification (Hansen et al., 1999). The personalisation strategy assumes that tacit knowledge is shared through interpersonal communication. Codification assumes that knowledge can be effectively extracted and codified. In this approach, knowledge artifacts are stored and indexed in databases for later retrieval and use. As such, it can serve as evidence and proof of an idea, decision or action taken by individuals, organisations and governments.

Following the principles of codification, Pederson (2002) proposed a comprehensive framework for building a society's cumulative "explicit" knowledge base. This framework suggests that the process starts with identifying critical documentable knowledge. This may include individual and group ideas, actions, decisions and transaction worth preserving. Once identified as such, these documentable "acts" are then codified, organised, stored and kept together with relevant meta-knowledge for as long as required. Typically, only a small portion of recorded knowledge has long term significance and becomes part of the society's cumulative memory and of concern to public authorities.

Pederson (2002) provides numerous examples of knowledge records from the world's public archives available on the Internet. Such web-based collections of digital content represent an exciting development full of promise for users for research, education and practice purposes (Henninger, 2003). The following sections illustrate some notable Australian web sites as examples that are particularly significant for empowering justice and attaining wisdom in the society.

Achieving a Fairer Society

Accumulated knowledge records can be viewed as an important societal tool for establishing facts and a way to validate human memory. Typically they include personal documents, corporate knowledge bases, industry and government reports and statistics, technical and specialist literature, databases and internet resources, academic journals, scholarly and reference books, general knowledge compilations, popular books and magazines, and info-tainment. *Founding Documents* is an Australian project in social history realised by a partnership of eight government archives, for the Centenary of Federation celebration. The project is available at the URL http://www.foundingdocs.gov.au/. Since documented knowledge often serves as proof of an idea, decision or action taken by individuals, organisations and governments, it is of vital importance that records are constructed with care, and that they are complete, reliable and unchanging.

Knowledge records are also important in ensuring the protection of individual rights. One of the first and most important protective documents in this category is The Universal Declaration of Human Rights proclaimed by the newly formed United Nations after World War II. Thirty clauses of the declaration can now be easily accessed and read from the United Nations website by all those who may wish to remind themselves or teach others about human rights, and ensure their fulfillment. On a different level, personal documents are especially crucial to individuals seeking to establish their identity and ensure their entitlements. The intentional destruction of one's vital personal records can be extremely disruptive and often life threatening to those affected. The stories of Kosovars found at web pages of the United Nations High Commissioner for Refugees, and various government councils give a graphic insight into the experiences and deprivation suffered by people whose identity documents were systematically destroyed and who were forced to become refugees. The Australian Government provides instruction and help to refugees through *The Refugee Council of Australia,* available at the URL http://www.refugeecouncil.org.au/.

Progressive societies demand that governments and individuals demonstrate great responsibility and accountability in the conduct of their public and personal affairs. Typically, governments enact laws and regulations which define the structures and sets of rules governing the relations and activities of all legal entities within their jurisdictions. Written laws and regulations represent infrastructural archives that support the rule of law and enable society to hold people and institutions accountable for their actions. They also help to achieve improved stability and fairer distribution of society's resources. Despite all these measures, keeping those in charge honest still represents a major challenge for democratic societies. The Australian Government has recently awarded a major research grant to the Records Continuum Research Group at Monash University to investigate the issue of accountability in public services (URL http://rcrg.dstc.edu.au/publications/recordscontinuum/ smoking.html). The group's web site contains numerous reports and analyses of recent crises, scandals and risks faced by the Australian public sector that all have their roots in inadequate knowledge record management.

Achieving a Wiser Society

The capacity to construct and transfer culture has always been considered as an essential social function. Recorded knowledge has an important cultural value too. It links us to the ideas and activities which have lasting importance for symbolic or concrete reasons. Bodies of recorded knowledge constitute a society's "cultural capital". Cumulative layers of evidence legitimise and witness the development of significant ideas and activities within a society over time. When cultural treasures do not survive, it is hard to reclaim the lost wisdom and skills and the ability of the society to progress is hindered. It gradually loses its memory and capacity to sustain itself. Stories of recent attempts to destroy cultural treasures, as well as international conventions and safeguarding measures designed to protect them can be found at UNESCO's web site. One of the recent Australian contributions to preserving society's achievements is *Bright Sparcs*, an Australian Science Archives Project, available at the URL http://www.asap.unimelb.edu.au/bsparcs/bsparcshome.htm. It is a register of over 3,000 people involved in the development of science, technology and medicine in Australia. The site also includes references to scientists' materials and bibliographic resources.

Governments represent an important source of knowledge needed to facilitate citizen and business orientated services. The Australian Government Entry Point http://www.fed.gov.au shown in Figure 3.1 is a comprehensive government web site that currently signposts over 700 Australian Government web sites and over 1 million pages of text. It is the Australian Government's aim to provide efficient access to its expertise, and the variety of access approaches available on this site

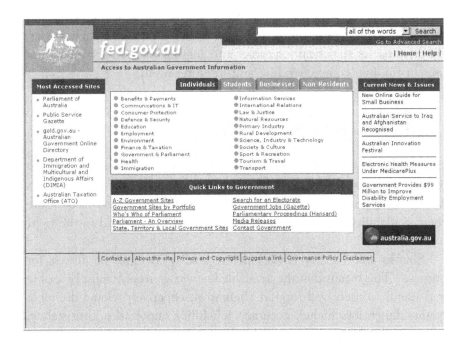

Figure 3.1 The Australian Government Website

allow users to choose the method that best suits their needs. Customised links are provided for different types of users including individuals, students, businesses and non-residents. For example, the site points to relevant places where best advice on benefits and payments may be obtained for individuals, education related information for students, taxation help for businesses, and immigration tips for non-residents.

The public administration and government work is often delivered in the form of strategic knowledge products. The Australian Bureau of Statistics (ABS), Australia's official statistical organisation http:// www.abs.gov.au assists and encourages informed decision-making, research and discussion within governments and the community, by providing a high quality, objective and responsive national statistical service on its web site. ABS organises its statistical products around the broad themes including: economy, environment and energy, industry, people and regional statistics. Each of these is further divided into more specific categories. For example, industry theme includes agriculture and rural, building and construction, information technology, manufacturing, mining, retail, science and innovation, service industries, tourism and transport statistics. At the next level are related data and publications. By dividing its statistical expertise into logical blocks, ABS helps the user in finding, comprehending and interpreting it.

3.5 Issues and Challenges

Due to the power of recorded knowledge as a resource of wisdom and justice in society, knowledge management must ensure that government's knowledge repositories are of high quality and integrity and also ensure their availability to the right people, at the right time, and in the right form.

Shanks and Tansley (2002) define quality in terms of "fitness for purpose". This means that the available knowledge records must be usable and useful to users and support their work effectively. Some desirable quality dimensions include accuracy, reliability, importance, consistency, precision, timeliness, understandability, conciseness and usefulness (Ballou and Pazer, 1985; Wand and Wang, 1996). More complete perspectives on quality are provided by a number of proposed frameworks that organise and structure the concept of quality.

For example, the framework by Strong et al., (1997), based on a survey of opinions of expert practitioners, suggests four quality dimensions: intrinsic, contextual, representational and accessibility. The framework of Shanks and Darke (1998) is based on semiotic theory and Bunge's ontology and consists of quality goals and measures for consumer stakeholders. Quality goals include syntactic, semantic, pragmatic and social levels. Syntactic quality concerns the form, semantic quality concerns the meaning, pragmatic quality concerns the usage, and social quality the shared understanding. Other frameworks include Wand and Wang (1996), which is also based on Bunge's ontology, and Kahn et al., (1997), which is based on product and service quality theory.

The Australian standard for records management (Standards Australia, 2002) lists several important characteristics that records should have in order to ensure society's need for evidence, accountability and information. First, a record's content should correctly reflect an idea that was communicated, or a decision that was made or an action that was taken. In addition to the content, the record should also contain the metadata describing its structure, context and links to other relevant records. Furthermore, the record should be authenticated, that is proven to be what it purports to be, shown to have been created or sent by the person purported to have created or sent it, and verified as having been created or sent at the time purported. The record should also be reliable, so that its contents can be trusted as a complete and accurate representation of knowledge. The integrity of a record should be preserved by protection from an unauthorised alteration. Finally, it should be useable, easy to locate, retrieve, present and interpret.

The failure to address the issues of quality and integrity of records in government's knowledge repositories may lead to serious impairment of functioning of society and its institutions, the loss of evidence of the rights of people as citizens, the inability of societal watchdogs to call to account governments and individuals, the loss of collective and individual identity and memory, and the inability to authenticate and source critical knowledge. These issues pose a great challenge to governments. One possible way forward is in standardisation of relevant policies and procedures. Such standards may ensure that appropriate attention and protection is given to all records and that the evidence and information they contain can be retrieved more efficiently and effectively. The Australian government's response to this challenge is described in the following section.

3.6 Australian Standard Guidelines

Australian Standard provides a methodology that specifically aims at facilitating the implementation of knowledge records management in organisations (Standards Australia, 2002). One of the first recommendations to institutions intending to implement the knowledge records system is to define and document relevant policies. A policy statement can be understood as a statement of intentions. It also sets out programmes and procedures that will achieve those intentions. The standard describes a step-by-step procedure for designing and implementing records systems, that includes (1) preliminary investigation, (2) analysis of activities, (3) identification of requirements, (4) assessment of existing systems, (5) identification of strategies, (6) systems design, (7) systems implementation and (8) post-implementation review.

The purpose of the first step is to provide an understanding of relevant administrative, legal and social contexts. The next step involves building of a conceptual model of institutional activities. The purpose of the third step is to identify requirements to create, receive and keep knowledge records. The following steps involve reviewing of the existing system; determining the most appropriate policies, procedure, standards, tools and other tactics; and converting these strategies into a plan that fulfils requirements and remedies deficiencies identified in earlier steps; and putting in place an appropriate mix of strategies to implement the designed plan. The purpose of the final step is to evaluate and maintain the effectiveness of the system, and to establish a monitoring regime for the duration of the life of the system.

Another Standard recommendation specifies required operational processes and controls. Theoretically, these processes include a linear sequence of capture, registration, record classification, access and security classification, identification of disposition status, storage, use and tracking, and implementation of disposal activities. In practice, however, some operations may take place simultaneously. Certain operations may depend on the existence of controls. Controls include the instruments needed for different operations, and factors that may affect these operations. The principal instruments are classification schemes, the disposition authority and the security and access scheme. Additional instruments include specific tools such as a thesaurus and a glossary of terms, as well as regulatory and risk frameworks, formalised delegation of authority and the registry of permissions.

Finally, the Standard specifies the need to define responsibilities and authorities. The overriding objective of this recommendation is to establish and maintain the regime that meets the needs of all stakeholders. The likely authorities and responsibilities of senior managers include ensuring the success of the overall knowledge records management programme. Specialised professionals have primary responsibility for the implementation of policies, procedures and standards. Other knowledge workers may have a variety of specific duties, including responsibility for security, responsibility for design and implementation of information and communication technology based systems, or creation, receipt and storage of knowledge records.

By establishing proper management of knowledge records, governments may prevent serious impairment of the functioning of society and its institution, avoid the loss of evidence of the rights of people as citizens, avert the inability of societal watchdogs to call to account governments and individuals, stop the loss of collective and individual identity and memory, and hinder the inability to authenticate and source critical knowledge, and create a wiser and fairer society.

3.7 Conclusions

This chapter addresses the role of web technology in facilitating the preservation and dissemination of society's accumulated knowledge to the public. Recorded and documented knowledge is seen as an important societal tool for establishing facts, and a way to validate human memory, protect human rights, support the rule of law, and preserve culture. The case study of the selected Australian government web sites further highlights the importance of the availability of high quality and timely knowledge records to their seekers in order to ensure a better and fairer society. A systematic approach to managing knowledge records is essential to protect and preserve evidence, support decision-making and ensure accountability to present and future stakeholders.

References

Alavi, M. and Leidner, D.E. (2001), "Knowledge Management and Knowledge Management Systems: Conceptual Foundations and Research Issues", *MIS Quarterly*, 25(1), 107–136.

Ballou, D.P. and Pazer, H.L. (1985), "Modeling Data and Process Quality Multi-input Multi-output Information Systems", *Management Science*, 31(2), 150–162.

Becerra-Fernandez, I., Gonzalez, A. and Sabherval, R. (2004), *Knowledge Management: Challenges, Solutions and Technologies*, Pearson Education, New Jersey.

Davenport, T.H. and Prusak, L. (1998), *Working Knowledge*, Harvard Business School Press, Boston.

Davenport, T.H., DeLong, D.W. and Breers, M.C. (1998), "Successful Knowledge Management Projects", *Sloan Management Review*, Winter, 43–57.

Devlin, K. (1999), *Infosense: Turning Information into Knowledge*, W.H. Freeman, New York.

Edvinsson, L. (2003), "The Intellectual Capital of Nations", in Holsapple, C.W. (ed.), *Handbook on Knowledge Management*, Vol. 1, Springer, Berlin, pp. 153–163.

Edwards, J. (2004), *Supporting Knowledge Management with IT*, (paper submitted to DSS 2004 conference).

Grayson, C.J. and O'Dell, C. (1998), "Mining Your Hidden Resources", *Across the Board*, 35(4), 23–28.

Hahn, J. and Subramani, M.R. (2000), "A Framework of Knowledge Management Systems: Issues and Challenges for Theory and Practice", in *Proceedings of the International Conference on Information Systems, ICIS' 2000*, Brisbane, Australia, pp. 302–312.

Handzic, M. (2004), "The Role of Knowledge Mapping in Electronic Government", in Wimmer, M.A. (ed.), in *Proceedings of the 5th IFIP International Working Conference (KMGov 2004)*, Krems, Austria, May 17–19 (forthcoming).

Handzic, M. (2003), "Empowering Society through Knowledge Records", in Wimmer, M.A. (ed.), in *Proceedings of IFIP International Working Conference Knowledge Management in Electronic Government (KMGov 2003)*, Rhodes, May 26–28, pp. 262–267.

Handzic, M. and Van Toorn, C. (2002), *Penetration of KM Practices in a Non-Profit Organisation: A Case of Academia*, working paper, UNSW.

Hansen, et al. (1999), "What's Your Strategy for Managing Knowledge?", *Harvard Business Review*, March–April, pp. 106–116.

Henninger, M. (2003), *The Hidden Web*, UNSW Press, Sydney.

Huang, F.T. et al. (1999), *Quality Information and Knowledge*, Prentice Hall, New Jersey.

Kahn, B., Stong, D.M. and Wang, R.Y. (1997), "A Model for Delivering Quality Information as Product and Service", in *Proceedings of the International Conference on Information Quality*, MIT, Boston, pp. 80–94.

Laudon, K.C. and Laudon, J.P. (1998), *Management Information Systems: New Approaches to Organisation and Technology*, Prentice Hall, New Jersey.

Lowe, D. (2003), "Emergent Knowledge in Web Development", in Aurum, et al., *Managing Software Engineering Knowledge*, Springer, Berlin, pp. 157–175.

NOIE (2002), http://www.noie.gov.au.

Nonaka, I. (1998), "The Knowledge-Creating Company", in *Harvard Business Review on Knowledge Management*, Harvard Business School Press, Boston.

Nonaka, I. and Takeuchi, H. (1995), *The Knowledge Creating Company: How Japanese Companies Create the Dynamics of Innovation*. Oxford University Press, New York.

Pederson, A. (2002), http://john.curtin.edu.au/society.

Polanyi, M. (1966), "The Logic of Tacit Inference", *Philosophy*, 41(1), 1–18.

Quinn, J.B., Anderson, P. and Finkelstein, S. (1996), "Managing Professional Intellect: Making the Most of the Best", *Harvard Business Review*, March–April, pp. 71–80.

Shanks, G. and Darke, P. (1998), "Understanding Metadata and Data Quality in a Data Warehouse", *Australian Computer Journal*, November.

Shanks, G. and Tansley, E. (2002), "Data Quality Tagging and Decision Outcomes: An Experimental Study", in *Proceedings of Decision Support in Internet Age Conference (DSIage2002)*, Cork, July.

Standards Australia (2002), *Australian Standard: Records Management*, Parts 1 & 2, Standards Australia, Sydney.

Stephens, D. (2001), "Knowledge Management in the APS: A Stocktake and a Prospectus", *Canberra Bulletin of Public Administration*, 100, 26–30.

Strong, D.M., Lee, Y.W. and Wang, R.Y. (1997), "Data Quality in Context", *Communications of the ACM*, 40(5), 103–110.

Van Krogh, G. (1998), "Care in Knowledge Creation", *California Management Review*, 40(3), 133–153.

Wand, Y. and Wang, R. (1996), "Anchoring Data Quality Dimensions in Ontological Foundations", *Communications of the ACM*, 39(11), 86–95.

CHAPTER 4

Structured Knowledge Repositories:

Building Corporate Memories

We're drowning in information and starving for knowledge.
— Rutherford D. Rodgers

This chapter investigates ways of building more effective knowledge repositories and tests empirically the impact of a massaging technique on people's ability to process and use stored knowledge in a judgmental decision-making task context. The main findings indicate that knowledge massaging in the form of aggregation had a significant positive effect on people's knowledge assimilation and utilisation. This, in turn, led to enhanced decision accuracy. These findings have important implications for practice as they point to a proven way to enhance the effectiveness of corporate memories in organisations, but warn of the dangers of overdependence on tools.

4.1 Introduction

Knowledge has been widely recognised as a critical organisational resource for success in the new economy. Many organisations are trying to capitalise on their organisational knowledge in order to maintain their competitive advantage. This requires mobilising the collective assemblage of all intelligences that contribute towards building a shared vision, renewal process and direction for the organisation (Liebowitz, 2000).

In Chapter 1, we identified that one of the important objectives of knowledge management is to capture, codify, organise and store relevant organisational knowledge. Capturing and storing knowledge into knowledge repositories is an important part of building organisational memory. The assumption is that tacit knowledge needs to be made explicit and formilised to be shared and used more easily by organisational members. By capturing experiences, anecdotes, war stories, case studies, lessons learnt, best practices, failures and success, heuristics and valuable relationships organisations also begin to evolve into true knowledge organisations.

Technology can be used as an enabler to support these KM efforts via building computer-based knowledge repositories. The Interim Australian KM standard (Standards Australia, 2003) proposes a number of technologies including databases, textbases, data warehouses and data marts as useful in building organisational knowledge repositories. A knowledge management systems framework (Hahn & Subramani, 2000) suggests that the availability of a KM system, such as a codified knowledge repository, should lead to an increase in organisational knowledge and result in improved performance. Other researchers argue that knowledge repositories contribute to knowledge and performance by facilitating knowledge processes such as assimilation (O'Leary, 2003).

Currently, there is ample of evidence to show that organisations do implement various storage technologies as part of their best KM practices (AA, 1998). However, there is little empirical evidence regarding the impact of these initiatives on organisational performance (Alavi and Leidner, 2001). The existing KM research is mainly limited to anecdotal stories and descriptive case studies. Some researchers point out that our ability to accumulate and store knowledge artefacts has by far surpassed our ability to process them, and warn of the danger that vast institutional memories may easily become tombs rather than wellsprings of knowledge (Fayyad & Uthurusamy, 2002). Thus, we argue here that one of the most challenging research questions with respect to building effective knowledge repositories for organisations is to find technologies (tools and methods) that make stored knowledge more effective. The purpose of this chapter is to address the issue through a series of laboratory experiments. The specific aim is to determine those technologies that best facilitate knowledge extraction and assimilation.

4.2 Concept of Knowledge Repository

A knowledge repository can be viewed as a form of organisational memory, that is a set of stored artifacts that organisations acquire and retain, and to bear on their present activities in order to avoid future mistakes. A knowledge repository can be studied from two perspectives. The "content" perspective focuses on the knowledge that is captured and the context in which it is used. The "repository" perspective focuses on how knowledge is stored and retrieved (Jennex and Olfman, 2003).

In general, repositories store two types of knowledge: 1) structured concrete information and knowledge in databases, documents and artifacts (e.g., standards, rules), and 2) the representation of unstructured abstract information and knowledge of human actors (e.g., conceptual lenses, frameworks). They serve two basic functions: representation — presenting the knowledge for a given context, or interpretation — providing the frames of reference and guidelines for knowledge application. With the aggressive rate of growth of disk storage in the last decade, organisations are increasingly relying on computer-based repositories, as opposed to more traditional paper based repositories or human memory. Computer-based repositories incorporate a variety of knowledge forms ranging from data and text-based documents and models, to digital images, video and audio-recordings.

Some researchers anticipate that applying corporate knowledge repositories will result in improved organisational effectiveness. Jennex and Olfman (2002) put forward a number of propositions to define the beneficial outcomes of the use of organisational memories. These range from improved decisions, through reduced decision resistance, to more successful change efforts. However, these may or may not happen. Some researchers (O'Leary, 2003) argue that while knowledge may be gathered, created and converted, if it is not assimilated, the organisations will not be able to take action on that knowledge or actualise its potential value. As a result, corporate memories will have only limited impact on an organisation.

Other researchers (Fayyad and Uthurusamy, 2002) warn that the increasing ability to capture and store data may produce a phenomenon called the "data tombs". These are effectively write-only stores where knowledge artifacts are deposited to merely rest in peace never to be accessed again. Such stores represent missed opportunities to support exploration in a scientific activity or commercial exploitation by a business organisation. If knowledge captured in organisational stores stays unused, most opportunities to discover, profit, improve service or optimise will be lost.

Given that much of the previous research on knowledge management has ignored the issues associated with extraction and internalisation of knowledge from corporate stores, this chapter will particularly focus on factors that promote effective use of corporate knowledge repositories. The challenge is to find ways to turn them from tombs into wellsprings of knowledge (Handzic and Bewsell, 2003).

4.3 Facilitating Knowledge Extraction from Repositories

The prime function of a knowledge repository is to store captured artifacts in forms that can be retrieved and applied effectively. O'Leary (2003) suggested a number of technologies for assimilation that may assist in achieving this goal. They include knowledge storage, massaging, organising, linking, filtering and navigating. In this chapter, we will take a closer look at storage, massaging and filtering approaches. The common characteristic of these three approaches is that they all deal with different ways of "structuring" knowledge content in repositories. The other three approaches, namely organising, linking and navigating deal more with the issues of "guiding" users towards knowledge stored in repositories. This issue will be addressed in more detail in the following chapter.

Structuring Knowledge Content

According to O'Leary, knowledge storage and thus availability provides a basis to facilitate knowledge assimilation. Knowledge can be stored in a variety of forms: documents, rules, cases, diagrams etc. For decision making, the value of stored environment, organisation and cause-effect knowledge may be seen primarily in its ability to explain past and anticipate future changes in the behaviour of the variable of interest. This enables the decision maker to deal more competently with his or her decision task.

O'Leary (2003) suggested that massaging knowledge into an appropriate format by a KM system could help the user better understand and use knowledge. One approach is to provide knowledge in a summarised rather than in a detailed format. For decision making purposes, aggregated knowledge can be produced by modeling systems that combine existing knowledge into single integrated responses. It is assumed that processing of smaller amounts of task information induces lower demands on the mental resources of the decision maker and reduces the complexity of the decision problem. This in turn may have a positive effect on performance.

Furthermore, knowledge can be filtered to facilitate assimilation. Filtering tries to get the right knowledge to the right people at the right time. One possible approach is to package single workgroups' critical knowledge into smaller knowledge marts as opposed to storing collective knowledge across functional teams, departments, divisions and subsidiaries in enterprise wide knowledge warehouses. The assumption is that filtering prevents the negative effect of irrelevant information on human judgment. Filtering can be done manually, using human experts who determine if knowledge is relevant, and take responsibility for filtering it for others. Alternatively, technology can be used to help users directly monitor and determine high quality content from a broader knowledge base.

Providing Guidance to Knowledge

Alternative ways to facilitating extraction and assimilation of knowledge from repositories is by providing guidance to relevant knowledge by making it more visible and accessible to the user. O'Leary (2003) suggests that one possible way of achieving improved assimilation is by developing knowledge taxonomies or ontologies. An ontology is defined as an explicit specification of a concept. Linking knowledge to other knowledge or people is another way suggested to improve assimilation. Technology can be used to determine who knows who or what. Finally, knowledge navigation may facilitate assimilation by helping the user better visualise the world. Many different approaches for assisting knowledge navigation have been suggested including hyperbolic browsing, table lens, and intelligent agents. Knowledge maps or k-maps are alternative terms used to denote the above ideas (Wexler, 2001). They will be addressed in a greater detail in Chapter 5.

To summarise, all of the above approaches have been suggested as methods to improve knowledge extraction and assimilation. However, there has been very little empirical evidence to support such propositions. Recent findings indicate that both storage and filtering are beneficial. One paper reported that people managed to extract between 40% and 60% of the knowledge stored in codified repositories depending on quantity, quality and diversity of the content available (Handzic and Bewsell, 2003). As a result they improved the quality of their decisions compared to those without such repositories, but failed to achieve what was theoretically possible. In another study Handzic and Parkin (2000) found out that providing people with a knowledge mart instead of a knowledge warehouse resulted in improved knowledge use and performance.

The main objective of the current study was to examine the impact of one knowledge massaging technique (aggregation) on the effectiveness of knowledge absorption from repositories, and its subsequent effect on people's performance in a decision making task. The knowledge repository in this study was a prototype data warehouse. This is relatively new and immature, but promising KM technology (Finnegan and Sammon, 2002). It was hoped that the current research would provide a deeper insight into the potential and limitations of the knowledge massaging approach to improving the effectiveness of knowledge repositories in supporting decision making.

4.4 Empirical Study

Experimental Task

The experimental task in the current study was a simple production planning activity in which subjects made decisions regarding daily production of fresh ice cream. The participants assumed the role of Production Manager for a fictitious dairy firm that sold ice cream from its outlet at Bondi Beach in Sydney, Australia. The fictitious company incurred equally costly losses if production was set too low (due to loss of market to the competition) or too high (by spoilage of unsold product). The participants' goal was to minimise the costs incurred by incorrect production decisions. During the experiment, participants were asked at the end of each day to set production quotas for ice cream to be sold the following day. Subjects were required to make thirty production decisions over a period of thirty consecutive days. Before commencing the task, participants had an opportunity to make five trial decisions (for practice purposes only).

From pre-experiment discussions with actual store owners at Bondi Beach, three factors emerged as important in determining local demand for product: the ambient air temperature, the amount of sunshine and the number of visitors/tourists at the beach. This knowledge was presented to the subjects in two different forms. One half of the participants received it in a massaged form as one aggregated cue (i.e., index), and another half received it in a raw form as three separate contextual cues (i.e., temperature, sunshine, visitors).

The task provided a challenge because it did not stipulate exactly how this knowledge should be translated into specific judgment. The participants were provided with a meaningful task context, sequential historic information of task relevant variables to provide some clues to causal relationship, and their forecast values to suggest future behaviour.

However, they were not given any explicit analysis of the quality of their knowledge artifacts, or rules they could use to apply the available knowledge.

At the beginning of the experiment, task descriptions were provided to inform subjects about the task scenario and requirements. The given text differed only with respect to the form of knowledge presented. In addition, throughout the experiment instructions and feedback were provided to each participant to analyse earlier performance and to adjust future strategies.

Experimental Design and Variables

A laboratory experiment with random assignment to treatment groups was used, since it allowed greater experimental control. This made it possible to draw stronger inferences about causal relationships between variables due to high controllability. The only independent variable was *knowledge form* (raw vs massaged).

The raw knowledge form was operationalised by providing the participants with three cues of decision relevant contextual information (e.g., temperature, sunshine and visitors) in a computerised database. The massaged knowledge form was operationalised in terms of one aggregated cue (e.g., sales index). All information cues were equally predictive irrespective of the form to control for the potential confounding effects of quality and diversity.

Individual performance was evaluated in terms of *processing efficiency* of the available knowledge and *decision accuracy* achieved as a result. Processing efficiency was operationalised by a relative to optimal error (ROE) and was calculated as a ratio of an absolute error of a person's decision to the corresponding error of the "optimal strategy". The optimal strategy was modeled using stepwise regressions with three (or one) cues as independent variables and sales data as the dependent variable. R-square values were 0.87 ($F(3,26)=56.82$, $p=0.000$) for the raw form, and 0.66 ($F(1,28)=55.62$, $p=0.000$) for the massaged form. The optimal response integrated individual variables into a single response using regression weights and produced the best possible performance given the available cues. ROE were calculated to assess how much of the maximum knowledge potential was extracted and used by the subjects. Scores equal to 1 indicate maximal, while scores greater than 1 indicate suboptimal processing efficiency.

Decision accuracy was operationalised by a relative to naive error (RNE) and was calculated as a ratio of an absolute error of a person's decision to the corresponding error of the "random walk" (naive) strategy (for details see Amstrong and Collopy, 1992). A naive strategy is one that simply determines the next day sales as equal to the current day's sales. Such strategy makes no use of any contextual knowledge and typically produces poor performance. RNE was used to assess improvement in the quality of decisions due to knowledge use. Scores equal to 1 indicated no improvement, while scores smaller than one indicated improved accuracy.

Subjects and Procedure

The subjects were 28 graduate students enrolled in the Master of Commerce course at the University of New South Wales, Sydney. Subjects participated in the experiment on a voluntary basis and received no monetary incentives for their performance. Graduate students are generally considered to be appropriate subjects for this type of research (Ashton and Kramer, 1980; Remus, 1996; Whitecotton, 1996). The experiment was conducted in a microcomputer laboratory. On arrival, subjects were assigned randomly to one of the treatment groups by picking up a diskette with an appropriate version of the research instrument to be used. The instrument was specifically developed by the author in Visual Basic. Subjects were briefed about the purpose of the study, read the case descriptions and performed the task. The session lasted about one hour.

Results

The analysis of collected data was performed using a series of T-tests to examine the effects of knowledge form on two dependent variables of interest (processing efficiency and decision quality). The results are presented graphically in Figures 4.1 and 4.2. They were all significant at $p=0.05$.

The results of the analysis shown in Figure 4.1 indicate a significant positive effect of knowledge massaging on processing efficiency. The mean ROE of the subjects provided with knowledge in the aggregated form was significantly lower than that of the subjects presented with knowledge in a raw form (2.70 vs 4.00). Mean values greater than 1 indicated that subjects assimilated knowledge less efficiently than they could have irrespective of variations in knowledge form.

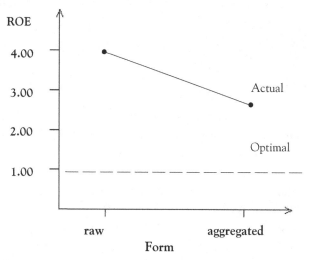

Mean processing efficiency (ROE) by knowledge form

Figure 4.1 Decision efficiency graph

Figure 4.2 shows a significant positive effect of knowledge massaging on decision accuracy. The subjects with the aggregated knowledge form had a significantly lower mean RNE than their counterparts with the raw knowledge form (0.94 vs 1.15). Mean values less than 1 indicate marginal improvement in decision accuracy compared to naive strategy due to information utilisation.

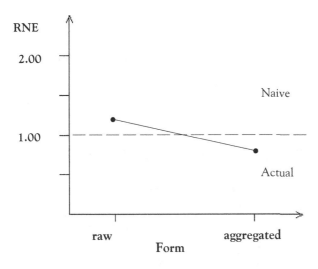

Mean Decision quality (RNE) by knowledge form

Figure 4.2 Decision accuracy graph

4.5 Lessons Learned

Main Findings

The main findings of this study provide important empirical support for the proposition that knowledge massaging will enhance knowledge extraction and assimilation, and improve performance in a decision-making task context. The study demonstrated that knowledge massaging had a beneficial effect on processing efficiency. Subjects provided with aggregated knowledge tended to assimilate their available knowledge relatively more efficiently compared to those with raw knowledge. This was demonstrated by significantly smaller processing errors found among the subjects from the aggregated than from raw knowledge form groups. Consistent with a substantially improved processing efficiency, the study revealed that knowledge massaging resulted in enhanced decision accuracy. This was evidenced by significantly lower decision errors found among the subjects with aggregated than raw knowledge forms.

In general, these findings are consistent with the theoretical expectations from the KM literature (O'Leary, 2003) that suggest a positive effect of knowledge massaging approach on assimilation. They also agree with the earlier work done in the psychology field on the impact of cognitive load (Schroder et al., 1967) and task complexity (Beach and Michell, 1978; Christensen-Szalanski, 1978; Payne, 1982; Wood, 1986) on performance. Finally, they confirm our own earlier empirical evidence of enhanced efficiency and accuracy (Handzic, 1997) with reduced volumes of stored artifacts.

With respect to overall performance, the study revealed relatively inefficient use of the available knowledge across both treatments, which consequently resulted in little or no real improvement in decision accuracy over naive strategy. The relatively poor overall performance could be potentially attributed to the lack of monetary incentives. Other Handzic (1997) study provided participants with a substantial monetary reward for their performance. It is possible that without monetary incentives, the subjects in this study were not as motivated to use the full potential of their information to improve decisions. This is offset by the assumption that graduates chosen from the pool of students attending an advanced Master's level course should be motivated to do their best on the task by their intrinsic interest in the subject matter.

Alternatively, poor overall performance could be attributed to the characteristics of the task information and the task performers. Computerised knowledge repositories available to participants in the current study contained only factual knowledge with little analysis, and had no procedural information. Conversion of explicit factual knowledge into personal tacit knowledge was insufficiently achieved to perform well on the task. The participants also needed analytical information such as an evaluation of the predictive validity of each contextual factor, as well as the relevant know-how to integrate factual information into a decision response. This crucial information was assumed to be a part of an individual's "tacit" knowledge. However, non-expert participants appear not to have had high levels of the required "tacit" knowledge to perform well on the task without prior training or experience.

Limitations and Implications

While the current study provides a number of interesting findings, some caution is necessary regarding their generalisability due to a number of limiting factors. One of the limitations refers to the use of a laboratory experiment that may compromise external validity of research. Another limitation relates to artificial generation of information that may not reflect the true nature of real business. The subjects chosen for the study were students and not real life decision makers, although the fact that they were mature graduates may mitigate the potential differences. Also, no incentives were offered to the subjects for their effort in the study. Consequently, subjects could have found the study tiring and unimportant and may not have tried as hard as possible. Most decisions in real business settings have significant consequences which contributes to motivate the decision makers.

Although limited, the findings of the current study may have some important implications for organisational KM strategies. They indicate that aggregation as a form of knowledge massaging is a very useful means of improving decision performance in organisations. Some researchers predict that the adoption of aggregation and other similar model-based tools in organisations will increase over time (Snowden, 2003). The main danger is seen in promoting an over-reliance on the tools at the cost of human judgment. One of the distinguishing characteristics of humans from other life forms is their ability to create means to hold knowledge and organise the world. Overdependence on tools can destroy these human capabilities by breeding in conformity. This is of major concern to KM that seeks to empower and not to enslave human judgment.

Filtering and storage approaches are also not without shortcomings. Filtering requires reliance on other people or tools for selection of relevant knowledge, and involves a substantial cost and time to realise. Uncontrolled storage, on the other hand, may produce an overload effect. These concerns call for devising alternative measures aimed at improving the depth of understanding as well as knowledge consumption in KM. Further research is necessary to address the issue.

4.6 Conclusions

The main objective of this chapter is to examine ways of building more effective knowledge repositories. It described an empirical test of the effect of knowledge massaging on people's ability to process and use stored knowledge to improve performance in a specific decision-making context. In summary, the findings of the study indicate that an aggregated knowledge form had a beneficial effect on both processing efficiency and decision accuracy of individual decision makers. These findings have important implications for practitioners, as they point to one proven way of enhancing performance in organisations by alleviating the detrimental effect of cognitive overload. However, further research is required that would look at alternative ways to improve performance through knowledge management.

References

AA (1998), *The Knowledge Management Practices Book*, Arthur Andersen.

Alavi, M. and Leidner, D.E. (2001), "Knowledge Management and Knowledge Management Systems: Conceptual Foundations and Research Issues", *MIS Quarterly*, 25(1), 107–136.

Amstrong, J.S. and Collopy, F. (1992), "Error Measures for Generalising about Forecasting Methods: Empirical Comparisons", *International Journal of Forecasting*, 8, 69–80.

Ashton, R.H. and Kramer, S.S. (1980), "Students as Surrogates in Behavioural Accounting Research: Some Evidence", *Journal of Accounting Research*, 18(1), 1–15.

Beach, L.R. and Mitchell, T.R. (1978), "A Contingency Model for the Selection of Decision Strategies", *Academy of Management Review*, July, 439–449.

Christensen-Szalanski, J.J.J. (1978), "Problem Solving Strategies: A Selection Mechanism, Some Implications, and Some Data", *Organisational Behaviour and Human Performance*, 22, 307–323.

Fayyad, U. and Uthurusamy, R. (2002), "Evolving into Data Mining Solutions for Insight", *Communications of the ACM*, 45(8), 28–31.

Finnegan, P. and Sammon, D. (2002), "Fundamentals of Implementing Data Warehousing in Organisations", in Barnes, S. (ed.), *Knowledge Management Systems: Theory and Practice*, Thomson Learning, London, pp. 195–209.

Hahn, J. and Subramani, M.R. (2000), "A Framework of Knowledge Management Systems: Issues and Challenges for Theory and Practice", in *Proceedings of the International Conference on Information Systems, ICIS'2000*, Brisbane, Australia, pp. 302–312.

Handzic, M. (1997), "Decision Performance as a Function of Information Availability: An Examination of Executive Information Systems", in *Proceedings of the 2nd New South Wales Symposium on Information Technology and Information Systems*, Sydney: UNSW.

Handzic, M. and Bewsell, G. (2003), "Corporate Memories: Tombs or Wellsprings of Knowledge", in *Proceedings of the Information Resources Management Association International Conference (IRMA 2003)*, Philadelphia, May 18–21, pp. 171–173.

Handzic, M. and Parkin, P. (2000), "Knowledge Management Technology: Examination of Information Diverse Repositories", *South African Computer Journal*, 26, 125–131.

Jennex, M. and Olfman, L. (2003), "Organisational Memory", chapter 11 in Holsapple, C.W. (ed.), *Handbook on Knowledge Management*, Vol. 1, Springer, Berlin, pp. 207–234.

Liebowitz, J. (2000), *Building Organisational Intelligence*, CRC Press, Boca Raton, Florida.

O'Leary, D.E. (2003), "Technologies for Knowledge Storage and Assimulation", chapter 34 in Holsapple, C.W. (ed.), *Handbook on Knowledge Management*, Vol. 2, Springer, Berlin, pp. 29–46.

Payne, J.W. (1982), "Contingent Decision Behaviour", *Psychological Bulletin*, 92(2), 382–402.

Remus, W. (1996), "Will Behavioural Research on Managerial Decision-Making Generalise to Managers?", *Managerial and Decision Economics*, 17, 93–101.

Schroder, H.M., Driver, M.J. and Streufert, S. (1967), *Human Information Processing*, Holt, Rinehart and Winston.

Snowden, D. (2003), "Innovation as an Objectve of Knowledge Management. Part I: The Landscape of Management", *Knowledge Management Research & Practice*, 1(2), 113–119.

Standards Australia (2003), *AS5037(Int)-2003, Interim Australian Standard, Knowledge Management*, Standards Australia International Limited, Sydney.

Wexler, M.N. (2001), "The Who, What and Why of Knowledge Mapping", *Journal of Knowledge Management*, 5(3), 249–263.

Whitecotton, S.M. (1996), "The Effects of Experience and a Decision Aid on the Slope, Scatter, and Bias of Earnings Forecasts", *Organisational Behaviour and Human Decision Processes*, 66(1), 111–121.

Wood, R.E. (1986), "Task Complexity: Definition of the Construct", *Organisational Behaviour and Human Decision Processes*, 37(1), 60–82.

CHAPTER 5

Knowledge Maps:

Locating and Acquiring Expert Advice

Without geography, you are nowhere.
— Jimmy Buffet

This chapter focuses on knowledge mapping technology. First, it examines the concept and types of knowledge maps. Then it reports the development effort and results of an empirical examination of the usefulness of a competency map in locating and acquiring expert knowledge to support decision-making. Results indicate that the expert competency map was quite useful in enhancing user's knowledge of the decision task and led to improved decision performance. Subjects tended to perform significantly better with the map irrespective of expert group, but needed less time to do the task with a group of similar experts.

5.1 Introduction

According to some analysts, the capacity of digital storage in the last decade has increased worldwide at twice the rate predicted for the growth of computing power (Fayyad and Uthurusamy, 2002). The gap between the two trends represent an interesting pattern in the state of technological evolution. Our ability to capture and store data has by far outpaced our ability to process and utilise it. The proliferation of knowledge artefacts in organisational stores creates an overload that is threatening to inhibit the efficient functioning of these organisations. As more artefacts are added to an organisational store, it becomes clear that there need to be some sort of mechanism to help organise and search for useful knowledge from these stores. Otherwise it may remain invisible and unused. This poses a major challenge for knowledge management (KM).

Some authors point to "knowledge mapping" as a feasible KM method to coordinate, simplify, highlight and navigate through complex webs of knowledge possessed by institutions (Wexler, 2001). Knowledge maps or k-maps point to knowledge but they do not contain it. They are guides, not repositories (Davenport and Prusak, 1998). One of the main purposes of k-maps is to locate important knowledge in an organisation and show users where to find it (Kim et al., 2003). Effective k-maps should point not only to people but to documents and databases as well. K-maps should also locate actionable information, identify domain experts, and facilitate organisation-wide learning (Eppler, 2003). They should also trace the acquisition and loss of knowledge, as well as map knowledge flows throughout the organisation (Grey, 1999).

Knowledge mapping can offer many benefits including economic, cultural, structural and knowledge returns (Wexler, 2001). Indeed, empirical findings indicate that knowledge mapping has been successfully used in education to facilitate students' learning (Chung et al., 1999). Knowledge mapping tools have also been used in the medical field (Miller, 1999) and aerospace industry (Despres and Chauvel, 1999, Gordon, 2000). Despite its many possible beneficial applications in industry, a recent survey shows that knowledge mapping is a relatively rarely used knowledge management method in business organisations (Stanford, 2001).

The purpose of this chapter is to analyse how knowledge mapping can be used to facilitate the visibility of and access to organisational knowledge resources required by its employees. In addition, results of an empirical study will be presented to illustrate the level of use and benefits achievable from a specific competency map application in a decision-making task.

5.2 Understanding Knowledge Maps

A review of the literature reveals a variety of definitions and categories of knowledge maps proposed and used by industry and academia. Most definitions circle around the idea of tools or processes that help users navigate the silos of artefacts that reside in an organisation, while determining meaningful relationships between knowledge domains (Grey, 1999; Speel et al., 1999; Wexler, 2001). For the purpose of this paper, knowledge map or k-map is understood as the visual display of knowledge and relationships using text, stories, graphics, models or numbers (Eppler, 2003; Vail, 1999a,b).

K-map examples provided by Eppler (2003) include knowledge application, knowledge structure, knowledge source, knowledge asset and knowledge development maps. Wexler (2001) identifies concept, competency, strategy, causal and cognitive maps. Plumley (2003) suggests that knowledge maps can be procedural, concept, competency and social network maps. A more abstract set of categories focusing primarily on cognitive maps is used by Huff (1990). The analysis of similarities and differences among various types of maps mentioned in the KM literature led us to the following three-class categorisation: concept, competency and process based k-maps.

Concept Based k-maps

The group of concept-based k-maps or taxonomies includes conceptual k-maps (Plumley, 2003) and knowledge structure maps (Eppler, 2003).

Both these maps provide a framework for capturing and organising domain knowledge of an organisation around topical areas. They represent a method of structuring and classifying content in an hierarchical manner. Concept based maps also allow for internal experts' knowledge to be made explicit in a visual, graphical representation that can be easily understood and shared. Mind maps (Wexler, 2001) as special forms of concept or cognitive maps provide further ability to express and organise a person's thoughts about a given topic.

Concept maps improve both the visibility and usability of organisational knowledge. The visibility is typically enhanced by the structure of the concept maps and the use of the visual symbols. The visual symbols can be quickly and easily recognised, while the minimum use of text makes it easy to scan for a particular word or phrase. In short, visual representation allows for development of a more holistic understanding of the domain that words alone cannot convey. Concept maps also improve the usability of knowledge as they organise knowledge artefacts around topics rather than functions. Thus, they provide the ability to cross functional boundaries.

Competency Based k-maps

Competency based k-maps cover a group of similar maps including competency k-maps (Plumley, 2003), knowledge source and knowledge assets maps (Eppler, 2003). These maps provide an overview of expertise that resides in the organisation along with the identification of entities that possess such expertise. They act as "yellow pages" or directories which enable people to find needed expertise; visually qualify the existing stock of knowledge of an individual, team or whole organisation; and document the skills, positions and career paths. Essentially, they are simple graphic balance sheets of a company's intellectual capital (Eppler, 2003).

One of the major benefits of competency based k-maps is that they make the human capital of the organisation highly visible. They can be used to profile a company's workforce across a number of criteria such as domains of expertise, proximity, seniority or regional distribution. They can also be used to depict the stages of development of a certain competence. This can be used to help project managers in assessing the available knowledge for projects, jobs as well as to make decisions about personal development and training (Eppler, 2003). Competency based maps can also greatly improve the usability of intellectual capital within the organisation. When converted into "yellow pages" and directories these maps can enable employees to easily find needed expertise within an organisation (Plumley, 2003).

Process Based k-maps

Process based k-maps are one of the most commonly used types of knowledge maps in organisations. They include procedural maps (Plumley, 2003) and knowledge application maps (Eppler, 2003). They are similar in that they both focus on work/business processes. Essentially, process based k-maps present business processes with related knowledge sources in auditing, consulting, research and product development. Any type of knowledge that drives these processes or results from execution of these processes can be mapped. For example, this could include tacit knowledge in people, explicit knowledge in databases, and customer of process knowledge (Plumley, 2003).

Process k-maps have several benefits. They help to improve the visibility of knowledge in organisations by showing which type of knowledge has to be applied at a certain process stage or in a specific business situation. These maps also provide pointers to locate that specific knowledge (Eppler, 2003). Process based k-maps help to improve the usability of knowledge in organisations by forcing participants to identify key knowledge areas that are critical to their business. The analysis of the knowledge map generates ideas for sharing and leveraging knowledge most suited to the organisation and the business context. Finally, the clear and simple visual format is easy to update and evolve over time (Plumley, 2003).

Research Objectives

While researchers have suggested that all three types of knowledge maps improve knowledge access and visibility, there has been very little empirical research to support such claims. One recent study found out that providing people with a concept map or ontology resulted in improved weather forecasting. Similarly, a study on the effectiveness of a procedural map in sales forecasting revealed less frequent use of heuristics and more accurate forecasting with such a map (Handzic, 2004). The current study builds on recent research by Handzic and Li (2003) and examines competency maps.

In view of the general lack of empirical evidence, the main objective of the study was to develop and examine the impact of a competency map on locating and accessing advisors' expertise, and its subsequent impact on users' performance in a decision-making task. It was hoped that the current research would provide a deeper insight into the potential and limitations of knowledge mapping technology in managing-knowledge for decision making purposes.

5.3 Competency Map Description

A computer-based competency map was devised as a KM tool to facilitate decision-makers' access to and evaluation of the available expertise. Several features have been implemented in the simulation software to aid users in locating and accessing different advisors' opinions, and subsequently making their predictions as accurate as possible. These features were based on two concepts: regression analysis and graphical visualisation. In addition, a simple questionnaire was included in the simulation software, asking primarily about the tool usefulness.

One of the features involved line curves. Time series of sales events for twenty days was initially provided in order to guide the decision-making process. The series data were presented in the form of a line curve. With the line curve described above, the users had a reasonable amount of knowledge to make fairly accurate decisions. However, in a knowledge-based economy, "fairly good" is not enough. Therefore an extra K-map was provided in one software version to help users locate and access experts knowledgeable on the subject matter.

Since different advisors in our simulation had different opinions about the next day's sales, it was important to know their forecasting ability. To do so, the linear regression modeling technique was employed. A new graph was produced containing several components. The first was the three regression lines calculated from historic figures recorded in a repository. Only lines of best fit and no scatter graphs were presented. The second component in the graph was three dotted lines extended from the three regression lines. These dotted lines extended to both *x* and *y* axes. The value cut at the *x* axis refers to estimated values by the three advisers, while the value cut at the *y* axis refers to the best estimated values based on the advisors' past accuracy. The third component included sample correlation coefficients for all independent variables. These three components jointly provided users with a very good idea of how good different advisors were at sales forecasting task.

5.4 Empirical Test

Experiment Description

We tested the competency map developed in a simulated forecasting exercise. As part of the forecasting task, the participants were instructed to assume the Role of the Sales Manager for a fictitious Dream Cream dairy company. They were required to make a series of predictions of the expected product sales over a given period of thirty simulated days. The company was assumed to incur substantial costs from inaccurate forecasts, therefore the goal of the exercise was to minimise forecast errors and save cost.

Subjects performed the task with or without a competency map, so that any difference in performance due to the tool could be determined. In addition, subjects had available a group of similar or diverse advisors to ask for help. The first group was composed of three advisors with similarly moderate levels of forecasting expertise. The second group was composed of advisors with unequal forecasting expertise, one with very high and two with very low levels. The intention was to create varying degrees of uncertainty and complexity in the business environment in order to examine the potential contingent effect of a competency map upon the context.

Experimental research design was used for this investigation as it allowed us to have greater control and made possible drawing of stronger inferences about causal relationships among the variables examined. We carried out the experiment with sixty-eight student-subjects from the Business Intelligence Systems course at UNSW. These subjects participated in the exercise on a voluntary basis, and received no monetary incentives.

The effectiveness of the competency map was evaluated in terms of its users' accomplishment. To explore what the competency map users could actually accomplish with the tool, the total cost of errors incurred by each subject was calculated. It was obtained as a sum of absolute difference between subjects' forecasts and actual sales over a period of thirty trials (Makridakis, 1993), and expressed in dollar terms. In addition, the total time taken to complete the task was calculated for each subject to evaluate the efficiency effect of the map.

Results

Mean performance scores (total cost, total decision time) of four experimental groups are presented in Table 5.1. The collected data were further analysed statistically by a t-test. The analysis found some significant results at $p = 0.1$ or better.

Table 5.1 Summary results for total cost and decision time

Dependent Variable	Similar Without Map	Advisors With Map	Diverse Without Map	Advisors With Map
Cost (Std.Dev.)	$9,455.18 (2,332.71)	$8,160.18 (2,877.45)	$12,628.19 (7,544.68)	$9,321.53 (5,028.91)
Time (Std.Dev.)	12.38 min (4.72)	8.19 min (4.84)	10.75 min (4.52)	10.61 min (4.87)

With respect to the total cost incurred, the results of the analysis performed indicate significant differences in error scores between subjects in different k-map groups. Subjects with the k-map tended to make significantly smaller forecast errors than their counterparts without the k-map irrespective of the advisor group ($8,741 < $11,042). Smaller errors indicated better knowledge and greater improvement in the quality of actual forecasts over naive forecasts.

With respect to the total decision time spent, the results of the analysis indicated different effects of k-map in different advisor groups. Subjects with the k-map tended to take a shorter decision time than their counterparts without the k-map only in a similar advisor group (8.2 min vs. 12.4 min). Shorter time indicated faster knowledge acquisition in addition to greater improvement in the quality of actual forecasts. However, the availability of the k-map made no significant difference in the decision time spent by subjects with diverse advisor group (10.6 min vs. 10.7 min).

Effectiveness Impacts

It was predicted that the use of a competency k-map such as the regression graph applied in the experiment above would improve the ability of decision makers to locate and acquire experts' opinions and increase the performance of a decision task.

Table 5.1 supports the predicted hypothesis in two ways. Firstly, the average sales cost of subjects working on the simulation with a k-map tool is much less than those working without such a tool: by 13.70% for the equally competent advisors and 26.18% for the unequally competent advisors. The effects are quite significant when taking into account that the k-map tool was quite simple. Another important fact that can be observed from these figures is that the positive effect of a k-map increases with the increased diversity in the advisor set (26.18% > 13.70%).

An additional observation from Table 5.1 is the much smaller standard deviation of total sales cost for k-map subjects with diverse set of advisors. The smaller standard deviation value means that most subjects consistently out-perform those who worked without the aid of the k-map. It implies that k-maps help to increase both performance accuracy and consistency of users, the latter is particularly evident in a more complex diverse advisor situation that is hard for users to deal with.

Similar
Quality

Diverse
Quality

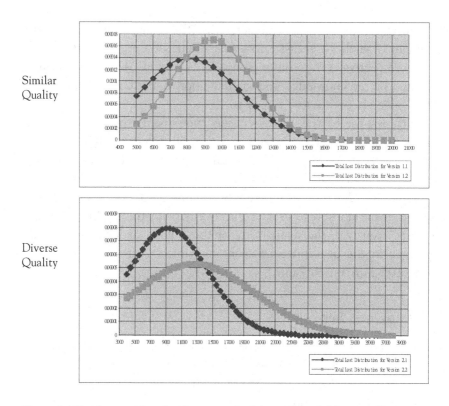

Figure 5.1 Total cost with and without map for (a) equally and (b) unequally competent advisors

Frequency distribution graphs presented in Figure 5.1 provide further support for the above analysis. The graphs reveal that more subjects with the map showed improved performance irrespective of the advisor set.

Efficiency Impacts

As stated earlier, the time consumed to make decisions is also an important factor when considering the effectiveness of a k-map. It is predicted that with the aid of a tool, the time required to locate and acquire needed knowledge should be less than the time required without the tool. The correctness of this hypothesis can be justified by Table 5.1.

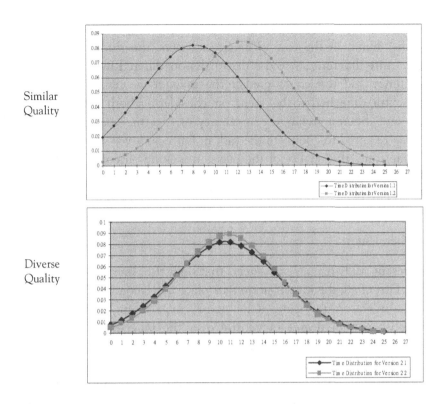

Figure 5.2 Total time with and without map for (a) equally and (b) unequally competent advisors

Similar to the case for sales cost, the average time required to finish the task was 33.89% and 1.36% less for subjects who worked with the simulation accompanied by k-map, with similar and diverse advisor sets, respectively. The difference is significant for the similar advisor set, but not for the diverse one.

These results are further supported by the frequency distribution graphs presented in Figure 5.2. These graphs show that more subjects required less time to complete the task for the similar advisor set only.

The explanation for this phenomenon may lie in the different level of effort required to interpret the mixed information provided by the regression based k-map tool in different cases. In the case of similar advisors, the three sales figures suggested by the set were usually quite close to one another. This enabled subjects to make quick decisions. On the other hand, in the case of diverse advisors, the three values were usually quite different since the three advisors differed in their level of competency and tended to predict the sales of ice-cream differently. Thus, extra time had to be spent on considering both the suggested values and different relative competency of the three advisors. While the time required to complete the task in both cases was comparable, at the same time, the quality of the decision making outcome was higher with k-map use. Thus, k-map still improved the overall process of decision-making.

Other Issues

The present study has several aspects that limit the generalisability of its results. First of all, the investigation took place in a laboratory experiment. The main reason for using a laboratory experiment design was to accomplish a high degree of control over the independent variables. High control maximises the internal validity of the research and enables drawing of stronger inferences about causal relationships (Huck et al., 1974; Judd et al., 1991). However, it may compromise external validity. Data were artificially generated from statistical processes. This was done to allow internal control of different advisor characteristics, such as their predictive ability of the variable of interest, but makes it difficult to generalise to more realistic settings. Finally, the subjects in the study were students. Their lack of real-life experience on decision making tasks implies that different strategies may be chosen when comparing with decision makers in industry domains. They also had to learn how the system works. Despite making a serious effort to ensure its ease of use, it is possible that five practice trials were not sufficient to completely familiarise subjects with the system and allow optimal performance.

Due to the above limitations, the present study should be considered exploratory and its conclusions tentative. Replications using real experts in their domain as subjects in applied settings are needed to gain deeper insight into people's knowledge acquisition process. Additional insight may also be obtained by using real world data. Several further extensions to the current research are also possible. This study has examined the tool effectiveness in noisy but stable data patterns. In addition, the current study has investigated only the extreme situations when all available advisors were either very similar or very different. Further studies should incorporate less extreme situations. In particular, one may examine whether moderate contrasts would dilute the effect of a k-map on performance.

With respect to tool presentation, the present study used only two-dimensional (regression line) graphs for displaying different advisor competencies. Future research may investigate whether multi-dimensional graphs would facilitate faster and better understanding of the situation and possibly further help to improve performance. A preliminary study conducted by Stephens and Handzic (2004) indicates that a virtual reality tool may be useful for visualising social networks and identifying paths to right people. Finally, decision performance analysis was employed as a primary method to evaluate the effectiveness of a k-map. Although this method is unobtrusive and robust, other techniques, such as verbal protocols or eye fixation movement, may provide deeper insight into the users' knowledge acquisition processes. The results may also be utilised to further validate inferences made in this study.

5.5 Conclusions

The study showed the ability of a competency k-map to improve people's ability to locate and acquire expert knowledge and enhance performance of a forecasting task. From our research findings one may conclude that using k-maps can effectively enhance decision makers' working knowledge and performance while at the same time reduce the time required to finish the task. However, the study is not without limitations. Different technologies will have advantages and disadvantages under different situations, and thus careful consideration of different combinations of technologies is necessary. Further empirical research is recommended that would address some of these issues.

References

Andreassen, P.B. (1991), *Causal Prediction versus Extrapolation: Effects on Information Source on Judgmental Forecasting Accuracy*, working paper, MIT.

Ashton, R.H. and Kramer, S.S. (1980), "Students as Surrogates in Behavioural Accounting Research: Some Evidence", *J. Accounting Research*, 18(1), 1–15.

Chung, G., Osmundson, E., Herl, H. and Klein, D. (1999), "Knowledge Mapping in the Classroom, A Tool for Examining the Development of a Student's Conceptual Understanding", *CSE Technical Report 507*, UNSW, August.

Dalrymple, D.J. (1987), "Sales Forecasting Practices: Results from a United States Survey", *International Journal of Forecasting*, 3, 379–391.

Davenport, T.H. and Prusak, L. (1998), *Working Knowledge: How Organisations Manage What They Know*, Harvard Business School Press, Boston.

Depres, C. and Chauvel, D. (1999), "Knowledge Management(s)", *Journal of Knowledge Management*, 3(2), 110–120.

Eppler, M. (2003), "Making Knowledge Visible through Knowledge Maps: Concepts, Elements, Cases", in Holsapple, C.W. (ed.), *Handbook on Knowledge Management*, Vol. 1, Springer-Verlag, Berlin, pp. 189–205.

Fayyad, U. and Uthurusamy, R. (2002), "Evolving into Data Mining Solutions for Insight", *Communications of the ACM*, 45(8), 28–31.

Gordon, J. (2000), "Creating Knowledge Maps by Exploiting Dependent Relationships", *Knowledge Based Systems*, 13, 71–79.

Grey, D. (1999), "Knowledge Mapping: A Practical overview", URL: http://www.smithweaversmith.com/knowledg2.htm

Handzic, M. (2004), "Decision Support through Knowledge Management: Empirical test of Two Strategies", in *Proceedings of DSS' 2004*, Prato, Italy, July 1–3.

Handzic, M. and Li, W. (2003), "Discovering Predictive Quality of Knowledge Artefacts in Organisational Repositories", in *Proceedings of the Australian Conference for Knowledge Management and Intelligent Decision Support (ACKMIDS 2002)*, Australian Scholarly Publishing, Melbourne, pp. 133–144.

Handzic, M., Aurum, A., Lam, B. and Oliver, G. (2002a), "A Comparative Study of Two Knowledge Discovery Tools: Barchart versus Scatterplot", in

Proceedings of the International Conference on Data Mining (DM'2002), Bologna, September.

Handzic, M., Aurum, A., Oliver, G. and Logenthiran, G. (2002b), "An Empirical Study of a Knowledge Discovery Tool", in *Proceedings of the European Conference on Knowledge Management (ECKM'2002)*, Dublin, September.

Handzic, M. (2003), "Empowering Society through Knowledge Records", in Wimmer, M.A. (ed.), in *Proceedings of IFIP International Working Conference Knowledge Management in Electronic Government (KMGov 2003)*, Rhodes, May 26–28, pp. 262–267.

Handzic, M. and Aurum, A. (2001), "Knowledge Discovery: Some Empirical Evidence and Directions for Future Research", in *Proceedings of the 5th International Conference on Wirtschafts Informatics (WI'2001)*, September 19–21, Augsburg, Germany.

Harvey, N., Bolger, F. and McClelland, A. (1994), "On the Nature of Expectations", *British Journal of Psychology*, 85, 203–229.

Huck, S.W., Cormier, W.H. and Bounds, W.G., Jr. (1974), *Reading Statistics and Research*, Harper and Row, London.

Huff, A. (ed.) (1990), *Mapping Strategic Thought*, Wiley, New York.

Judd, C.M., Smith, E.R. and Kidder, L.H. (1991), *Research Methods in Social Relations*, 6th ed., Harcourt Brace Jovanovich College Publishers.

Kim, S., Suh, E. and Hwang, H. (2003), "Building the Knowledge Map: An Industrial Case Study", *Journal of Knowledge Management*, 7(2), 34–45.

Makridakis, S. (1993), "Accuracy Measures: Theoretical and Practical Concerns", *International Journal of Forecasting*, 9, 527–529.

Offsey, S. (1997), "Knowledge Management: Linking People to Knowledge for Botton Line Results", *Journal of Knowledge Management*, 1(2), December.

Plumley, D. (2003), "Process-based Knowledge Mapping: A Practical Approach to Prioritising Knowledge in Terms of its Relevance to a Business or KM Objective", *Knowledge Management Magazine*, March 03. http://www.destinationkm.com/articles

Remus, W. (1996), "Will Behavioural Research on Managerial Decision Making Generalise to Managers?", *Managerial and Decision Economics*, 17, 93–101.

Sanders, N. and Manrodt, K. (1994), "Forecasting Practices in US Corporations: Survey Results", *Interfaces*, 24, 92–100.

Speel, P.H., Shadbolt, N., deVries, W., vanDam, P.H. and O'Hara, K. (1999), "Knowledge Mapping for Industrial Purposes", in *Proceedings of the 12th Workshop on Knowledge Acquisition (KAW'99)*, Alberta, 16–21 October. http://sern.ucalgary.ca/KSI/KAW/KAW99/papers/Speel1

Stanford, X, (2001), "Who's Mapping", *Knowmap*, 1(4).

Stephens, G. and Handzic, M. (2004), "Knowledge Discovery through Visualising Using Virtual Reality", in *Proceedings of the 37th Annual Hawaii International Conference on System Sciences – HICSS37* (CD/ROM), January 5–8, 2004, Computer Society Press.

Vail, E. (1999a), "Mapping Organisational Knowledge", *Knowledge Management Review*, 8, 10–15.

Vail, E. (1999b), "Knowledge Mapping: Getting Started with Knowledge Management", *Information Systems Management*, 16(4), 16–23.

Wexler, M. (2001), "The Who, What, Why of Knowledge Mapping", *Journal of Knowledge Management*, 5(3), 249–263.

Whitecotton, S.M. (1996), "The Effects of Experience and a Decision Aid on the Slope, Scatter, and Bias of Earnings Forecasts", *Organisational Behaviour and Human Decision Processes*, 66(1), 111–121.

CHAPTER 6

Knowledge Discovery Tools:

Application in Associations Analysis

The real voyage of discovery consists not in seeking new lands,
but in seeing with new eyes.
— Marcel Proust

This chapter focuses on tools and technologies for knowledge discovery from data. First, it examines the process, approaches and techniques of knowledge discovery. Then it reports results of an empirical examination into the effectiveness of two knowledge discovery tools (barchart and scatterplot) in the context of a sales forecasting task. The main results of the study indicate that both tools were reasonably suitable for well conveying associations among task variables and offering improvements in prediction accuracy when compared to a naive predictor. In addition, findings show that a scatterplot was significantly more beneficial than a barchart in enhancing forecasters' knowledge and performance of the task. This superiority can be potentially explained in terms of the favorable aspects of Cartesian graphs and the greater concentration required for using the tool.

6.1 Introduction

We have already established the fact that we live in a world of rapid change. Experts predict that the turbulence brought about by mega trends of globalisation, digitalisation and transformation will continue to increase over the next few decades, the complexity of business will be even higher, and uncertainty worse than ever (Raich, 2000, Tiwana, 2001). Ongoing economic, technical and social transformations are placing enormous pressure on organisations to better manage their knowledge in order to successfully compete or even survive in the new-age economy (Drucker, 1993; Stewart, 1997).

In Chapter 1, knowledge management (KM) is presented as an emergent response to the need to accelerate both the creation and application of knowledge for successful competitive advantage. Various disciplines are contributing to the academic literature on the subject (Devlin, 1999; Earl, 2001). The common task of all concerned is to determine best ways to cultivate, nurture and exploit knowledge at both the individual and collective levels. We have argued that technology may play an important role in supporting KM effort. The focus on this chapter is on tools for knowledge discovery.

The growing amount of data being generated by electronic and traditional business transactions represents a potentially valuable source of new knowledge for organisations. A central issue for these organisations is the discovery of potentially useful patterns implicit in their electronically recorded transactions with their customers, and their trading partners. Once discovered, this new knowledge can then be utilised to support organisational decision-making (Blanning, 2000). Graph- and text-based web content is another vast source of knowledge, offering opportunities for Web-mining (Smyth et al., 2002).

The purpose of this study is to address the issue of knowledge discovery from organisational data in the context of product sales forecasting. Considering that decision-makers often must rely on enterprise systems for their work activities, it is critical that they better understand the knowledge available in these systems. The proposition made here is that an appropriate knowledge discovery tool may help such organisational members to improve their task performance by enhancing their understanding of the patterns implicit in the stored knowledge artifacts. The main objective of this chapter is to examine whether and how different knowledge discovery tools may help decision-makers to better recognise associations among multiple events, and whether and how this impacts their decision performance.

6.2 Knowledge Discovery from Data

Process

Knowledge discovery (KD) is the nontrivial process of identifying valid, novel, potentially useful and ultimately understandable patterns in data (Fayyad et al., 1996). The twin goals of knowledge discovery are description and prediction. Description is concerned with identifying patterns for the purpose of presentation to users in an understandable form. Prediction is concerned with forecasting future values of some variables. If discovered knowledge is going to be used for judgment and decision-making, then comprehensibility of the extracted pattern is considered to be crucial (Adamson and Venerable, 1998).

The term knowledge discovery is often used interchangeably with data mining. The view adopted here is that KD refers to the overall process of discovering useful knowledge from data, while data mining refers to a particular step in this process. Fayyad et al. (1996) describe KD as an explorative and iterative process over one or more of the following steps: defining the objectives, data preparation, data transformation, data mining, analysis of results, and assimilation of knowledge. Objectives drive the entire process. They are the basis on which the process is established and final results measured and evaluated. Data preparation involves the selection of data subset and its preprocessing in terms of resolving the problems of missing data and noise. Data transformation translates data into the format required by the mining algorithm. The data mining step involves the choice and application of the appropriate algorithm for searching patterns in data. Analysis comprises interpretation and evaluation of the mining output obtained.

Finally, assimilation consolidates the discovered knowledge and integrates the insights from the KD process into existing knowledge. The usefulness and the relevance of the discovered patterns are typically measured in terms of 'interestingness' (Hilderman and Hamiton, 1999).

Approaches and Technologies

Knowledge discovery approaches can be classified by the function they perform into four major categories: classification, association, sequence and cluster (Marakas, 1999). Classification seeks the rule that defines whether an item or event belongs to a particular class or set. Association analysis searches for a rule that correlates one set of events or items with another set of events or items. Sequencing is used to relate events in time. Through this analysis various hidden trends can be discovered that are often predictive of future trends. Clustering groups a set of objects together by virtue of their similarity or proximity to each other.

Technologies associated with these approaches are numerous (Lee and Siau, 2001). They cover statistics, mathematics, database technology, artificial intelligence, economic and decision theory, and visualisation. Statistics can help to detect noise and trends, and traditional modeling techniques such as regression analysis are appropriate for building linear predictive models. Multidimensional and relational analytical processing technologies help analysis across multiple dimensions and in drilling down data sets. Neural networks deal with non-linear relationships and have the ability to learn. Other learning algorithms such as genetic algorithms and fuzzy logic can extract patterns and detect trends within highly complex and imprecise sets. Decision trees refer to simple mathematical tools for problem structuring. This technology generates tree-shaped structures that assist in the classification of data. Finally, visualisation enables clearer representation of the found patterns using colors, shapes, sound and virtual reality.

According to Beccera-Fernandez et al. (2004), the many KD techniques fall under one of three basic categories: symbolic; connectionist and statistical. Symbolic techniques use inductive algorithms to build decision trees. Connectionist techniques consist of several processing elements called neurons to perform the tasks. The result is a neural network. Statistical methods cover linear regression, k-means, basket analysis, discriminant analysis and logistic analysis. These KD systems have made a significant contribution in scientific fields for years, and have become increasingly popular in business applications over the last decade or so. Typical applications of KD include customer, product and market analysis in retail and banking, fraud detection in government, actuarial modeling in insurance, patient and therapy analysis in health care, risk and portfolio analysis in asset management (Marakas, 1999).

The suggested benefits range from being better informed about a customer's needs, to higher efficiency, productivity, accuracy in prediction, and better decision-making. Our own empirical studies reveal that neural networks indeed were helpful in supporting loan officers' application decisions (Handzic et al., 2003). Statistics assisted in discovering predictive quality of knowledge artifacts in organisational repositories (Handzic and Li, 2003) and forecasting sales trends (Handzic et al., 2002a). Finally, visualisation using virtual reality was useful in social network analysis (Stephens and Handzic, 2004). In the next section we report one empirical study (Handzic et al., 2002b) conducted as part of the on-going research program in knowledge management at UNSW.

6.3 Empirical Study

Research Objectives

The main focus of this study is on association analysis using visualisation and statistics. Such analysis can uncover highly useful and informative relational patterns among sets of data that can be used to develop predictive models of behavior in a wide variety of knowledge domains. Given that most business forecasting is conducted judgmentally (Dalrymple, 1987; Sanders and Manrodt, 1994) forecasters who have better understanding of external causal influences would have a potential advantage in that they can take into account the effect of these influences to make better judgments. Most empirical findings from unaided knowledge discovery studies cast doubts regarding the ability of people to correctly discover causal influences (Andreassen, 1991; Harvey et al., 1994; Handzic and Aurum, 2001). Contingent factors affect this ability. They include the amount, predictive power, regularity and frequency of data (Goodwin and Fildes, 1999).

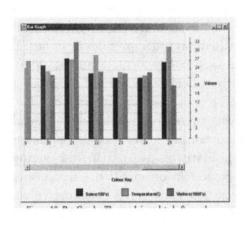   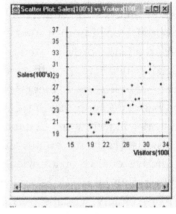

(a) BarChart   (b) ScatterPlot

Figure 6.1 Knowledge discovery tools

The integrated KM framework (Handzic, 2001, 2003) suggests that a computer based Knowledge Data Discovery (KDD) tool may facilitate data analysis and presentation, and thus help people better discover potentially useful associations among recorded events or items. The following study based on Handzic et al. (2002b) empirically tests this proposition. In particular, the study examines the comparative effectiveness of two popular KDD tools (barchart and scatterplot) in helping people to discover associative patterns among related contextual and sales data recorded in electronic databases, and to translate this knowledge into improved product sales forecasts.

Research Methodology

The experimental task in the current study was a simulated forecasting activity in which participants made estimates of daily sales of fresh ice cream. Participants assumed the role of Manager of a fictitious firm that sold ice cream products in the beach suburb of Bondi in Sydney. The manager made daily sales forecasts as a part of the production planning process. The company incurred equally costly losses if production was set too high (due to spoilage of unsold product) or too low (due to loss of market to competition). The manager's goal was to minimise the company's total loss, by minimising forecast errors.

During forecast preparation, the manager could consult the company's database containing a series of data on past sales. The database also contained the history and regular forecasting of local temperature and visitor data obtained from the Meteorology Bureau and Tourist Board respectively. Temperature and visitor data was used to simulate the effects of continuous contextual factors on the sales time series. All participants received the same sales, temperature and visitors data. In addition, one group of participants was provided with a barchart, while the other half received a scatterplot tool to aid their knowledge extraction from data. It was assumed that by using the KDD tool, a participant would be able to better discover valid associations between past sales and two contextual variables, and use this knowledge to more accurately predict future sales of ice-cream based on weather and tourist forecasts.

The participants could inspect the information presented by their respective KDD tool as long as they wished, and when satisfied they made their forecast for the day by typing in their estimated number of sales units. They then initiated the screen for the next forecast. Participants repeated the task for thirty consecutive simulated days. Prior to commencing the real task, participants were allowed a practice of five trial forecasts. Throughout the experiment instructions were provided to inform participants of the task scenario and of requirements. Performance feedback was provided to enable participants to analyze their earlier performance and to adjust their future strategies.

Experimental Design and Variables

A laboratory experiment with random assignment to treatment groups was used, as it allowed greater experimental control and made possible drawing of stronger inferences about causal relationships between variables. The only independent variable was the *KDD tool* (barchart or scatterplot).

Experimental data were artificially generated for control purposes. Sales figures were produced by drawing random values from a normal distribution with a mean of 25 and a standard deviation of 5 (in hundred units). Contextual data were created by adding error terms to sales series data. Error terms were produced by drawing random values from normal distributions each having a mean of 0 and a standard deviation of 3.75. This standard deviation provided a theoretical correlation coefficient $r = 0.80$ between contextual and sales variables.

Task performance was evaluated in terms of forecast accuracy operationalised by Mean Absolute Error (MAE). It was calculated as an average absolute difference between participants' forecast and actual sales over a period of thirty trials (Marakas, 1999). For comparison purposes, the corresponding errors of naive and optimal strategies were calculated. A naive strategy simply determines the next day's sales as equal to the current day's sales. Such a strategy makes no use of any contextual knowledge and typically produces poor performance. This measure was used to assess improvement in the quality of forecasts due to knowledge extracted.

In addition, optimal forecast errors were calculated to assess how much of the maximum hidden knowledge was extracted and used by the participants. Optimal strategies were modeled using stepwise regressions with two contextual variables (temperature and visitors) as independent variables, and sales data as the dependent variable. The optimal response integrated both variables into a single response using regression weights and produced the best possible performance given the available patterns in data.

Participants and Procedure

The participants were forty-one graduate students from the University of New South Wales, Australia. They participated in the experiment on a voluntary basis, and received no monetary incentives. Some previous studies indicated that postgraduate students were appropriate participants for this type of research (Ashton and Kramer, 1980; Remus, 1996; Whitecotton, 1996).

The experimental session was conducted in a microcomputer laboratory. On arrival, participants were assigned randomly to one of the two treatment groups, by choosing a microcomputer from a number of units set for the experiment. Before commencing the task, participants were briefed about the purpose of the experiment and read case study descriptions incorporated in the research instrument. They then performed the task. The session lasted about one hour.

Results

Mean performance scores (MAE) of experimental participants by KDD tool groups are presented graphically in Figure 6.2. Mean values of naive and optimal forecast errors are also presented for comparison purposes. The collected data were further analysed statistically by t-test. The analysis found some significant results at $p < 0.05$.

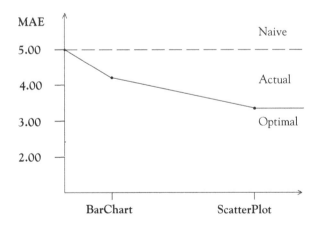

Figure 6.2 Subjects' performance (MAE) by KDD tool

Firstly, error scores of all actual participants were lower than those of their notional naive counterparts. Actual participants tended to make smaller than naive forecast errors both in barchart (4.33 < 4.98) and with scatterplot (3.32 < 4.98) groups. These results indicate real improvement in performance due to knowledge extracted. The analysis found that error scores dropped on average by 13% and 34% in barchart and scatterplot groups, respectively.

Secondly, the results of the analysis performed indicate significant differences in error scores between participants in the two KDD tools groups. Participants in scatterplot condition tended to make significantly smaller forecast errors than their counterparts in the barchart group (3.32 < 4.33). Smaller errors indicated better knowledge extraction and greater improvement in the quality of actual forecasts over naive forecasts.

Thirdly, Figure 6.2 shows that participants tended to make greater than optimal errors in both the barchart (4.33 > 2.34) and the scatterplot (3.32 > 2.34) KDD tool groups. Further analysis showed that participants discovered and extracted on average 27% of the hidden knowledge in barchart, and 67% in scatterplot KDD tool groups.

6.4 Lessons Learned

Main Findings

In summary, both KDD tools (barchart and scatterplot) helped people reasonably well at discovering and utilising valid knowledge about associative patterns in data, and in improving their subsequent forecasting performance. Nevertheless, gains were less than theoretically possible given the objective relationships among data provided. In addition, participants tended to make significantly better forecasts when provided with scatterplot than barchart.

The fact that the participants made better than naive forecasts irrespective of the tool used indicates that both tools were able to convey to users the associations between the values of scale and temperature, and also between sales and visitors reasonably well. Users appeared to interpret that there was a high degree of association between these task variables. This interpretation of the relationship allowed reasonably correct predictions and improvement over naive forecasts. In real terms, error scores dropped by 13% and 34% in barchart and scatterplot groups, respectively. It is possible that a graphical form of presentation by the tools facilitated discovery of associations and enabled the participants to better judge the right direction and the magnitude of future changes in sales. These findings are consistent with the general notion that it is the ability to perceive relations among the elements of graphs that make them so powerful tools (Spence, 1990). This is also consistent with (Levy et al., 1996) empirical findings that graphical presentation enhances the forecast accuracy of novices.

Further analysis revealed that in terms of the accuracy of the predictions made and the consistency of predicted values, those made using a scatterplot appeared to be superior to those predictions deriving from a barchart. In most cases the direction of the error for both tools were similar, but the magnitude of the absolute error made by those using barchart were usually greater. This suggests that both types of graphs convey the same information, only at different levels of effectiveness. Considering the fact that barchart is the most preferred type of graph that people will use to visualise patterns in order to understand the available information (Levy et al., 1996), this is an important finding.

One possible reason for the inferior performance found in this study resulting with the barchart found in this study could be the use of a pattern matching strategy. In pattern matching, which can be seen as a form of the representativeness heuristic, a single past case which will contain an element of noise, is used as the basis for the prediction, while general tendencies such as long-run time series trends are ignored. Hoch and Schkade (1996) found evidence of pattern matching in a judgmental time series forecasting task and suggested that pattern matching is a fairly good strategy in highly predicable environments, but is deficient when the environment contains high levels of noise.

In contrast, scatterplot has a number of properties from which their usefulness and superior effectiveness arise. Poulet (2000) argues that in explorative data analysis, a scatterplot is an ideal tool for examining two variables. Murdoch (2000) discusses scatterplot matrices as geometric techniques which reveal many different features of the associations between two variables. The favorable aspect of Cartesian graphs of two variables x and y, is that it allows values of x and y to be visually extracted by perceiving position along the scale (Cleveland and McGill, 1984). Perception of direction is what enables the connection between x and y to be made. Also, humans are able to imagine slopes and curves through the points on a scatterplot. An interesting finding from the questionnaire responses was that the users' perceived difficulty in processing the available information was higher with a scatterplot than with a barchart. This could be another possible factor for the superiority of the scatterplot, whose users were required to apply greater effort and concentration in order to understand the displayed information. This produced more effective results.

Finally, the overall results indicate room for further improvement. Participants were found to make greater forecast errors than optimal, irrespective of the KDD tool used. Greater than optimal errors indicate that the participants tended to uncover less knowledge from the available data than they possibly could with the help of their KDD tools. Further analysis revealed that on average they extracted and used 27% and 67% of the maximum knowledge in barchart and scatterplot conditions, respectively. This would suggest that perhaps the graphical displays given by the tool were not comprehensible to their full extent. Effectiveness of a visual tool assumes syntactic simplicity and easy interpretation of the output (Wong, 1999). Also, an observation of the signed prediction errors for each attempted prediction revealed a pattern of oscillating errors between over and under estimation. This could be an indication of user uncertainty regarding a predictor. It is debatable whether the scatterplot with the true regression line plotted through the data points would increase prediction accuracy, because the process of fitting data points in a graph into a particular model already takes place in the mind (Cleveland and McGill, 1984).

Other Issues

While the current study provides a number of interesting findings, some caution is necessary regarding their generalisability due to a number of limiting aspects. One of the limitations refers to the use of a laboratory experiment that may compromise external validity of research. Another limitation relates to artificial generation of data that may not reflect the true nature of real business. The participants chosen for the study were students and not real life forecasters. The fact that they were mature graduates may mitigate the potential differences. No monetary incentives were offered to the participants for their effort. Consequently, they might not have been motivated to try as hard as they could. Most decisions in real business settings have significant rewards. Further research is necessary that would address these limitations and extend the study to other participants and environmental conditions in order to ensure the generalisability of the present findings.

Although limited, the findings of the current study may have some important implications for research and practice of knowledge discovery. First, they suggest that visualisation and its application in knowledge discovery tools holds much promise for the future. They also suggest that the effective knowledge discovery systems in practice may need to integrate various different techniques and approaches rather than focus on a limited set of features. This should increase their usefulness in analysing and understanding large collections of data. In addition, findings suggest that sales and marketing personnel could potentially benefit from other knowledge management initiatives that would enhance their understanding of the existence and the form of relationships in data. These may include training in analytical and statistical reasoning, and encouraging culture of knowledge sharing (Nonaka, 1998; Nonaka and Takeuchi, 1995). Combining and integrating various knowledge management initiatives may create synergy effect and even higher levels of knowledge. According to (Davenport and Prusak, 1997) only by taking a holistic approach to managing knowledge, it is possible to realise the full power of information ecology. Future research may look at some of these issues.

6.5 Conclusions

The main objective of this study was to empirically examine the comparative effectiveness of two commonly used KDD tools, barchart and scatterplot, in a specific sales forecasting task context. The findings indicate that both tools were able to convey reasonably well associations among task variables hidden in data. As a result, participants achieved some performance improvement, however they fell short of what was possible to accomplish. The findings also indicate that scatterplot was more effective, although more complex, compared to barchart. Important implications of these findings for research and practice include the awareness of the future potential of visualisation in knowledge discovery and the recognition of the need to integrate various different techniques and approaches into the effective knowledge discovery system. Further research is recommended to address the current study limitations and ensure the generalisability of its findings.

References

Adamson, C. and Venerable, M. (1998), *Data Warehouse Design Solutions*. Wiley, New York.

Alavi, M. and Leidner, D.E. (2001), "Knowledge Management and Knowledge Management Systems: Conceptual Foundations and Research Issues", *MIS Quarterly*, 25(1), 107–136.

Andreassen, P.B. (1991), *Causal Prediction versus Extrapolation: Effects on Information Source on Judgmental Forecasting Accuracy*, working paper, MIT.

Ashton, R.H. and Kramer, S.S. (1980), "Students as Surrogates in Behavioral Accounting Research: Some Evidence", *Journal of Accounting Research*, 18(1), 1–15.

Becerra-Fernandez, I., Gonzales, A. and Sabherwal, R. (2004), *Knowledge Management: Challenges, Solutions, and Technologies*, Pearson Education, New Jersey.

Blanning, R.W. (2000), "Knowledge Management and Electronic Commerce", in *Position Papers on Future Directions in Decision Support, IFIP WK8.3 Working Conference on DSS*, Stockholm.

Cleveland, W.S. and McGill, R. (1984), "Graphical Perception: Theory, Experimentation and the Application to the Development of Graphical Models", *Journal of the American Statistical Association*, 79, 531–554.

Dalrymple, D.J. (1987), "Sales Forecasting Practices: Results from a United States Survey", *International Journal of Forecasting*, 3, 379–391.

Davenport, T.H. and Prusak, L. (1997), *Information Ecology*, Oxford University Press, Oxford.

Devlin, K. (1999), *Infosense: Turning Information into Knowledge*, W.H. Freeman, New York.

Drucker, P.F. (1993), *Post-Capitalist Society*, Harper Business, New York.

Earl, M. (2001), "Knowledge Management Strategies: Toward Taxonomy", *Journal of Management Information Systems*, 18(1), 215–233.

Fayyad, U., Piatetsky-Shapiro, G. and Smyth, P. (1996), "Knowledge Discovery and Data Mining: Towards a Unifying Framework", in *Proceedings of 2nd International Conference on Knowledge Discovery and Data Mining, KDD-96*, Oregon.

Goodwin, P. and Fildes, R. (1999), "Judgmental Forecasters of Time Series Affected by Special Events: Does Providing a Statistical Forecast Improve Accuracy?", *Journal of Behavioural Decision Making*, 12, 37–53.

Handzic, M. (2001), "Knowledge Management: A Research Framework", in *Proceedings of the European Conference on Knowledge Management*, Bled.

Handzic, M. (2003), "An Integrated Framework of Knowledge Management", *Journal of Information and Knowledge Management*, 2(3), September.

Handzic, M., Tjandrawibawa, F. and Yeo, J. (2003), "How Neural Networks Can Help Loan Officers to Make Better Informed Application Decisions", in *Proceedings of Informing Science and IT Education Conference (InSITE 2003)*, Pori, June 24–27, pp. 97–108.

Handzic, M. and Li, W. (2003), "Discovering Predictive Quality of Knowledge Artefacts in Organisational Repositories", in *Proceedings of the Australian Conference for Knowledge Management and Intelligent Decision Support (ACKMIDS 2002)*, Australian Scholarly Publishing, Melbourne, pp. 133–144.

Handzic, M., Aurum, A., Oliver, G. and Logenthiran, G. (2002a), "An Empirical Investigation of a Knowledge Discovery Tool", *European Conference on Knowledge Management (ECKM 2002)*, Dublin, September.

Handzic, M., Lam, B., Aurum, A. and Oliver, G. (2002b), "A Comparative Analysis of Two Knowledge Discovery Tool: Scatterplot versus Barchart", *International Conference on Data Mining (DM 2002)*, Bologna, September.

Handzic, M. and Aurum, A. (2001), "Knowledge Discovery: Some Empirical Evidence and Directions for Future Research", in *Proceedings of 5th*

International Conference on Wirtschafts Informatics (WI'2001), September 19–21, Augsburg, Germany.

Harvey, N., Bolger, F. and McClelland, A. (1994), "On the Nature of Expectations", *British Journal of Psychology*, 85, 203–229.

Hoch, S.J. and Schkade, D.A. (1996), "A Psychological Approach to Decision Support Systems", *Management Science*, 42, 51–64.

Lawrence, M., Edmundson, B. and O'Connor, M. (1985), "An Examination of Accuracy of Judgmental Extrapolation of Time Series", *International Journal of Forecasting*, 1, 25–35.

Lee, S.J. and Siau, K. (2001), "A Review of Data Mining Techniques", *Industrial Management & Data Systems*, 101(1), 41–46.

Levy, E., Zacks, J., Tversky, B. and Schiano, D., (1996), "Gratuitous Graphics? Putting Preferences in Perspective", *Proceedings of CHI'96*, Vancouver, ACM Press, pp. 42–49.

Makridakis, S. (1993), "Accuracy Measures: Theoretical and Practical Concerns", *International Journal of Forecasting*, 9, 527–529.

Marakas, G.M. (1999), *Decision Support Systems in the 21st Century*, Prentice Hall, New Jersey.

Murdoch, D.J. (2000), "Drawing a Scatterplot", *Chance*, 13(3), 53–55.

Nonaka, I. (1998), "The Knowledge-Creating Company", *Harvard Business Review on Knowledge Management*, HBS Press, Boston.

Nonaka, I. and Takeuchi, H. (1995), *The Knowledge Creating Company: How Japanese Companies Create the Dynamics of Innovation*, Oxford University Press, New York.

Poulet, F. (2000), "Comprehensibility in Data-Mining", *International Symposium on Data Mining and Statistics*, November 19–22, University of Augsburg, Germany.

Raich, M. (2000), *Managing in the Knowledge-Based Economy*. Raich Limited, Switzerland.

Remus, W. (1996), "Will Behavioral Research on Managerial Decision Making Generalise to Managers?", *Managerial and Decision Economics*, 17, 93–101.

Sanders, N. and Manrodt, K. (1994), "Forecasting Practices in US Corporations: Survey Results", *Interfaces*, 24, 92–100.

Smyth, P., Pregibon, D. and Christos, F. (2002), "Data-Driven Evolution of Data Mining Algorithms", *Communications of the ACM*, 45(8), 33–37.

Spence, I. (1990), "Visual Psychophysics of Simple Graphical Elements", *Journal of Experimental Psychology: Human Perception and Performance*, 16(4), 683–692.

Stephens, G. and Handzic, M. (2004), "Knowledge Discovery through Visualising Using Virtual Reality", in *Proceedings of the 37th Annual Hawaii International Conference on System Sciences – HICSS37* (CD/ROM), January 5–8, 2004, Computer Society Press.

Stewart, T.A. (1997), *Intellectual Capital: The New Wealth of Organisations*, Doubleday, New York.

Tiwana, A. (2001), *The Essential Guide to Knowledge Management: E-Business and CRM Applications*, Prentice Hall, New Jersey.

Whitecotton, S.M. (1996), "The Effects of Experience and a Decision Aid on the Slope, Scatter, and Bias of Earnings Forecasts", *Organisational Behavior and Human Decision Processes*, 66(1), 111–121.

Wong, P.C. (1999), "Visual Data Mining", *IEEE Computer Graphics and Applications*, September/October.

PART III

Personalisation Technologies:

Supporting Knowledge Creation and Sharing

CHAPTER 7

Interactive Idea Generator:

Stimulating Creative Thinking

The ancestor of every action is a thought.
— Ralph W. Emerson

This chapter describes and empirically evaluates a specific KM technology aimed at stimulating creative thinking. An interactive idea generator system was built to allow users to collect stimulating material from various sources in preparation for ideation, relate ideas to peers and mentors, create potential solutions to problems, and donate results to the idea bank or disseminate them to people. An empirical test of the brainstorming feature of the system was conducted using volunteer student subjects who performed a creative decision-making task. The test revealed a highly beneficial effect of technology on participants' ability to generate ideas.

7.1 Introduction

The need to improve decision-making is a longstanding concern in DSS research. As we enter the 21st century, accelerated technological development and fierce competition coming from global sources are becoming more apparent, and enhanced decision-making capabilities are required more than ever before to enable organisations to meet the new challenges.

At the same time, there is a growing recognition that the organisation's capability to deal with change, improve services and quality, cut costs and compete in the global market is dependant on the level of creative and innovative thinking of its workforce (Covey, 1989). Futurists propose that we are entering an era of great uncertainty. The quest to stay competitive in the global and rapidly changing world will force businesses to constantly pursue new strategies to differentiate themselves from their competition. One way companies can distinguish themselves is by offering new products and providing new services (Satzinger et al., 1999). In short, organisational success in a new age is defined by continuous profitable growth, and creativity has been recognised as a key factor to growth or survival (Tomas, 1999).

To meet the challenge, new age decision-makers will need to discover new resources and implement new pathways, realising new solutions in situations where conventional methods of decision analysis and decision support may not apply. It will be no longer enough to do the same things better. There is a growing need to develop relevant creative and innovative capabilities to enable employees to work more productively and contribute to economic growth. In order to enhance the innovativeness of an organisation, the creative decision-making performance of employees also needs to be improved (Shalley and Perry-Smith, 2001). In general, creative decision-making on an individual and group level is seen to be the key to job success and decision-making performance in the new era.

7.2 Creativity in Decision-Making

Decision-making can be viewed as a dynamic and iterative process during which a final solution evolves. It includes exploring, defining and framing problems, as well as generating, evaluating and selecting options. The well-known Mintzberg's model of decision-making includes three major phases of the decision process: (i) identification phase, which involves decision problem recognition and diagnosis activities, (ii) development phase, which concerns search and design activities, and (iii) selection phase, which comprises screening, evaluation and authorisation activities (Mintzberg et al., 1976). Several other popular process models use different labeling or further refine these activities (Simon, 1960; Nutt, 1984; Smith, 1989).

Problem identification or formulation is used to initiate the decision-making process and frame the problem in terms of its major issues. In most cases, the diagnosis activity requires gathering of background information on the problem area, calling experts, or examining histories of similar cases in the organisation. In this way, the existing problem is clarified and the decision-makers can start looking for solutions. However, in situations where the problem is novel, and no prior experience exists, decision-makers must determine relevant issues by generating creative ideas (Aurum and Handzic, 2001). The subsequent steps of decision-making will depend on the nature of the issues generated during problem formulation.

Creative ideas are also important in finding possible courses of actions because they increase the number of available options which may determine the boundaries of a decision. These boundaries may potentially influence the later phases of decision-making and, over time, may become a source of direction for thinking and behavior within the organisation. Finally, the ability of key decision-makers to make creative decisions may influence the efficiency and productivity of the organisation and affect its chances for survival and progress in the new era.

The literature offers diverse conceptual definitions of creativity. Tomas (1999) defines it in terms of an original idea. In contrast, Shalley and Perry-Smith (2001) argue that it is not enough to only be original. Also, appropriateness is vital in order to distinguish creative ideas from surreal ideas that may be unique, but have unlawful or highly unrealistic implications. Furthermore, a restricted definition of the concept focuses solely on rare revolutionary and paradigm shifting ideas, while a looser definition includes useful evolutionary contributions that refine and apply existing paradigms (Shneiderman, 2000). In decision-making, appropriateness and contribution aspects are particularly important, as the idea may be a part of the policy formulation and strategic planning process within an organisation.

There are also differences among researchers with respect to the way in which creative ideas are generated. Three major perspectives offered by Shneiderman (2000) include: inspirationalist, structuralist and situationalist views. The inspirationalist approach emphasises dramatic breakthrough and intuitive aspects of creative idea generation. The structuralist perspective emphasises the importance of previous work and methodological techniques to explore possible solutions. The situationalist view focuses on the social context as a key part of the creative idea generation process. Another classification of various theories recognises psychoanalytical, behavioral and process orientated perspectives on creative decision-making (Marakas, 2003). The psychoanalytical perspective maintains that creative idea generation is a preconscious mental activity, whereas the behavioural perspective argues that it is a natural response to stimuli; and the process oriented view sees it as a thought process that can be improved through instruction and practice.

We hold the view that there is a need for an integrated approach to creative decision-making to bring together these various perspectives. An integrated framework would provide researchers with a holistic view of creative decision-making that would enhance our understanding of creative decision processes and their facilitators. Such a framework could also help practitioners to better understand what sort of support initiatives are possible and to identify those that make sense in their context. In the following sections we have attempted to develop such an approach based on descriptive and inductive inquiry.

Creative Processes and Techniques

Consistent with the view that creative thinking can be learnt by appropriate stimulation and instruction, a variety of formal techniques have been developed to assist the production of novel ideas for decision-making. Some of these techniques are limited to only the idea generation aspect of the creative process, while ignoring previous work, consulting with others or disseminating solutions. Other techniques primarily aim to increase the production of novel ideas by enhancing the creative environment as well as the interaction within a group.

Most techniques are based on the notion that one may lose many creative ideas by evaluating them prematurely. Therefore, separation of the creation of ideas from their evaluation is an important aspect. De Bono takes the view that "Unless we can imagine something, we cannot undertake to achieve it" (quoted in Sunderland, 2000). The fundamental rules of creative thinking are: "Have a positive outlook; Build on group ideas; Think of as many ideas as possible; and don't stop to review your ideas" (Morais, 2001). Tomas (1999) also asserts that in order to be creative, decision-makers must not constrain themselves by rules when generating ideas. A popular expression that highlights this scenario is the need to 'think out of the box'. In general, it is believed that idea generation methods are an important source of encouragement for decision-makers (Satzinger et al., 1999).

There are many idea-generation techniques available. Handzic and Cule (2002) reviewed and summarised some of the most popular ones. Those applicable in decision support can be classified into three basic categories: free association, structured relationships, and group techniques (Marakas, 2003). One of the most popular free association techniques is brainstorming. Brainstorming is used to uncover ideas without being constrained, as the outcome is not permanent. Brainstorming also allows individuals or groups to capture all of their thoughts. One of the underlying rules of brainstorming is that external factors will influence the ideas generated. Also, brainstorming sessions can be conducted electronically, manually, or verbally. Mind mapping is a method of recording the free flow of ideas by drawing up a map that iterates your ideas. Mind mapping is a valuable technique for individuals, as creative ideas can be generated effectively and because the ideas captured are limitless (Tomas, 1999). In the category of structured relationship techniques, the focus is on the generation of new ideas via forced combinations of diverse ideas or concepts to produce new ideas.

Group brainstorming enables all group members to build upon their own and group member's ideas. Thus, each group member's ideas stimulate their own and others' thinking and each individual produces new ideas. Group support systems (GSS) have become a popular group technique for electronic brainstorming. A GSS has three vital components: anonymity, group memory and parallelism. Anonymity allows individuals to take part without attaching their name. Group memory contains the ideas generated by all individuals during the idea generation session. Parallelism allows the group to suggest ideas simultaneously (Satzinger et al., 1999). Other widely used group techniques include nominal group technique which builds upon the concept of brainstorming, and the delphi method, which involves a series of question-answer iterations until a convergence of responses is noted. Anonymity and consensus are very important aspects of the delphi technique.

Most empirical studies investigating the effects of creative thinking and idea generation techniques on the ideas generated, suggest a highly contingent nature of individual and group creative performance upon a variety of socio-technological factors.

Socio-Technological Influences

The variety of factors has been suggested to influence creative thinking. Handzic and Cule (2002) grouped them into two broad categories: social and technological. An extensive review and analysis of past literature (Paulus et al., 2002; Paulus and Yang, 2000; Shalley and Perry-Smith, 2001) identified a series of social and cognitive influences on both individual and group oriented creative processes. In summary, this analysis revealed that those left to their own devices are not likely to be very productive, particularly when involved in a verbal exchange of ideas. However, when processes are structured as to limit the inhibitory processes and facilitate stimulation, high levels of ideas generation can be achieved.

Mixture of individual and group processes appeared to be the optimal approach. In short, social initiatives such as educational programs, organisational culture and structure, and government policies are seen as fundamental in establishing a climate conducive to creative performance (Handzic and Cule, 2002).

The role of information technology, on the other hand, is seen primarily in terms of facilitating the creative process, including generation, exploration, communication, and dissemination of ideas (Sridhar, 2001; Shneiderman, 2000). An extensive analysis of existing tools by Shneiderman (2000) revealed that most available tools provide support only for some parts of the creative decision-making process. These activities may include searching and browsing libraries, consulting with peers, visualising data, developing ideas, what-if analysis, composing artifacts, reviewing and replaying histories, or disseminating results. He pointed out that by combining all of them into an integrated decision support system a workbench for creative decision-making can be achieved. However, he did warn about potential limitations of such a workbench as it may restrict imagination to only what is possible within the toolset. In summary, in pursuing an integrated approach to creative decision support, an understanding of the positive possibilities and of the dangers is important.

Following the above recommendations, this author and her colleague have proposed and empirically tested an integrated and interactive idea generator system (Handzic and Loy, 2004). The following sections describe the development effort and the results of the empirical test conducted to evaluate the tool in the context of creative decision-making.

7.3 Tool Description

The proposed system can be viewed as a personal knowledge management tool that primarily aims to support the individual in their daily exercise of creative thinking. It has been constructed using the Shneiderman's (2002) integrated "genex" framework. Essentially, the system supports the activities of searching and browsing digital libraries for sources of stimulating material; consulting with peers and mentors for intellectual and emotional support; thinking by free associations to generate new ideas; composing artefacts and performances; reviewing and replaying session histories to support reflection; disseminating results to gain recognition and add to the searchable resources.

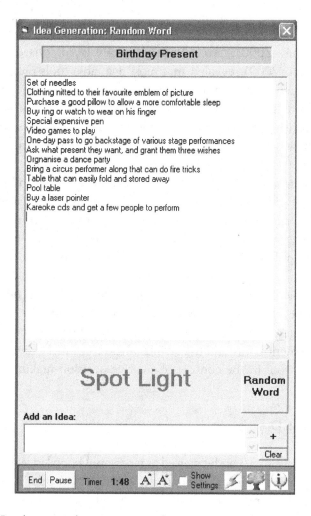

Figure 7.1 Random input brainstorming tool

To support the activity of thinking by free associations, a brainstorming session shown in Figure 7.1 is incorporated based on the "random input" creativity technique (De Bono, 1992). This is a commonly used method for generating new ideas particularly in situations such as developing new products. The assumption is that a random word will stimulate thoughts on associated objects, related concepts and functions suggested by the word. Random words are chosen from concrete nouns and manipulative verbs. Concrete nouns can be objects that can be touched or seen, e.g., cat, plane, stereo. Manipulative verbs imply an action that can be applied to an object to cause an effect, e.g., minimise, solidify, rotate, stretch. These types of words are suggested to be more effective than adjectives or abstract concepts because they can be vividly imagined.

Furthermore, the system includes a personal idea storage system for managing ideas, pop-up search utility to explore prior ideas to reconsider and elaborate; mechanism to allow incidental ideas to be registered quickly and modified or classified later on, and evaluation procedures to assess the number of ideas and their quality. These features were suggested as necessary to support the long term and non-intentional idea generation as they allow users to record useful ideas that may surface accidentally outside the brainstorming sessions (Shibata and Hori, 2002). They also allow users to confidently evaluate competing idea and compare them in a deliberate, systematic and transparent process (Asensio, 2001).

The evaluation tool included in the system is based on a grid analysis approach (Gabora, 2002). It involves producing a table that lists and scores various ideas or options to choose from, and specifies various factors that need to be taken into consideration together with their relative importance. Thus, the tool allows the users to verify that an acceptable selection and number of useful creative solutions have been presented. The highest overall scoring option is considered to be the best choice.

The idea generator tool described above was built primarily with the intention to empower the process of creative decision-making. The following empirical test was carried out to evaluate the tool from the users' point of view.

7.4 Tool Evaluation

Study Description

The current study tested only the random input brainstorming component of the idea generator system. The tool was empirically tested in a simulated business situation. It involved a fictitious organisation, a small ice-cream shop named Dream Cream and located on Bondi Beach. Subjects adopted the role of the shop owner/manager eager to boost his business through innovation.

The subjects' task was to generate ideas with respect to product, planning, potential and people aspects of the business. To aid their task, one half of the subjects were provided with the brainstorming technology. These subjects were asked to interact with the technology, read stimulating material available in the form of random words (nouns and verbs), and produce a written document listing their generated ideas and comments. The other half of subjects were asked to identify and record a range of innovations they believed were important for boosting the ice-cream business based solely on their past knowledge and experience.

A total of 56 subjects participated in the study on a voluntary basis. The participants were drawn from the pool of students attending a course in computer information systems at a large Australian university. They received no monetary incentive for their participation. The experimental session was conducted as part of a tutorial on special purpose systems. On arrival, subjects were randomly assigned to one of two treatment groups and worked alone. They received instructions regarding the case study and task requirements. They also had an opportunity for asking questions before and during the experiment. The session lasted about half an hour.

Subjects' accomplishment in the task was evaluated in terms of the total number of relevant ideas generated (denoted total ideas), as well as the number and percentage of relevant categories of issues (out of 4) addressed as assessed by an expert judge. The judge was an academic with over 30 years of experience in the field of IS. The judge examined the students' ideas for relevance and assigned them to appropriate categories (i.e., product, planning, potential, people). The classification scheme enabled examination of the differences in the quantity, as well as the quality of ideas generated by the students due to technology use.

Results

In order to understand the effects of the technology on individual participants' creative performance we analysed statistically the differences in the number and the categories of ideas generated between those with and without technology. The T-test was selected as the most suitable method for the analysis (Huck et al., 1974). Results of the analysis are shown in Table 7.1.

Table 7.1 Results of T-test analyses on dependant variables

Dependent Variable	Unit of Measure	Without Tool	With Tool	Difference
Total Ideas	Number	6.82	13.50	+ 6.68*
Total Categories	Number	2.39	2.57	ns
	(%)	(59.82)	(64.28)	

$*p < 0.001$

Overall, the results of the analysis performed indicate a significant positive impact of the technology on the quantitative, but not qualitative aspects of the participants' creative performance. Table 7.1 shows significant effects on total ideas, but not idea categories.

With respect to the quantitative aspect of performance, the results indicate a highly significant positive impact of technology on the total number of relevant ideas generated by the participants. As shown in Table 7.1, there was a significant increase in the number of relevant ideas generated due to using the technology. More specifically, the mean value for total ideas increased by 6.68 (from 6.82 to 13.50) due to technology use.

However, the results indicate no significant impact of technology on the qualitative aspect of participants' performance. Table 7.1 shows that there was no significant difference in the number of relevant categories addressed by the participants as a result of their use of the technology. The mean number of different categories addressed by the subjects with technology was similar to that of their counterparts without technology (2.57 or 64.28% versus 2.39 or 59.82%).

Further results presented in Figure 7.2 indicate that about one half (55%) of all ideas generated were related to planning. Examples include "beach delivery" and "mood creation". About one-third (35%) of the ideas were product related, including phrases such as "cheesy flavour", "hot topping" and "ice-cream sandwich". Only 9% of the ideas were people related, and typically addressed "colorful uniforms". The remaining 1% were about potential.

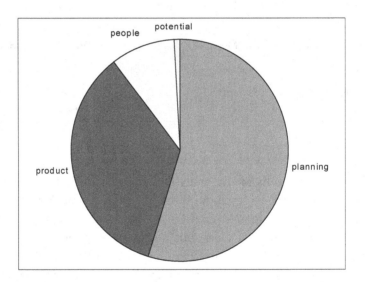

Figure 7.2 Categories of generated ideas

Discussion

The experimental results clearly indicate that an electronic brainstorming technology had a powerful effect on the students' creative performance in the specific decision-making task. The effect was evident primarily in the quantitative, but not qualitative aspects of the performance evaluated. Users were found to generate significantly greater number of relevant ideas, but similar number of categories of issues as the result of their interaction with technology.

The results of this study provide substantial support for the view that creative performance can be enhanced by appropriate stimulation, as suggested by some theorists (Ford, 1996; Marakas, 1998). The stimulating technology studied here was found to contribute to a significant improvement in the quantity of ideas generated by the participating students. This result agrees with our earlier findings from an empirical study conducted in the software engineering context (Aurum and Handzic, 2001). Essentially, the results support the idea that creative applications can be developed, learnt, practiced and used to generate ideas. Thus, they can enable an individual to think, provided that the principles are clearly understood.

It has also been suggested in the literature (Satzinger et al., 1999) that the idea generation method is one of the most important sources of encouraging creativity. The results of our study indicate that the brainstorming technique underlying our proposed technology was a highly appropriate method for stimulating creative thinking and idea generation in a creative decision-making task. Students were found to generate a significantly greater number of relevant business ideas when supported by the idea generator tool. Essentially, the system helped students stimulate their own thinking by external influences and to capture all of their thoughts.

The findings of the study also support the proposition that an electronic tool following a specific creativity technique can assist the creative process (Sridhar, 2001). One of the main advantages of such a tool is the speed at which ideas can be produced. Furthermore, the ideas can be stored and revisited at a later time. The tool can also provide a variety of stimuli that enhance imagination. The electronic technology implemented in this study provided all of the above, plus a written protocol that brought a formal structure to the idea generation process.

Our findings may have some important implications for KM practice. The results of this study suggest that the technology tested here may be useful in a variety of situations involving creative thinking and problem solving. They also suggest that it is likely to be most valuable in situations where the problem is unstructured, goals indistinct, and the outcome of an action cannot always be clearly identified. The tool is a rather generic one, since it uses a technique that can be applied to a variety of scenarios.

While the current study provides a number of interesting findings, some caution is necessary regarding their generalisability due to a number of limiting factors. The application of experimental conditions is a limitation of this study. We believe that in field work, the users' individual achievements would improve even further. The emphasis of the present study was on individuals. It would be interesting to examine the effect of the technology on creative performance of groups. Future research may address some of these issues.

7.5 Conclusions

The objective of this chapter was to explore the potential of technology to support creative and innovative idea generation. A specific idea generator system was built that allowed users to collect stimulating material from various sources in preparation for ideation, relate ideas to peers and mentors, create potential solutions to problems, and donate results to the idea bank or disseminate them to people. The electronic brainstorming component of the system was empirically tested in the context of a creative decision-making problem. The results of the test indicated that the tool was quite helpful. Users were able to substantially improve their creative performance and generate a greater number of relevant ideas. These empirical findings suggest that such KM tools may be useful in facilitating learning and performance in tasks involving creative thinking and problem solving. Future research is recommended to address current research limitations.

References

Asensio, A. (2002), "The Process of Idea Management", *Executive Update*, May issue.

Aurum, A. and Handzic, M. (2001), "Technology for Managing Professional Knowledge of Future Software Developers", in *Proceedings of the 16th IAIM International Conference on Informatics Education and Research (IAIM'2001)*, December 14–16, 2001, New Orleans, Louisiana.

Covey, S.R. (1989), *The 7 Habits of Highly Effective People*, Simon & Schuster, New York.

DeBono, E. (1992), *Serious Creativity*, Advanced Practical Thinking Publishing.

Ford, C.M. (1996), "Theory of Individual Creative Action in Multiple Social Domains", *Academy of Management Review*, 21(4), 1112–1142.

Gabora, L. (2002), "Cognitive Mechanisms Underlying the Creative Process", in *Proceedings of the Creativity and Cognition Conference*, October.

Handzic, M. and Cule, M. (2002), "Creative Decision Making: Review, Analysis and Recommendations", in *Proceedings of the Conference Decision-Making in Internet Age (DSIage 2002)*, Cork, July, pp. 443–452.

Handzic, M. and Loy, A. (2004), *Electronic Brainstorming Technology Evaluation*, working paper, UNSW, April.

Huck, S.W., Cormier, W.H. and Bounds, W.G. Jr. (1974), *Reading Statistics and Research*, Harper and Row, New York.

Marakas, G. (2003), *Decision Support Systems for 21st Century*, 2nd ed., Prentice Hall, New Jersey.

Mintzberg, H. et al. (1976), "The Structure of Unstructured Decision Process", *Administration Science Quarterly*, 21(2), 246–275.

Morais, R.J. (2001), "Analytical Ideation: Power Brainstorming", *Brandweek*, 42(3), 22–23.

Nutt, P. (1984), "Types of Organisational Decision Processes", *Administrative Science Quarterly*, 29, 414–450.

Paulus, P.B. and Yang, H. (2000), "Idea Generation in Groups: A Basis for Creativity in Organisations", *Organisational Behaviour and Human Decision Processes*, 82(1), 76–87.

Paulus, P.B. et al. (2002), *Social and Cognitive Influences in Group Brainstorming: Predicting Production Gains and Losses*, working paper, 2002, University of Texas at Arlington.

Satzinger, J.W., Garfield, J.M. and Nagasundaram, M. (1999), "The Creative Process: The Effects of Group Memory on Individual Idea Generation", 14(4), 143–160.

Shalley, C.E. and Perry-Smith, J.E. (2001), "Effects of Social-Psychological Factors on Creative Performance: The Role of Informational and Controlling Expected Evaluation and Modelling Experience", *Organisational Behaviour and Human Decision Processes*, 84(1), 1–22.

Shibata, H. and Hori, K. (2002), "A System to Support Long-term Creative Thinking in Daily Life and Its Evaluation", in *Proceedings of the Creativity and Cognition Conference*, October.

Shneiderman, B. (2000), "Creating Creativity: User Interfaces for Supporting Innovation", ACM *Transactions on Computer-Human Interaction*, 7(1), 114–138.

Simon, H.A. (1960), *The New Science of Management Decision*, Prentice Hall, New Jersey.

Smith, C.G. (1989), "Defining Managerial Problems: A Framework for Prescriptive Theorising", *Management Science*, 35(8), 963–981.

Sridhar, R. (2001), "India: Software for Breaking Mental Blocks!", *Business Line, India*, February, pp. 1–3.

Sunderland, K. (2000), "The Power of a Silly Idea", *Charter*, 71(6), 49–51.

Tomas, S. (1999), "Creative Problem-Solving: An Approach to Generating Ideas", *Hospital Material Management Quarterly*, 20(4), 33–45.

CHAPTER 8

Electronic Mentor:

Fostering Knowledge Development

Teachers open the door, but you must enter by yourself.
— Chinese proverb

This chapter explores the potential of an electronic mentoring system to foster the development of knowledge. The system was developed to provide performance guidance and/or feedback. The impact of the tool on learners' knowledge and performance was tested empirically in the judgmental decision-making task context. The results indicate that guided learners tended to make smaller decision errors than their feedback counterparts. These results suggest that future knowledge management initiatives need to consider these forms of interactive learning systems in response to environment pressures for faster and more effective learning.

8.1 Introduction

Knowledge management literature suggests that to remain competitive, or even to survive, in today's uncertain economy with shifting markets, proliferating technology, multiple competitors and shortening product life, companies will have to invent new business processes, new businesses, new industries, and new customers. This will require a major shift in focus from tangible resources such as financial capital to intangible resources such as intellectual capital (Davenport and Prusak, 1998; Davenport et al., 1998; Drucker, 1993; Grayson and Dell, 1998; Stewart, 1997). In general, there seems to exist a widespread recognition in the literature of the importance of organisational learning (Garvin, 1998), knowledge-creating processes (Nonaka, 1998), and knowledgeable workers (Drucker, 1998) for a new age economy.

However, the complexities of learning and the large number of interacting factors which affect individual and group learning present many challenges. Learning entities (individuals and organisations) are expected to be skilled at creating, acquiring and transferring knowledge and modifying their behaviour accordingly (Garvin, 1998); to continually expand their capacity to create desired results, nurture new thinking patterns, set free collective aspirations and learn how to learn together (Senge, 1990). It is also suggested that inventing new knowledge should become a way of behaving or being (Nonaka, 1998).

So far, these concerns have not been adequately addressed by Management Education (Seufert and Seufert, 1999). One of the major criticisms is that a large amount of knowledge is imparted to the learner without any attempt to interlink it with reality. Another widespread weakness lies in the neglect of process-oriented learning, that is, making the learning and thought process visible in order to develop learners' meta-cognition (Joyce and Weil, 1986).

Organisations' demands for new skills and capabilities for future professional and managerial knowledge workers necessitate a corresponding change in education. This implies a need for a balance between the imparting of knowledge to the learner and the learner's own construction of it. A suggestion is made that the quantity of material to be learnt by telling should be reduced to a minimum and that the lesson time should instead be devoted to the cultivation of qualities such as problem-solving, decision-making and creativity through self-directed and collaborative learning.

The main purpose of this chapter is to explore the potential of an electronic mentoring system in fostering experiential learning and performance in a decision-making context. The chapter attempts to answer the following questions: whether and how an electronic mentoring system may affect individual knowledge workers' learning, and what impact it will have on their subsequent decision performance.

8.2 Learning from Feedback and Guidance

Learning theorists suggest that people should learn from experience through task repetition to adjust their behaviour and improve performance over time. In decision-making, some authors (Payne et al., 1988) claim that adaptivity in decision behaviour may be important enough to individuals for them to guide themselves to it without the need for an external intervention.

Empirical studies from judgement research indicate mixed findings. A number of studies involving learning to purchase information where its value outweighs its cost, given multiple pieces of information of varying accuracy, have reported only modest learning over trials (Connolly and Serre, 1984; Connolly and Gilani, 1982; Connolly and Thorn, 1987). In order to explain how people learned to adjust their acquisition strategies over time, Connolly and his associates devised a simple hill-climbing algorithm (Connolly and Wholey, 1988). A computer simulation reliably reproduced information acquisition behaviour of real subjects in earlier empirical studies. Although the improvement was real, a serious deviation from optimality remained. In contrast, a study conducted in a similar multivariate judgement task reported no learning at all (Connolly and Wholey, 1988), while the results of a judgemental adjustment study (Lim and O'Connor, 1996) indicated that information acquisition strategies even worsened and consequently performance declined over time. Many studies performed in the multiple cue probability learning (MCPL) paradigm have concluded that people cannot learn effectively when multiple cues are involved or non-linear cue-criterion relationships exist (for a review see Brehmer, 1980).

Some authors (e.g., Hogarth, 1981) suggest that the availability of immediate feedback, in addition to the opportunity to take corrective action, is critical for effective learning. Adequate feedback is considered especially important for the correct assessment of the previous responses in situations where the subject is unfamiliar with the task or topic (O'Connor, 1989). It has been suggested that feedback may enhance learning by providing information about the task, task outcome, individual's performance and/or decision process. From this information, through task repetition, an individual may learn to adapt, i.e., maintain, modify or abandon their strategy to improve task performance.

Different dimensions of feedback have been shown to result in varied success in supporting learning and consequent decision-making. In his review of a number of laboratory and field studies on the impact of feedback on task performance, Kopelman (1986) reported that objective feedback (defined as information about task behaviour or performance that is factual and inconvertible), had a positive effect on performance. But it was stronger and more sizeable in the field than in the laboratory. In the choice task setting, Creyer et al. (1990) also indicate that feedback on accuracy led to more normative-like processing of information and improved performance. The role of accuracy feedback was greater when the decision problem was more difficult. Effort feedback, on the other hand, had no impact on processing or performance regardless of the difficulty of the problem.

Feedback was also found to have induced learning in the so-called cue discovery tasks (Klayman, 1988). People were found to perceive the existence and direction of a cue-criterion relationship, but have difficulties in learning its shape. A significant improvement in predictive success over time was attributed to cue discovery rather than accurate weighting. Most findings from MCPL studies with feedback indicate that while people have difficulties learning from outcome feedback in these tasks, they can learn more effectively when they are provided with cognitive feedback, such as summary analysis of how their past predictions differed from optimal (Klayman, 1988).

In contrast, some studies have found a detrimental effect of feedback on performance. In a complex probability task a large error on a particular trial might imply poor strategy or merely the fact that occasional errors can be expected in an uncertain task. As a consequence, outcome feedback may sometimes have a detrimental effect on strategy selection. Peterson and Pitz (1986) discovered that outcome feedback increased the amount by which the decision-maker's estimates deviated from the model. These findings were further reinforced by Arkes et al. (1986) who found that the omission of feedback was effective in raising performance with a helpful classification rule.

In a more recent study examining the impact of several types of learning aids on the accuracy of forecasts of time series with structural instabilities, Remus et al. (1996) found that task information (showing the underlying structure of the task) with or without cognitive feedback gave significantly better forecasting performance than the baseline simple outcome feedback. Adding cognitive information feedback to task information feedback did not improve forecasting accuracy. The results for task and cognitive feedback largely replicated those by Balzer et al. (1992, 1994). These findings suggest that task guidance in a form of feed-forward information (e.g., task or method) may be more beneficial to learning than information on past performance provided by feedback (e.g., outcome or cognitive). The purpose of this chapter is to test this proposition.

Research Questions

In summary, findings concerning learning in multivariate judgement and choice tasks are mixed and inconclusive. The findings suggest that the quality of performance may be conditional upon the type of feedback/guidance, task difficulty, time period, and whether participants are allowed to experiment or not. In view of the equivocal prior findings, the objective of this chapter is to empirically examine whether there will be any difference in learning and performance between users of guidance and feedback types of electronic mentoring systems. The empirical study reported is a part of the author's ongoing research into KM support for learning and decision-making (Handzic, 2004; Handzic and Tolhurst, 2002).

8.3 Empirical Study

We chose to investigate the above question by undertaking an experimental study. A quantitative approach was chosen to allow clear and strong statements to be made regarding empirical findings (Judd et al., 1991) and offer some more conclusive evidence to the body of literature in this area. We are aware, however, that qualitative methods would also support an understanding of the complex aspects of learning. Supplementing the quantitative results to provide greater depth and dimension to these results remains our future research goal.

Experimental Task

A forecasting task simulation was created for the purpose of studying the effect of electronic mentoring systems in fostering knowledge development and supporting decision-making. It was implemented in Microsoft Visual Basic language. The mentoring system was developed and incorporated into the simulation in order to give users a clearer and more understandable knowledge guidance and/or feedback that could lead to higher quality decisions.

Users assumed the role of the Production Manager for the Dream Cream dairy company in Sydney. One of their responsibilities was to make decisions on daily production of ice creams sold from the company's outlet at Bondi Beach. Users were required to make accurate sales estimates for ice cream which was to be sold the following day. Users completed the task for thirty-five consecutive days.

All participants were provided with sequential historic information on the task relevant variable (product sales) to provide some cues to suggest future behaviour. The task differed with respect to the KM support received. One half of the subjects was provided with performance feedback to analyse earlier performance and to adjust future strategies. The other half made decisions with additional guidance on how to perform the task.

Financial remuneration was based on users' performance. Users incurred costs depending on the accuracy of daily estimates. Therefore, minimisation of cost, or in other words, maximisation of accuracy was the goal of the task. Over and under estimation errors were equally costly. At the beginning of the experiment, task descriptions were provided to inform all subjects about the task scenario and requirements.

Experimental Design and Variables

The experiment had a factorial design with a single independent factor: electronic mentoring system (feedback vs guidance). The manipulation was achieved by developing two different versions of the system. In one version, learners were provided with feedback support in the form of decision errors made in each trial. The other version provided learners with guidance support in the form of a method to follow when solving the problem.

Decision performance was evaluated in terms of *cost* operationalised by absolute error (AE) and expressed in dollar terms and *accuracy* operationalised by symmetric absolute percentage error (SAPE). AE was calculated for each trial as an absolute difference between subjects' forecasts and actual sales values. SAPE was calculated by dividing AE by an average of actual and forecast values, and multiplying by 100% (for details and justification see Makridakis, 1993). Subjects' decision behaviour was evaluated in terms of self-reported dominant *forecasting strategy*. Individual subjects' *confidence* in the quality of decisions and *satisfaction* with their KM support were collected for control purposes and to supplement the measures of actual performance. These were rated on seven-point Likert scales with 1 as least and 7 as most end points.

Time Series Generation

For the purpose of this study, the product sales time series was artificially generated as a seasonal series with an upward trend in order to take into account days of the week and the holiday time influences. The error term was added to account for irregular or random events. The intention was to create a decision task that is "knowable" but "complicated". According to Kurtz and Snowden (2003) such tasks require sensing of incoming data, analysis of that data using a method which seeks to identify the patterns, and response in accordance with interpretation of that analysis or in accordance with expert advice. In the current study, the optimal response required subjects to detect and decompose the time series into trend, season and noise elements, and take these into account when making future predictions. Kurtz and Snowden suggest that a simple error in an assumption can lead to a false conclusion and result in poor performance. Thus, the detection of peak seasonal demands often can mean the difference between effective and ineffective decision.

Subjects and Procedure

Twenty-four graduate students enrolled in the Master of Commerce course "Knowledge Management Systems and Technology" at UNSW took part in the experiment. They participated on a voluntary basis, and received no monetary incentives. Some previous studies indicated that graduate students are appropriate subjects for this type of research (Ashton and Kramer, 1980; Remus, 1996; Whitecotton, 1996).

The experimental session was conducted in a microcomputer laboratory. On arrival, subjects were randomly assigned to one of the two treatments by choosing a microcomputer from a number of units set for the experiment. Before commencing the task, subjects were briefed about the purpose of the experiment and read case study descriptions incorporated in the research instrument. They then performed the task. The session lasted about one hour.

Results

Descriptive results (means or frequencies) for cost, accuracy, strategy, confidence and satisfaction variables by experimental groups are presented in Table 8.1. The collected data were further analysed by a series of parametric (T-test) and non-parametric (Mann-Whitney) statistical tests. The analyses found some significant results ($p < 0.05$).

Table 8.1 Descriptive results by type of electronic mentor

Dependent Variable	Feedback System	Guidance System	N
Cost (AE)	$761.73	$698.45	840
Accuracy (SAPE)	7.8%	7.0%	840
Strategy (Simple/Complex)	8/4	3/9	24
Confidence (Score)	2.9	3.5	24
Satisfaction (Score)	5.2	4.2	24

As expected, the results indicate significant positive effects of an electronic mentoring system on cost, accuracy, strategy and confidence, but not satisfaction. The mean AE of the subjects with guidance was significantly smaller compared to those with feedback only (698.45 vs 761.73). Similarly, the mean SAPE of the subjects with guidance was significantly smaller than that of their counterparts with feedback (7.0% vs 7.8%). Consistently, the subjects with guidance tended to feel more confident in their performance than those without guidance, as shown by their higher mean score (3.5 vs 2.9). Better performance suggested greater knowledge of the decision problem and the subsequent application of a more appropriate forecasting strategy. Indeed, subjects with guidance compared to feedback tended to use less often simple heuristics such as random or naive (3 vs 8), and more often complex strategies such as averaging or trend analysis (9 vs 4) as their dominant approach. However, guidance had less favourable impact on satisfaction. To our surprise, subjects tended to like less the system providing guidance than that providing feedback only (4.2 vs 5.2).

Discussion

This study demonstrated that guidance improved decision accuracy, reduced related cost, discouraged heuristics and enhanced confidence over that achieved by feedback support. However, it reduced user satisfaction with the system.

Subjects provided with guidance were found to better understand the decision task, apply more appropriate forecasting strategy and consequently make more accurate decisions and incur less cost than those performing the task without such guidance. Subjects were also found to be more confident in the quality of their decisions. Interestingly, guidance made less favourable impact on user satisfaction.

The beneficial effect of guidance is consistent with the theoretical expectations suggested by the knowledge mapping literature (Plumley, 2003; Eppler, 2003; Wexler, 2001). The form of guidance used in this study presented critical stages of the decision-making process and pointed to key knowledge areas required at each stage. Thus, it improved the visibility of knowledge in the time series data, and helped participants to identify and locate it. The "reuse" economics (Hansen et al., 1999) can also explain the beneficial effect of the guidance system found in this study. Once the guidance method was developed and made available, it could allow fast and reliable reuse across the repetitive experimental trials.

The positive effect of guidance can also be attributed to the nature of the task domain at hand. According to Kurtz and Snowden (2003), in ordered task domains, patterns are knowable and the only issue is whether we can afford the time and resources to move from knowable to known. Applying methodology which seeks to identify the patterns through study of task properties is considered both legitimate and desirable. The form of guidance in this study provided such a methodology. It facilitated the analysis and led to more appropriate responses in accordance with interpretation of that analysis.

The impact of guidance on perceived satisfaction is quite interesting. One would hope that the users provided with the more helpful tool would also have more favourable attitudes towards it. However, according to Straub et al. (1995), perceptual and behavioural scores can be radically different. This finding can be potentially attributed to the characteristics of the task context in which the investigation was carried out. The current study provided an iterative task context with the guiding method provided on the screen at all times. Constant reinforcement of the same guidelines could have irritated subjects and thus affected their satisfaction. In addition, subjects could have learnt the task over time through experience and from feedback and would not feel the need for such a reminder after a while.

In summary, the current study provides a number of interesting findings that may have some important implications for organisational KM strategies. In general, findings suggest that decision-makers faced with complicated decision tasks may greatly benefit from electronic mentoring systems. Guidance may enhance critical knowledge visibility and usability, and thus alleviate the negative effects of task difficulty and subsequent use of decision heuristics. This in turn may result in improved decision accuracy and lead to desired business outcomes.

However, some caution is necessary regarding the generalisability of these findings due to a number of limiting factors. One of the limitations refers to the use of a laboratory experiment that may compromise external validity of research. Another limitation relates to artificial generation of time series that may not reflect the true nature of real business. The subjects chosen for the study were students and not real-life decision-makers. The fact that they were mature graduates may mitigate the potential differences. No incentives were offered to the subjects for their effort in the study. Consequently, they could find the study tiring and unimportant and would not try as hard as possible. Most decisions in real business settings have significant consequences.

Further study is necessary that would address these limitations and extend current research to other tasks and contexts. Future research is also necessary to empirically investigate the potential of other individual or combined and integrated knowledge management initiatives to further enhance knowledge and enable optimal performance.

8.4 Conclusions

This study was able to demonstrate the potential of a specific electronic mentoring system to improve understanding and enhance performance of a forecasting task. From our research findings one may conclude that guidance is more beneficial to the performance of knowledge tasks than feedback. Guidance can more effectively enhance decision-makers' working knowledge and performance in the context of a complicated decision task, although at the cost of reducing satisfaction. However, the study is not without limitations. Different mentoring systems may have advantages and disadvantages under different situations, and thus careful consideration of different combinations of learning techniques is necessary. Further empirical research is recommended that would address some of these issues.

References

Arkes, H.R., Dawes, R.M. and Christensen, C. (1986), "Factors Influencing the Use of a Decision Rule in a Probabilistic Task", *Organisational Behaviour and Human Decision Processes*, 37, 93–110.

Ashton, R.H. and Kramer, S.S. (1980), "Students as Surrogates in Behavioural Accounting Research: Some Evidence", *Journal of Accounting Research*, 18(1), 1–15.

Balzer, W.K., Hammer, L.B., Sumner, K.E., Birchenough, T.R., Martens, S.P. and Raymark, P.H. (1994), "Effects of Cognitive Feedback Components, Display Format, and Elaboration on Performance", *Organisational Behaviour and Human Decision Processes*, 58, 369–385.

Balzer, W.K., Sulsky L.M., Hammer, L.B. and Sumner, K.E. (1992), "Task Information, Cognitive Information, or Functional Validity Information: Which Components of Cognitive Feedback Affect Performance?", *Organisational Behaviour and Human Decision Processes*, 58, 369–385.

Brehmer, B. (1980), "In One Word: Not from Experience", *Acta Psychologica*, 45, 223–241.

Connolly, T. and Gilani, N. (1982), "Information Search in Judgement Tasks: A Regression Model and Some Preliminary Findings", *Organisational Behaviour and Human Performance*, 30, 330–350.

Connolly, T. and Serre, P. (1984), "Information Search in Judgement Tasks: The Effects of Unequal Cue Validity and Cost", *Organisational Behaviour and Human Performance*, 34, 387–401.

Connolly, T. and Thorn, B.K. (1987), "Predecisional Information Acquisition: Effects of Task Variables on Suboptimal Search Strategies", *Organisational Behaviour and Human Decision Processes*, 39, 397–416.

Connolly, T. and Wholey, D.R. (1988), "Information Mispurchase in Judgement Tasks: A Task Driven Causal Mechanism", *Organisational Behaviour and Human Decision Processes*, 42, 75–87.

Creyer, E.H., Bettman, J.R. and Payne, J.W. (1990), "The Impact of Accuracy and Effort Feedback and Goals on Adaptive Decision Behaviour", *Journal of Behavioural Decision-making*, 3(1), 1–16.

Davenport, T.H. and Prusak, L. (1998), *Working Knowledge: How Organisations Manage What They Know*, Harvard Business School Press, Boston.

Davenport, T.H., DeLong, D.W. and Breers, M.C. (1998), "Successful Knowledge Management Projects", *Sloan Management Review*, Winter, 43–57.

Drucker, P.F. (1993), *Post-Capitalist Society*, HarperBusiness, New York.

Drucker, P.F. (1998), "The Coming of the New Organisation", *Harvard Business Review on Knowledge Management*, Harvard Business School Press, Boston.

Eppler, M. (2003), "Making Knowledge Visible through Knowledge Maps: Concepts, Elements, Cases", in C.W. Holsapple (ed.), *Handbook on Knowledge Management*, Vol. 1, Springer-Verlag, Berlin, pp. 189–205.

Garvin, D.A. (1998), "Building a Learning Organisation", *Harvard Business Review on Knowledge Management*, Harvard Business School Press, Boston.

Grayson, C.J. and Dell, C.O. (1998), "Mining Your Hidden Resources". *Across the Board*, 35(4), 23–28.

Handzic, M. (2004), "Decision Support through Knowledge Management: An Empirical Examination of Two Strategies", in *Proceedings of DSS'2004 Conference*, Prato, Italy, July 1–3.

Handzic, M. and Tolhurst, D. (2002), "Evaluating an Interactive Learning Environment in Management Education", *Educational Technology & Society*, *IEEE Journal*, 5(3), 113–122.

Hansen, M.T., Nohria, N. and Tierney, T. (1999), "What's Your Strategy for Managing Knowledge?", *Harvard Business Review*, March–April, 106–116.

Hogarth, R.M. (1981), "Beyond Discrete Biases: Functional and Dysfunctional Aspects of Judgemental Heuristics", *Psychological Bulletin*, 90(2), 197–217.

Joyce, B. and Weil, M. (1986), *Models of Teaching*. Prentice Hall, New Jersey.

Judd, C.M., Smith, E.R. and Kidder, L.H. (1991), *Research Methods in Social Relations*, 6th ed., Harcourt Brace Jovanovich College Publishers.

Klayman, J. (1988), "Learning from Experience", in Brehmer, B. and Joyce, C.R.B. (eds.), *Human Judgement. The SJT View*, North-Holland, Amsterdam.

Kopelman, R.E. (1986), "Objective Feedback", in Locke, E.A. (ed.), *Generalising from Laboratory to Field Settings*, Lexington Books.

Kurtz, C.F. and Snowden, D.J. (2003), "The New Dynamics of Strategy: Sense-making in a Complex and Complicated World", *IBM Systems Journal*, 42(3), 462–482.

Lim, J.S. and O'Connor, M.J. (1996), "Judgemental Forecasting with Interactive Forecasting Support Systems", *Decision Support Systems*, 16, 339–357.

Makridakis, S. (1993), "Accuracy Measures: Theoretical and Practical Concerns", *International Journal of Forecasting*, 9, 527–529.

Nonaka, I. (1998), "The Knowledge-Creating Company", *Harvard Business Review on Knowledge Management*, Harvard Business School Press, Boston.

O'Connor, M.J. (1989), "Models of Human Behaviour and Confidence in Judgement: A Review", *International Journal of Forecasting*, 5, 159–169.

Payne, J.W., Bettman, J.R. and Johnson, E.J. (1988), "Adaptive Strategy Selection in Decision Making", *Journal of Experimental Psychology: Learning, Memory and Cognition*, 14(3), 534–552.

Peterson, D.K. and Pitz, G.F. (1988), "Confidence, Uncertainty and the Use of Information", *Journal of Experimental Psychology: Learning, Memory and Cognition*, 14, 85–92.

Plumley, D. (2003), "Process-based Knowledge Mapping: A Practical Approach to Prioritising Knowledge in Terms of its Relevance to a Business or KM Objective", *Knowledge Management Magazine*, March 03.

Remus, W. (1996), "Will Behavioural Research on Managerial Decision Making Generalise to Managers?", *Managerial and Decision Economics*, 17, 93–101.

Remus, W., O'Connor, M. and Griggs, K. (1996), *Does Feedback Improve the Accuracy of Recurrent Judgemental Forecasts*, working paper, University of Hawaii, January.

Senge, P. (1990), *The Fifth Discipline*, Doubleday, New York.

Seufert, S. and Seufert, A. (1999), "Collaborative Learning Environments for Management Education", in *Proceedings of the 13th Annual Conference of the International Academy for Information Management*, pp. 279–284.

Stasser, G., Taylor, L.A., and Hanna, C. (1989), "Information Sampling in Structured and Unstructured Discussions of Three- and Six-person Groups", *Journal of Personality and Social Psychology*, 57, 67–68.

Stewart, T.A. (1997), *Intellectual Capital: The New Wealth of Organisations*, Doubleday, New York.

Straub, D., Limayem, M. and Karahanna-Evaristo, E. (1995), "Measuring System Usage: Implications for IS Theory Testing", *Management Science*, 41(8), 1328–1342.

Wexler, M. (2001), "The Who, What, Why of Knowledge Mapping", *Journal of Knowledge Management*, 5(3), 249–263.

Whitecotton, S.M. (1996), "The Effects of Experience and a Decision Aid on the Slope, Scatter, and Bias of Earnings Forecasts", *Organisational Behaviour and Human Decision Processes*, 66(1), 111–121.

CHAPTER 9

Knowledge Sharing Technology:

To E-talk or Not To E-talk?

Successful knowledge transfer involves neither computers
nor documents, bur rather interactions between people.
— Thomas H. Davenport

This chapter examines user acceptance of technology for knowledge sharing purposes in an organisation from the higher education sector. Both qualitative and quantitative analysis of data point to a low level of technology acceptance for knowledge sharing. People perceived technology as somewhat useful in supporting connectivity and collaboration, but not in idea exchange. They also perceived the technology as hard to use, felt discouraged, and tended to avoid using it. The chapter suggests a series of plausible actions to increase acceptance.

9.1 Introduction

A great deal of knowledge within organisations resides in the mind of its employees. To capitalise on individual knowledge, organisations need to turn it into organisational knowledge. Nonaka's (1998) SECI model describes organisational knowledge creation as a dynamic process involving a continual interplay between explicit and tacit dimensions of knowledge through processes of socialisation, externalisation, combination and internalisation. The model identifies socialisation as a mode that enables tacit knowledge to be transferred from one individual or group to another within the organisation. This concept is also found in some other process-orientated knowledge management frameworks under different names, including social learning, knowledge sharing, or knowledge transfer (Alavi and Leidner, 2001).

The assumption is that socialisation enables tacit knowledge to be transferred between individuals and groups through shared experience, space and time. Examples include spending time working together or in social meetings. Furthermore, knowledge sharing is considered as one of the most challenging processes for a knowledge-based enterprise due to employees' possible reluctance to share what they know. It is suggested that in its absence, the gap between individual and organisational knowledge can widen. It is also noted that knowledge sharing is the most susceptible process to the effects of various socio-technological factors (Ford and Chan, 2003). Technology for knowledge sharing is the main focus of this chapter.

The role of technology in KM and therefore in knowledge sharing is the source of major disagreement within the KM community (Holsapple, 2003; Edwards et al., 2003). "Nothing" and "all" to do with technology are the views on the two extreme ends of the spectrum (Snowden, 2003). The first is driven by the interest of those wishing to privilege the role of people in organisations, the second by those wishing to sell KM tools and systems (Swan, 2003). From the personalisation perspective on KM (Hansen et al., 1999) the main role of technology is seen in enabling and facilitating interaction among people for the purpose of knowledge sharing. The aim is to create a connected virtual environment for knowledge exchange by allowing knowledge seekers to identify and communicate with knowledge sources (Handzic and Hasan, 2003). The Interim Australian KM Standard (Standards Australia, 2003) recommends several types of technologies for consideration by organisations when developing KM solutions that support virtual socialisation including e-mail, bulletin boards, chat-rooms, whiteboards, audio and video-conferencing. They also cover various specialised groupware applications, and integrated portals, intranets and extranets.

A comprehensive survey of best KM practices (AA, 1998), reveals that most organisations implement some kind of technology to connect people and enable their interaction and collaboration. However, there are differences among researchers regarding the value of virtual (technology-mediated) interaction in comparison with real (face-to-face) interaction in knowledge management. Some researchers warn that technologies lack the emotional richness and depth of real, live, in-person interaction (Santosus, 2001), and are unable to fully develop relationships and an understanding of complex situations (Bender and Fish, 2000). Others argue that communication mediated by technology is no less effective than face-to-face communication (Warkentin et al., 1997). More and more cyber-communities are also beginning to challenge traditional ideas about communities' needs for a physical presence advocated by Nonaka and Konno (1998).

9.2 Technologies for Knowledge Sharing

Groupware is one of the most popular technologies that facilitate connections between people and transfer of knowledge between knowledge seekers and knowledge providers (Awad and Ghaziri, 2004). It is a type of technology specifically focused on issues related to collaborative processes among people (Marakas, 2003). People rely on groupware to communicate ideas and experiences, cooperate in problem-solving, coordinate work-flow, and negotiate solutions.

Groupware comprises a wide range of technologies including telephone, e-mail and messaging systems, newsgroups, work-flow systems, video conferencing, chat rooms, and scheduling systems. To make sense of this wide variety, groupware packages are usually categorised along the time (synchronous, asynchronous) and place (collocated, non-collocated) dimensions. For example, synchronous collocated systems include electronic meetings and presentation support, while synchronous non-collocated systems incorporate video and audio conferences. Examples of asynchronous collocated systems are shared computers and work-flow systems, while asynchronous non-collocated systems cover e-mail and collaborative writing.

Intranet is another popular type of technology that handles all kinds of communication needs with ease (Awad and Ghaziri, 2004). Intranet is a private, secure space on the web where all members of an organisation can communicate with each other, share information and collaborate on projects (Colmer and O'Brien, 2003). It is a vehicle for inexpensive, easy mass distribution of information. To be a successful enabler of knowledge sharing, an intranet needs to have a directory that structures the site content, search facility for access to all resources, and a news section that replaces organisation-wide email bulletins (Nielsen, 2002). In addition, it needs to have an open shared space where employees can post messages, questions, ideas, suggestions for improvements and request help or advice (Arnott, 2000).

It is believed that knowledge sharing technologies can provide many benefits. Technology can enhance the sharing of knowledge by reducing the restrictions pertaining to distance and time. The application of electronic mail, internet, collaboration technologies, bulletin boards, newsgroups can support the distribution of knowledge throughout an organisation. Technology also can provide a forum for employees to debate, discuss and interpret knowledge via multiple perspectives.

However, the vast array of technologies available to support organisations in their quest to engage in effective knowledge sharing can be overwhelming. An over-reliance on technology for the purposes of knowledge sharing can also lead to a free-for-all mentality where everything is important and everything is shared (Greco, 1999). Such mentality can lead to decreased employee knowledge performance due to overload and inability to distinguish valuable knowledge from what is not. Therefore organisations need to conduct an internal analysis of their existing strengths and weaknesses to determine the appropriate technological infrastructure to support their individual requirements.

9.3 Empirical Study

Study Description

The current study is a part of the larger research project aimed at exploring various socio-technical aspects of knowledge sharing (Handzic et al., 2004). The focus here is on user acceptance of technology for the purpose of knowledge sharing. The study was conducted using a case study method because it allows the phenomenon of interest to be explored in natural settings, facilitates exploratory type of research, and enables deeper understanding of complex situations (Yin, 1994). The case organisation selected was a highly renowned and respected tertiary and research institution established in the university community in 1991. University schools, although knowledge intensive organisations that can greatly benefit from knowledge management initiatives, have received relatively little attention from researchers compared to profit-making business organisations.

The subjects were 32 out of 36 possible staff members who participated in the study on a voluntary basis. The rate of 89% ensured that the sample was representative of the school. Out of 32 participants, 50% were teaching staff, 31% general staff, and 19% student services staff. With respect to the length of employment, 50% of the participants were with the school 5–10 years, 38% 1–5 years, 6% less than 1 year and the remaining 6% more than 10 years. Such distribution indicates that participants were familiar with their working environment.

The data collection was done by multiple methods. The methods were both quantitative and qualitative and included a general questionnaire followed by staff interviews, collection of school documents and direct site observations by one of the researchers. The questionnaire contained statements relating to the research model shown in Figure 9.1: perceived usefulness (connectivity, collaboration, idea exchange),

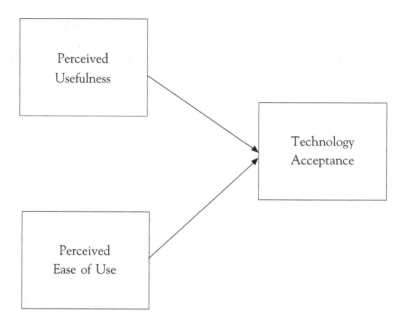

Figure 9.1 Technology acceptance model

perceived ease of use (real-time, integrated, efficient), and acceptance (encouragement, use) of knowledge sharing technology. Respondents were asked to evaluate each statement on a scale from (1) strongly disagree to (5) strongly agree. The questionnaire employed was based on similar instruments previously tested and used in the KM literature (Oliver et al., 2003). Modifications were made to reflect the specifics of the organisation being studied.

Follow-up interviews with 7 staff members were conducted and audio-taped with the aim to probe for culture-revealing elements as suggested by McDermott and O'Dell (2001). In addition, the school made available its existing documentation including agendas, minutes, actions, plans, reports and other records related to the school's structure, mission, principles and values. These were further supplemented with the researcher's own site observation notes taken during regular working hours over a period of 2 months.

Data analysis was done in several steps. First, a quantitative analysis of the questionnaire responses was carried out using statistical analyses. Then the qualitative analysis of interviews, documents and the researcher's diary was performed to identify and classify main themes from the recordings.

Quantitative Analysis and Results

A descriptive analysis of data was performed as suggested by Miles and Huberman (1994) to identify prevailing patterns and ensure plausibility of findings. In order to identify a central tendency in participants' perceptions, the average scores of their responses to relevant questionnaire items were calculated and presented in Figure 9.2.

The average score for the school's knowledge sharing (KS) conducted via technology (2.38 out of 5) indicates its low importance and acceptance within the school. The usefulness of technology in supporting collaboration (3.47) and connectivity (3.91) were the only aspects rated somewhat important. All other aspects evaluated were rated low including support for idea exchange (2.00), ease of use (2.91) and encouragement to use (2.78). These initial results suggest that the school's technology

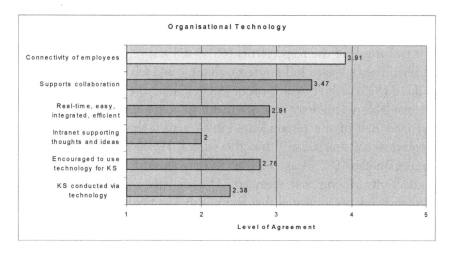

Figure 9.2 Mean results for technology acceptance variables

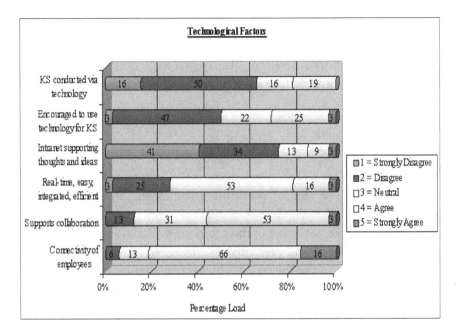

Figure 9.3 Individual responses for technology acceptance

did not provide sufficient support for knowledge sharing within the school. This, in turn, resulted in the low level of technology acceptance by the school employees for the purposes of sharing knowledge.

Further analysis of individual responses presented in Figure 9.3 shows that two-thirds of the respondents (66%) did not rely on technology at all when they engaged in knowledge sharing, and felt no encouragement to do so (50%). Over two-thirds of the respondents (75%) thought that the available technology was not useful in supporting ideas exchange. Just over half of the respondents (56%) agreed that it was useful for supporting collaboration within the school. However, the majority of the respondents (82%) agreed that technology was useful in providing connectivity among staff members. The analysis also highlighted that more respondents indicated that technology was hard to use (28%) than those who felt comfortable with it (19%). The remaining 53% of the respondents adopted a neutral position. The follow up interviews probed deeper into these findings.

Qualitative Analysis and Results

Qualitative analysis of collected data further confirmed that the level of user acceptance of technology for knowledge sharing purposes was low. The analysis found that the school utilised, or attempted to utilise, three main technologies in relation to their knowledge sharing activities. These were the Eudora e-mail system, WebCT, and a shared server. Technology was installed to facilitate communication and sharing among general staff, student services staff and the academics within the school. However, the quantitative analysis pointed out that technology was not a high priority for staff in terms of sharing knowledge and the interviews sought to uncover the reasons behind it.

The seven interviews with staff revealed that e-mail was used on a regular basis to keep the staff up-to-date with the latest activities and events. In contrast, very few people used a shared server to obtain required knowledge. Instead, most employees simply approached other staff in person to request the needed documents. When quizzed about the reasons why this may be the case, typical responses obtained were: 'there hasn't been any formal training to let people know what they can do', 'technology takes away personal relationships', and 'people are not technologically minded'. There was also an admission that the server was 'on a very rudimentary level'.

It appears that the lack of adequate functionality and literacy were the major inhibitors of greater reliance on technology for knowledge sharing within the school. However, the majority of the participants wholeheartedly agreed that the introduction of an open place on the shared server would indeed benefit the school. Some of the views expressed were along these lines: 'to get away from routine e-mails and get people thinking', and a 'scheme where everyone can contribute'. There was less support expressed for using collaborative technologies such as groupware 'given the small group where time and distance are not an issue', and 'when we are so close and can easily talk in person'. Physical proximity and the richness of the face-to-face medium of communication were responsible for the lack of greater reliance on technology for collaboration within the school. In summary, the technology was viewed as secondary to social methods. It was considered useful in situations when personal contacts were not possible or feasible.

Other Issues

Overall, this research study uncovered a distinct preference for people-orientated over technology-orientated means of knowledge sharing in the case organisation. The four major reasons identified were: personnel-related, method-related, and related to the fear of technology, and related to the technological promises vs actual deliverance. Lack of common language between IT and non-IT personnel, use of technology for discussing personal matters, unrealistic expectations from the technology, and forced use of new technologies were some of the most common problems identified.

In order to alleviate the existing problems, the study suggested a series of plausible actions. These include: organising face-to-face meetings with both IT and non-IT personnel on a regular basis to facilitate better understanding; considering the 'time' element involved, and the sensitivity of the knowledge to be shared; dealing with each situation on its merits (i.e., the personality of the recipient); understanding that technology will not and cannot, no matter how advanced or sophisticated, eradicate all organisational problems; implementing technological packages suitable to the requirements of the organisation; organising training and education as to the benefits of technology; and ensuring that on-going technical support is provided.

9.4 Conclusions

The main objective of this chapter was to examine user acceptance of technology for knowledge sharing purposes in a specific knowledge intensive organisation. Both qualitative and quantitative analysis of collected data point to a low degree of acceptance of technology as a medium for knowledge sharing within the organisation. The role of technology was found to be somewhat important in supporting connectivity and collaboration, but not in idea exchange. This could be potentially attributed to the early stage of the development and implementation of the relevant technology support. The study suggested a series of plausible actions to enhance the existing low level of acceptance.

References

AA (1998), *Best Practices in Knowledge Management*, Arthur Andersen.

Alavi, M. and Leidner, D.E. (2001), "Knowledge Management and Knowledge Management Systems: Conceptual Foundations and Research Issues", *MIS Quarterly*, 25(1), 107–136.

Arnott, D. (2000), *Corporate Culture: The Insidious Lure of the All-Consuming Organisation*, American Management Association, New York.

Awad, E.M. and Ghaziri, H.M. (2004), *Knowledge Management*, Pearson Education, New Jersey.

Bender, S. and Fish, A. (2000), "The Transfer of Knowledge and the Retention of Expertise: The Continuing Need for Global Assignments", *Journal of Knowledge Management*, 4(2), 125–150.

Colmer, M. and O'Brien, T. (2003), *InfoTrain Electronic Publishing on the Internet*, Module 3, University of South Australia, January.

Edwards, J., Handzic, M., Carlsson, S. and Nissen, M. (2003), "Knowledge Management Research and Practice: Visions and Directions", *Knowledge Management Research & Practice*, 1(1), 49–60.

Ford, D.P. and Chan, Y.E. (2003), "Knowledge Sharing in a Multi-cultural Setting: A Case Study", *Knowledge Management Research & Practice*, 1(1), 11–27.

Greco, J. (1999), "Knowledge is Power", *Journal of Business Strategy*, 20(2), 18–22.

Handzic, M. and Hasan, H. (2003), "The Search for an Integrated Framework of KM", chapter 1 in Hasan, H. and Handzic, M. (eds.), *Australian Studies in Knowledge Management*, UOW Press, Wollongong, pp. 3–34.

Handzic, M., Lazaro, O. and Van Toorn, C. (2004), "Enabling Knowledge Sharing: Culture versus Technology", in *Proceedings of the 5th European Conference on Organisational Learning, Knowledge and Capabilities (OKLC'2004)*, Innsbruck, Austria, April 2–3.

Hansen, M.T., Nohria, N. and Tierney, T. (1999), "What's Your Strategy for Managing Knowledge?", *Harvard Business Review*, 77(2), 106–116.

Holsapple, C.W. (2003), "Knowledge and Its Attributes", in Holsapple, C.W. (ed.), *Handbook on Knowledge Management*, Vol. 1, Springer, Berlin, pp. 165–188.

Marakas, G.M. (2003), *Decision Support Systems in the 21st Century*, 2nd ed., Pearson Education, New Jersey.

McDermott, R. and O'Dell, C. (2001), "Overcoming Cultural Barriers to Sharing Knowledge", *Journal of Knowledge Management*, 5(1), 76–85.

Miles, M.B. and Huberman, M.A. (1994), *Qualitative Data Analysis*. Sage, London.

Nonaka, I. and Konno, N. (1998), "The Concept of Ba: Building a Foundation for Knowledge Creation", *California Management Review*, 40(3), 40–54.

Nonaka, I. (1998), "The Knowledge-Creating Company", *Harvard Business Review on Knowledge Management*, Harvard Business School Press, Boston.

Nielsen, J. (2002), *Designing Web Usability: The Practice of Simplicity*, New Riders Publishing, Indianapolis.

Oliver, G., Handzic, M. and Van Toorn, C. (2003), "Towards Understanding Knowledge Management in Academia: The Shoemaker's Paradox", *Electronic Journal of Knowledge Management*, 1(2), Paper 13.

Santosus, M. (2001), *KM and Human Nature*, CIO.com "In the Know", http://www.cio.com/knowledge/edit/k121801_nature.html. [accessed 18/12/2001].

Snowden, D. (2003), "Innovation as an Objective of Knowledge Management. Part I: The Landscape of Management", *Knowledge Management Research & Practice*, 1(2), 113–119.

Standards Australia (2003), *Interim Australian Standard: Knowledge Management, AS5037 (Int)*, Standards Australia International Limited, Sydney.

Swan, J. (2003), "Knowledge Management in Action", in Holsapple, C.W. (ed.), *Handbook on Knowledge Management*, Vol. 1, Springer, Berlin, pp. 271–296.

Warkentin, M.E., Sayeed, L. and Hightower, R. (1997), "Virtual Teams versus Face-to-face Teams: An Exploratory Study of Web-based Conference System", *Decision Sciences*, 28(4).

Yin, R. (1988), *Case Study Research: Design and Methods*, Sage, London.

CHAPTER 10

Virtual Reality Model:

Visualising Social Networks

A picture is worth a thousand words.
— Napoleon

This chapter presents a three-dimensional virtual reality model aimed at assisting the user to visually explore social network structures and relationships. The three-dimensional model uses a combination of nodes and paths to represent actors and the strength and direction of their relationships. Virtual reality provides the mechanism for manipulation of the developed model in real-time. The effectiveness of this visual tool is demonstrated empirically by having postgraduate students, organised into focus groups, engage in a social network analysis exercise with data collected in an academic work environment.

10.1 Introduction

In knowledge intensive firms, people networks form an important part of the organisational social capital. According to Cohen and Prusak (2001), people often get things done through the people they know. Therefore it is important for individuals and collectives to develop an understanding of what expertise resides in each part of the organisation, and to have personal networks that are both trust based, wide reaching, and able to get to needed expertise within a small number of links.

Techniques for understanding the relationships between the net objects, nodes or actors as reflected in the transfer of assets, communication, or emotions, has long been the goal of the discipline of Social Network Analysis (SNA). SNA research suggests that the more people are aware of a network, the more power they have to achieve what they want to achieve. At the same time, it warns that people have a limited network horizon of about two. This means that they cannot see further than the people who know those they know (Townley, 2003).

Visual representations of these social or knowledge networks may help people to better understand the existing networks, as well as to plan the development of new ones. The purpose of this chapter is to examine the potential of a three-dimensional virtual reality model to assist users to visually explore social network structures and relationships. Subjects in the social network are viewed as a set of inter-dependent actors, rather than independent entities. Consequently, the focus of SNA is on the relationships between actors rather than the attributes of the actors themselves. The structure of their organisation is also important due to interdependence.

10.2 Visualisation

Visualisation is defined as the process by which numerical data such as surveys, measurements or simulations are converted into meaningful images (Marakas, 1999). The usefulness of visualisation lies in the basic assumption that large and normally incomprehensible amounts of data can be reduced to a form that can be understood and interpreted by a human through the use of visualisation techniques (Simoff, 2001). Human are known to be visual creatures with most of what they learn coming through sight (Whinston, 1995). It has also been recognised that visual pattern recognition skills exceed human ability to comprehend collections of texts and numbers (Ho and Azvine, 2000). This suggests that technologies and tools using visualisation techniques may be useful in analysing and understanding collections of data in various contexts.

Data visualisation models can be represented in different ways. They can be classified into geometric and symbolic representations. Geometric techniques include scatter-plots, lines, surfaces and volumes. Symbolic representations are showing the data using graphs (Fayyad et al., 2002). The simplest form of visualising data is using graphs, charts and tables, and indexing by colouring or symbol codes (Cabena et al., 1997). There are other forms that include digital images, geographic systems, graphical user interfaces, multi-dimensions, virtual reality, 3D presentations and animation.

So far, visualisation has been successfully used in many industries including credit scoring and risk analysis in banking, fraud analysis and drug enforcement in government, and customer behaviour analysis in marketing. Empirical findings from our own laboratory studies indicate that 2D visualisation tools were helpful in improving performance in forecasting trends (Handzic et al., 2002a), as well as in understanding relationships among multiple contextual cues (Handzic and Li, 2003). Our findings also show that scatterplots were more beneficial than barcharts in visualising two-way relationships among variables (Handzic et al., 2002b).

Two-dimensional (2D) and three-dimensional (3D) visualisations have always been some of the most popular design options when it comes to the layout of a semantic structure. It has been long debated whether a three-dimensional visualisation would indeed offer the user richer semantics and more informative and intuitive controls of the underlying information. Several projects have investigated the relative performance and preference of users for 2D and 3D non-interactive graphs. Some studies found no difference in performance between them

(Carswell et al., 1991), others found a general preference for 3D graphs particularly when they were used for making a memorable impression and when communicating information to others (Levy et al., 1996). 3D visualisations were also useful for examining interactions that could not be expressed by decomposing them into two-way relationships (Poulet, 2000). However, a disadvantage of some 3D visualisations was the difficulty of precisely locating an element in space.

The above review and analysis of previous research clearly demonstrates the usefulness of visualisation technology in a variety of contexts. It also suggests that the effectiveness of a particular tool may be contingent upon the task context. Stephens and Handzic (2004) proposed an interactive 3D visualisation tool using virtual reality as a potentially useful means to support social network analysis, particularly the discovery of relationships and network structures in an academic work environment. The following sections describe the proposed tool and its application.

10.3 Virtual Reality Model Description

Why VRML?

Users attempting to utilise visualisation tools are likely to face difficulties such as knowing and understanding the visualization tool, including the functionality provided by it; the implementation of the visualization paradigm; and usability problems introduced by the tool but independent of the visualization paradigm adopted. Providing a visualization tool that represents the data effectively while at the same time providing a suitable user interface is critical to the success of any system. Decision-makers also need the ability to collaborate with colleagues. Use of VRML provides a 3D environment, a graphical user interface (GUI) and interoperability (the ability of applications to work with other systems or applications without special effort). The 3D model produced is readily understood with respect to our visual spatial abilities. The ability to provide preset views of the 3D model (create viewpoints) assists collaboration by enabling the author to refer the user to particular views of interest.

Current visualisation techniques often require the viewer to be viewing from a distance 'looking in' at the entire network model. Although the model can be rotated around the vertical and horizontal axis the rotation is performed around the geometric centre of the network. This creates two problems. Firstly, it is difficult to visualise the network from an individual node's perspective, and, secondly, for large numbers of nodes it is difficult to enter the network perimeter. Entering the network perimeter enables the viewer to focus-in on groupings within the network. The application of the Virtual Reality Modelling Language (VRML) removes both of these restrictions.

The following have been suggested as features that would help an analyst comprehend the structural properties of relationships in data presented as a network: use of colour and different shapes to highlight properties; variations in colours or shapes to display various kinds of relations; use of animation to display time-dependent changes in network structure; and arranging points to draw attention to important structural features (Tufte, 1983; Freeman, 1998).

An experiment designed to look at a viewer's perceptions of patterns of leadership, coordination and sub-group organisation found that the subjects' perceptions were influenced by the form of the diagram (McGrath et al., 1997). Providing the user with a 3D space that can be manipulated easily will provide them with a model from which to investigate many of the aspects of relational data without relying solely on the way in which the author presents the images.

Various graphics packages, currently available, provide the following features to differing degrees: ability to use colour to highlight features; shape variation to highlight features; show linkages; user rotation of the 3D space; and zoom in/out. Given the current developments in computer power and graphics capabilities the following additional features should be viewed as desirable in a visualisation tool: user controlled rotation of the model; and interoperability. User controlled rotation of the model enables the user to specify viewpoints in the model and direct colleagues to them, at which point the view could be discussed. This could be implemented, for example, with a button embedded in an electronic publication. Morphing (i.e., the animation of the move from one fixed position to another) through a time series of node shifts is also a possibility. The desirable features of such a tool would include: animation; rotation of the model by the user as well as colleagues being able to specify set positions as an adjunct to discussion and interpretation; ability to interactively edit or re-position a node; colour and shape manipulation; view network specific metrics while exploring the model; and cross platform implementation.

VRML was chosen because it is a development environment designed to create and maintain virtual 3D spaces or worlds. Comprehending images presented in other packages may be restricted by the limitation of being able to rotate the image only about the centre and to zoom in or out of the world. VRML enables the viewer to inspect the world by these methods plus enabling the viewer to change the perspective of the world by selecting individual nodes or actors as the centre of the world, thus effectively viewing the network from the individual's standpoint. VRML allows the use of a variety of shapes and colours as well as the ability to attach labels to the shapes; clicking on a shape can display text to the viewer providing additional information such as who or what that node represents. This feature also enables other network specific metrics to be displayed which provides the user with useful information about the individual nodes while exploring the 3D space. As VRML is a 'plug-in' for a browser it is possible to create a frame in which to present this additional information.

It was felt that VRML should be able to provide most of the features indicated by commentators thus far and in addition provide a mechanism for electronic publication which would enable the author to specify movements of the 3D space that can be observed in real-time for illustrative purposes. The use of a high-level language such as Python to produce the VRML input allows a more efficient and tailored file than simply converting to VRML from other systems. This greater control also facilitates the inclusion of other network specific data.

Figure 10.1 provides an example of the 3D model plus the frame of additional information that can be provided. The bonds between the nodes (represented as 'sticks') are adjusted in thickness to highlight the strength of the bond (also indicated by the closeness of the nodes) and

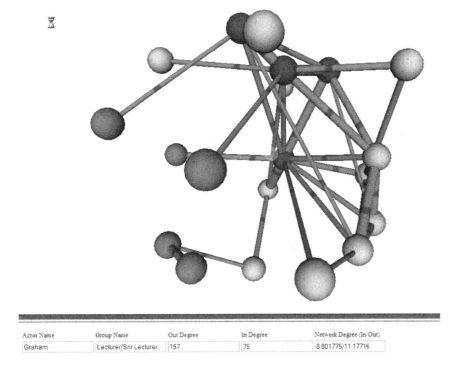

Actor Name	Group Name	Out Degree	In Degree	Network Degree (In/Out)
Graham	Lecturer/Snr Lecturer	157	75	8.801775/11.17716

Figure 10.1 VRML example screen shot

include a band which indicates the main direction of the communication. When the band is closer to one node it means that most of the communication was initiated by the other partner.

The Prototype

The original prototype was designed using a combination of three applications. The network was based on output from UCINET (i.e., a set of social network analysis tools including routines for multi-dimesional scaling) described in Borgatti et al. (2002). A visual basic application was used to collect author provided parameters such as input/output files, colours, shapes, and scaling factors. This application also produced the VRML coding for the model. COSMO Player 2 was used to view the network model. In the current prototype, visual basic has been replaced by Python — another high-level programming language. The most difficult part in setting up this application was the specification of an algorithm to place the bonds in the three-dimensional space, between two nodes.

This prototype was developed as an exploration of the suitability of VRML as a development platform for a network specific visualisation tool. It was decided, initially, that an interface would be developed between an existing social network analysis tool that would perform the required computation of network analysis specific metrics: UCINET VI was chosen as it seemed to provide the widest choice in generally accepted metrics (Borgatti et al., 2002). UCINET is also well accepted as a social network analysis tool.

The interface was built using Python. It was chosen for its ability to handle text strings, output ASCII text files, and ease of creating GUIs. This interface program basically reads in UCINET output from which it creates VRML compliant (.wrl) input files. The user interface provides the user with a number of choices that are incorporated as the VRML specification file is generated.

For instance, users are able to specify for the network: scaling factors, and threshold for viewing connections; and for each node: size, shape, colour, group membership, and diameter of the connections. The basic process is: data is collected and input into UCINET; output from UCINET is saved to an ASCII text file for input into the VRML generation application; as the VRML code is generated the user is requested to specify the parameters as indicated above; once the VRML code is produced it is saved to a .wrl file for processing by a viewer; in this case Cosmo Player Version 2.0; although any of the VRML viewers will suffice.

In fact three files are produced by the Python application — one VRML file and two HTML files. The initial anchor in the browser is to the first HTML file which has the other two embedded in it. The VRML file contains all the code required to produce the 3D model while the second HTML file contains the code necessary to create and maintain the frame in which the network specific data is displayed.

The potential of the developed visual tool was demonstrated by having postgraduate students, organised into focus groups, engage in a social network analysis exercise with data collected in an academic work environment.

10.4 Tool Application

Data Collection

The data that is used in the demonstration is based on recollections of the frequency of significant communication initiated with partners. Each individual was given a software tool designed to present a complete list of other staff members of the then School of Information Systems. Each individual was requested to specify how often in a typical month they initiated significant communication with the listed member of staff. Each member of staff was presented with the list of others randomly, that is, the software randomly selected from the 'not yet presented' list until that list became null.

This method of collection enabled the presentation of all staff names to each individual staff member without the risk of the order of presentation having an impact on results, although this was not considered to be a particular risk. More important was the functionality that was incorporated into the software that saved having to key-in the data manually.

The data was presented in summary form at the conclusion of the questionnaire and the staff member was requested to review it before finalising the session. At the conclusion of the session, the data was stored on a diskette and later transferred to a spreadsheet. A spreadsheet macro was developed to generate a file in the DL format required for UCINET.

The data was collected as part of a study of the impact of assumed organisational role on the social network maintained by an individual. Role was assigned by a committee of senior staff of the School as follows: Role 1 — those who generally participate in policy development; Role 2 — those who sometimes participate; and Role 3 — those who rarely, if ever, do. This is roughly analogous to the managerial hierarchy; strategic, tactical and operational. Those who do participate were assigned to Role 1 (strategic), those who do not ever participate were assigned to Role 3 (operational) and Role 2 (tactical) was assigned to the remainder. The data collected enabled the production of a valued square adjacency matrix.

Data Transformation

UCINET was used to process the collected data and produce the metrics used in the VRML visualisation tool. Multi-dimensional scaling was used to produce the three-dimensional coordinates for the individual nodes. The other social network measures that were of interest in the study included: centrality, flow betweenness, and information. However, for this demonstration only degree was presented as additional data.

The features incorporated into the demonstrated model were: a 3D virtual reality model that permits rotation on a centre point presented as a transparent spot; the ability to rotate the model on all axis; ability to zoom in/zoom out; ability to change the centre of rotation to one of the nodes; clicking on a node will change its colour (highlight) until another node is selected; clicking on a node displays the actor's name, group, inbound and outbound degree measures; thickness of the connectors is adjusted to enhance the indication of the strength of the bond; a black band on the connector indicates the direction and proportion of outbound degree; selection of a ViewPoint from a list; and ability to 'fly-through' and inspect the 3D model.

The basic methodology adopted for this prototype was to arrange the data into an adjacency matrix. This matrix was organised into an N by N matrix representing the communication on the left and the recipients along the top following the conventions adopted in social network analysis. The purpose of the visualisation tool was to enable the individual studying the data to identify groups and relationships by being able to manipulate a three-dimensional model in an Euclidean space. The model was developed with simplicity in mind. There are many different aspects of the data that could have been represented but to do so would have done nothing to help the user to discover knowledge — in particular the patterns of communication that existed in the network.

Consequently, the model has only a small number of variables represented (see Figure 10.2). These include the name (fictitious) of the individual that is represented by the ball, the direction and frequency of communication represented by the stick — the frequency being represented by the closeness of the nodes and the thickness of the stick; direction is indicated by a band on the stick; the proportion to the left and to the right of the band represents the proportion of total communication which emanates from that side. Where the band is closer to one node than the other then the majority of the communication comes from the node furthest away from the bar.

The values determined for the various measures employed in social networks such as betweenness and closeness are displayed in the frame

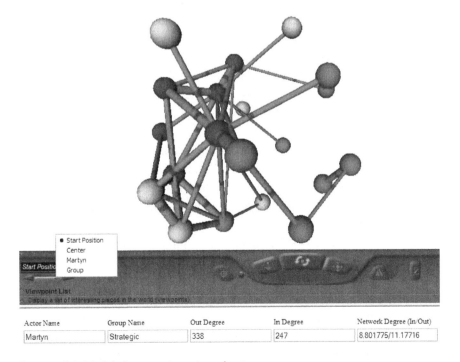

Actor Name	Group Name	Out Degree	In Degree	Network Degree (In/Out)
Martyn	Strategic	338	247	8.801775/11.17716

Figure 10.2 Model showing viewpoint selection

at the bottom of the diagram. This was done to reduce the clutter in the actual model and keep it free of text. In fact there is no text recorded in the model. The semi-transparent sphere is calculated as and positioned at the geometric centre of the network. Initially, the model spins around this axis. The centre point can be changed by seeking one of the actors — this enables the user to rotate the model about the node (and therefore the actor) which thus represents the network from the perspective of the selected node.

Tool Evaluation

The tool evaluation was carried out in an exploratory qualitative study using postgraduate commerce students as voluntary subjects. It is appropriate to include a warning here. The evaluation study reported here does not reflect the kind of scale, detail and rigour normally expected for a research study. At this stage, we were interested in quickly feeling the pulse of users, and therefore conducted a relatively informal study by engaging subjects in a knowledge discovery exercise with data collected in an academic work environment.

First, the adjacency matrix was presented to two classes with over 100 postgraduate Masters students enrolled in the Decision Support Systems course and the following seminars in data warehousing, data mining and knowledge management. These classes were used as focus groups that started by asking the question "what could be deduced from the valued square matrix presented". Some time was spent during the seminar discussing the matrix and what it represented. Additional information was also provided regarding the organisational role determined for each of the staff listed in the matrix. After some discussion the focus groups came to the conclusion that about all they could tell from what was presented was that some people communicated more than others. No one was able to detect or discuss any of the groupings, structure, etc. — this was the same for both classes.

Then, these same students were provided with an interactive 3D visual prototype described in the previous section. Following presentation of the virtual reality model both classes were able to identify a number of groupings, hierarchies, isolates and other structures present in the data. Although no formal quantitative data analysis was performed at this stage, the obvious conclusion to the deliberations of the two focus groups is that the tool provided the opportunity to identify structures and groupings in the data that were not possible without it. As one group member put it "it brought the data to life".

For example, in the screen image (Figure 10.3) of the model it is quite obvious that Martyn (yellow sphere), who has assumed a strategic role, is closely linked with three other staff (one acting in an operational role and two who have adopted a tactical role) — the banding on the sticks indicates that most of the communication in this group is initiated by Martyn. Also note the existence of the isolate in the top left of the

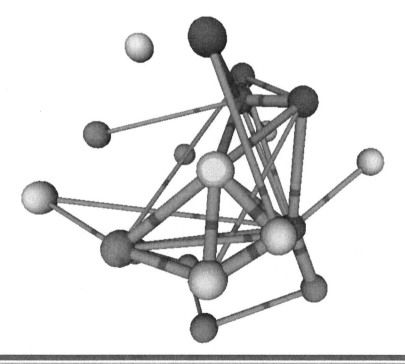

Actor Name	Group Name	Out Degree	In Degree	Network Degree (In/Out)
Martyn	Strategic	338	247	8.801775/11.17716

Figure 10.3 Model showing node selection and observation

model. None of this relational information is readily available from an inspection of the adjacency matrix from which the model was produced.

The representation of the network data in a three-dimensional model enabled the discovery of knowledge from the numeric data. This knowledge is not easily obtained without the assistance of the tool.

The results of this test demonstrate the ability of a 3D representation of relational data to enhance social network analysis. The viewers' ability to discover this knowledge was aided by the power to manoeuvre the model in a free-form fashion. In addition, the provision of the network specific metrics provided a check on the observations from the model itself. This technique is suitable to any data relationships that can be represented in a from/to exchange.

10.5 Conclusions

The main purpose of this chapter was to explore the ability of a three-dimensional model to assist in the task of social network analysis where the data being considered represents a relationship of the form of a transfer from/to objects/nodes/actors. This type of data is often presented in an adjacency matrix. However, this study found that a three-dimensional virtual reality model better assisted the users in exploring structures and relationships, visually. The combination of nodes and paths to represent objects/actors and the representation of strength/ direction of the measured characteristics provided the means by which the relationships and structures were discovered. The ability of virtual reality to provide the mechanism for real-time manipulation of the model assisted users in analysing the patterns.

Although the current evaluation study was rather informal, exploratory and qualitative in nature there was very strong feeling that the model enabled discovery of network structures and relationships that were not evident from the numeric data initially presented in a matrix. However, more rigorous research tests in controlled laboratory settings are needed to confirm the validity of these findings. Future research in this area may also consist of investigations into the usefulness of this type of modelling for presentation of relational data in other domains. Another line of investigation will involve developing an understanding of the best features to include and how these may relate to specific knowledge domains and/or relationships.

Subsequent versions of this application are being considered using Java as the development platform. This is being considered for the reasons: VRML is Java compliant and permits the use of Java objects as VRML objects; Java is suited to publishing on the Web; more interactive designs are achievable using Java; and the author of an electronic publication will be able to position the network at specific points to illustrate an argument.

References

Borgatti, S.P., Everett, M.G. and Freeman, L.C. (2002), *Ucinet for Windows: Software for Social Network Analysis*, Analytic Technologies, Harvard.

Cabena, P., Hadjinian, P., Stadler, R. and Zanasi, A. (1997), *Discovering Data Mining from Concept to Implementation*, Prentice Hall, New Jersey.

Carswell, C.M., Frankenberger, S. and Bernhard, D. (1991), "Graphing in Depth: Perspectives on the Use of Three-Dimensional Graphs to Represent Lower-Dimensional Data", *Behaviour and Information Technology*, 10(6), 459–474.

Cohen, D. and Prusak, L. (2001), *In Good Company: How Social Capital Makes Organisations Work*, Harvard Business School Press, Boston.

Fayyad, U., Grinstein, G.G. and Wierse, A. (2002), *Information Visualisation in Data Mining and Knowledge Discovery*, Morgan Kaufmann.

Freeman, L.C. (1998), "Using Molecular Modeling Software in Social Network Analysis: A Practicum", http://moreno.ss.uci.edu/groups.pdf.

Handzic, M. and Li, W. (2003), "Discovering Predictive Quality of Knowledge Artefacts in Organisational Repositories", in *Proceedings of the Australian Conference for Knowledge Management and Intelligent Decision Support (ACKMIDS 2002)*, Australian Scholarly Publishing, Melbourne, pp. 133–144.

Handzic, M., Aurum, A., Oliver, G. and Logenthiran, G. (2002a), "An Empirical Investigation of a Knowledge Discovery Tool", *European Conference on Knowledge Management (ECKM 2002)*, Dublin, September.

Handzic, M., Lam, B., Aurum, A., and Oliver, G. (2002b), "A Comparative Analysis of Two Knowledge Discovery Tool: Scatterplot versus Barchart", *International Conference on Data Mining (DM 2002)*, Bologna, September.

Ho, B. and Azvine, C. (2000), "Mining Travel Data with a Visualiser", in *Proceedings of ECML'01 Conference*, September.

Levy, E., Zacks, J., Tversky, B. and Sciano, D. (1996), "Gratuitous Graphics? Putting Preferences in Perspectives", in *Proceedings of CHI'96*, Vancouver, April, pp. 42–49.

Marakas, G.M. (1999), *Decision Support Systems in the 21st Century*, Prentice Hall, New Jersey.

McGrath, C., Blythe, J. and Krackhardt, D. (1997), "The Effect of Spatial Arrangement on Judgements and Errors in Interpreting Graphs", *Social Networks*, 19, 223–242.

Poulet, F. (2000), "Comprehensibility in Data Mining", *International Symposium on Data Mining and Statistics*, November, University of Augsburg, pp. 19–22.

Simoff, S.J. (2001), "Towards the Development of Environments for Designing Visualisation Support for Visual Data Mining", in *Proceedings of ECML'01*, September.

Stephens, G. and Handzic, M. (2004), "Knowledge Discovery Through Visualising Using Virtual Reality", in *Proceedings of the 37th Annual Hawaii International Conference on System Sciences — HICSS37* (CD/ROM), January 5–8, 2004, Computer Society Press.

Townley, C. (2003), "Knowledge Networks: A Case Study from Deloitte Touche Tohmatsu", in *Case Studies in Knowledge Management, Volume 2*, Standards Australia International Limited, Sydney, pp. 15–23.

Tufte, E.R. (1983), *The Visual Display of Quantitative Information*, Graphics Press, Cheshire, Connecticut.

Whinston, Z. (1995), *Business Information Visualisation*, Association for Information Systems Managerial Research, in progress.

PART IV

Complete KM Solutions:

Integrated Systems and Technologies

CHAPTER 11

Web Course Technology:

Creating Virtual Knowledge Spaces

All men by nature desire to know.

— Aristotle

This chapter introduces the concept of virtual knowledge space (k-space) and examines students' attitudes towards it in the context of an undergraduate IS course. The KM framework is used to guide the design of a conceptual model of the web-based k-space aimed at providing support for a variety of learning styles and processes. Data on students' perceptions of the importance of and their satisfaction with their k-space implementation were gathered by administering a survey questionnaire. Results indicate a clear preference for know-what (e.g., lecture notes and announcements) over know-how types (e.g., games and search engines) of knowledge management tools. Implications for online learning are discussed.

11.1 Introduction

Technology is currently driving a profound transformation of the learning industry. In response to the growing demand for education in the knowledge-based economy, universities and colleges are offering thousands of online courses, thus changing the traditional classroom-based methods of teaching and learning. Researchers and practitioners are predicting that the current trend will continue. However, while many institutions are developing and using web-based courses, little is known about their value in improving the quality of student's learning experiences. The underlying assumption is that technology can create conducive learning environments for students (Aurum et al., 2003).

A web-based virtual learning environment is usually defined as a computer-based environment that provides access to a wide range of resources and allows interactions and encounters among participants. Essentially, it combines the individualised learning experience with the communication dimension. Learners can access and utilise different available materials and follow different paths to them depending on their inquiry styles (Churchman, 1971; Vandenbosch et al., 2001). They can also interact and discuss electronically with other learners and instructors. Typically, online environments support learner-centered, modularised and self-paced learning. They may include group experiences, delivery anywhere, performance feedback and grades, and are usually developed by teams of theorists, designers, and content and IT specialists (Twigg, 2001).

The literature suggests that technology-mediated learning environments may improve students' achievement, their attitudes toward learning, and their evaluation of the learning experience. It also suggests that technology may help to increase teacher/student interaction and to make learning more student-centred. In addition, proponents of virtual learning environments suggest that they can potentially eliminate geographic barriers while providing increased convenience, flexibility, currency of material, retention of students, individualised learning and feedback over traditional classrooms. In contrast, other researchers suggest that technology-mediated learning environments may lead to the student feelings of isolation, frustration, anxiety and confusion. It may also result in reduced interest in the subject matter and questionable learner achievement (Piccoli et al., 2001).

Given the growing interest in online education and the general lack of empirical studies examining the effectiveness of the technology-mediated learning environments, the main purpose of this chapter is to address the issue in the context of undergraduate education. In particular, the chapter will first propose a conceptual model of a virtual knowledge space (or k-space) as a flexible learning environment to support multiple individual learning styles. Then, it will examine students' perceptions of and attitudes towards various features of their k-space in the context of an undergraduate IS course.

11.2 A Conceptual Model of Virtual k-Space

The complexities of learning and the large number of interacting factors which affect individual and group learning present many challenges. We argue here that a web-based system (or website) designed on the principles of knowledge management may provide necessary knowledge space to discover, obtain and share knowledge resources for a learner. It also may be a valuable virtual learning community for educators and students alike to share and discuss matters relating to the course. In short, it can enable or facilitate knowledge processes and enhance learning performance. The following sections describe the underlying knowledge management framework and the design philosophy of the proposed conceptual model.

The knowledge management framework presented in Figure 11.1 was adapted from Handzic and Jamieson (2001) and used as the underlying theoretical basis for the conceptual k-space model (Handzic et al., 2003; Handzic and Lin, 2003). The framework is essentially a two-by-two matrix with 'explicit' and 'tacit' knowledge as columns and 'what' and 'how' types of knowledge as rows of the matrix. Individual cells denote instances and sources of specific knowledge types. For example, 'explicit-what' comprises theories and concepts that may be found in lecture notes, databases or documents. 'Explicit-how' includes rules and patterns discovered by individual students while searching various resources. 'Tacit-what' consists of shared ideas and beliefs of course students and educators, while 'tacit how' represents their instincts and expertise gained through personal experience. The model suggests that students' course knowledge may be enhanced by enabling and facilitating availability, sharing and finding of relevant information, as well as learning by doing.

	Explicit	Tacit
What	**Availability of knowledge**	**Sharing of knowledge**
	• Lecture notes	• Discussion forums
	• Relevant resources	• Announcements
	• Databases	• News
How	**Finding of knowledge**	**Learning by doing**
	• Question and answers	• Assignments/Tutorials
	• Classifying summaries	• Online video & streaming
	• Search facilities	• Feed-back/guidance

Figure 11.1 A conceptual k-space model

In particular, the framework suggests that wider availability of relevant knowledge captured in information repositories such as lecture notes and databases will enhance students' learning of concepts, ideas and theories concerning the subject matter. Our preliminary empirical research also suggests that relevant information repositories may be helpful in enhancing students' knowledge. More specifically, our findings indicate that the availability of contextual information in a database increased management students' forecasting knowledge and improved their performance over that of nominal naives who had no such information (Handzic, 2001).

However, most past research also warns that people have difficulties in extracting knowledge due to the abundance, diversity and ambiguity of information often found in the available repositories (Handzic and Aurum, 2001). In order to minimise the detrimental effects of information complexity, the framework suggests that students should be supported by intelligent search and mining facilities. It is argued that such tools should help students extract and better understand and interpret knowledge from information repositories, as well as enable them to discover systematic patterns and rules of the discipline studied.

The framework also recognises the importance of the tacit knowledge of both educators and students. Graduate students often bring to class valuable and unique experiences from their work environments. The traditional class sessions provide only limited opportunity for sharing this knowledge with others. Yet, past research shows that students may benefit from interaction with their peers, particularly when faced with complex tasks (Handzic and Tolhurst, 2002; Handzic and Low, 2002). The proposed knowledge management framework addresses the need to devote more learning time to interaction and collaborative learning by suggesting a variety of information sharing support facilities.

Finally, responding to the need for cultivation of qualities such as problem-solving, decision-making and creativity (Shneiderman, 2000), the framework suggests the need for challenging assignments and self-paced online learning sessions with continuous guidance and feedback. However, one must not forget that learning through personal experience is a long and tedious process of trial and error (Klayman, 1988). Our own empirical research also shows modest learning through experimentation (Handzic, 2000). Therefore, a word of caution against high expectations and in favour of tolerance for failure is necessary here.

11.3 k-Space Design Features

The main objective of the virtual *k*-space or website is to provide students with a one-stop point of interaction for all their study needs, a portal that students can go to obtain lecture notes, assignments, reference materials, discussions, surveys, search facilities, links and many other useful tools. The idea is that different design features of the website accommodate different quadrants of the knowledge matrix. For example, search facilities support the 'explicit-how' quadrant and the discussion forum supports the 'tacit-what' quadrant. It is assumed that students respond differently to certain types of teaching methods, and if all sources are available, the productivity and enjoyment of the course will be increased.

Knowledge management tools are suggested as means to provide a convenient platform for students to access on-site materials as well as information on the World Wide Web. These tools are expected to cater to all students so they can serve themselves, whether it is seeking solutions to problems they have or downloading relevant information from sources. These tools are also suggested to create an environment in which students can comfortably share knowledge amongst one another and therefore create new knowledge concerning the subject. Likewise the tools are expected to provide the students with an ambience setting in which they can search around and play with the web site freely whilst being able to ask for support on subject matters at any time from anywhere.

The integration of these knowledge management tools on the course web site is suggested to bring added value to the traditional learning experience. Staff and students will be able to benefit from using these tools which will provide a means of communication and assessment. Sustained access to these tools will minimise the faculty's cost and time associated with the experience. Thus online education will benefit students greatly as it will provide them with much more interaction than a traditional classroom and with ever evolving Internet technology, the benefits can only increase. The following sections outline various web-course knowledge or k-tools suggested by Handzic and Chumkovski (2004). The idea or goal of the web site is to capture each quadrant of the framework matrix through the use of suitable knowledge management tools.

Explicit-What k-Tools

These tools make information available to students and hence act as great means of student and course content interaction. They explain theories, ideas, concepts and notions of which students would have probably been previously unaware. They act as knowledge repositories whose main purpose is to provide students with relevant information that they can absorb, interpret and hence turn into new and valuable knowledge. Therefore through the use of these tools and the availability of information that they allow for, students can enhance their learning and obtain a better understanding of the subject material. The 'explicit-what' tools that we will be concentrating on in this study are all great forms of knowledge repositories in their own right. These tools include:

❖ **Course Outline** gives students an insight into the course content, structure and assessments weighting.
❖ **Lecture Notes** aid in learning specific topics and increasing overall knowledge of the subject.
❖ **Reading Materials** come in the form of recommended texts, case studies and research papers. Knowledge about the subject may be gained from these readings.
❖ **Student Status Centre** is a means of gaining up-to-date confidential information such as assignment, quiz, and game and exam results. It also gives students an idea of their student ranking in relation to subject performance. It measures their progress and knowledge in the subject thus far.

Explicit-How k-Tools

Moving on to the second quadrant of the framework matrix, we introduce the 'explicit-how' tools. Otherwise known as 'finding of information tools', these tools enable students to search information on their own terms, as knowledge repositories can often create difficulties for students in extracting what they need, due to diversity and ambiguity of information. Unlike your standard knowledge repository, these tools allow students to search and find the information that is vital in solving a particular problem. It is of extreme importance that these tools are "intelligent" and easy to understand. This is because their purpose is to minimise the pernicious effects of information complexity which causes perplexity in people. Hence 'explicit-how' tools should let students understand and interpret knowledge from information repositories, whilst simultaneously providing them with a means of discovery and exploration.

Such 'explicit-how' tools are:

- ❖ **FAQ Page** is an efficient means of gaining knowledge about most important classes of issues, as well as additional clarifications of assignment queries.
- ❖ **Search Engine** is a direct means of access to what students are looking for. Its allows students to gain knowledge on relevant topics quickly, whether they are looking for course content or trying to find the details of a staff member.

Tacit-What k-Tools

The next quadrant captures the 'tacit-what' tools. These tools are also known as the sharing of information tools. Their role is to encourage both students and staff to interact with one another. By doing this, knowledge is transferred to and fro, retained by those who want it and transformed and transferred again. Unlike explicit tools, the value of tacit tools is still somewhat unclear to the fact that these tools are a newer phenomenon. But patterns from research are already starting to develop and are slowly but surely showing that students are stimulated by interaction with their peers, especially when they are faced with difficult and challenging tasks. By being able to share their ideas and beliefs with their peers online, students feel a sense of equality and belonging to the course. Hence, such tools are there to encourage and develop knowledge sharing amongst students and staff. The following 'tacit-what' tools are all great platforms for knowledge sharing amongst students and staff:

- ❖ **Discussion Forums** allow students to interact with each other. This is done by an asynchronous means and allows students to post questions regarding assignments, exams or even general queries in relation to the subject, thus allowing them to transfer and acquire knowledge amongst themselves.
- ❖ **Live Chat** is a synchronous means of student to student interaction in which posted messages can be answered instantaneously therefore servicing knowledge transfer and acquisition in real-time.

❖ **Online Announcements** allow students to keep up to date with everything that is going on in the course. They keep students informed of any changes on a 24-hour basis, therefore not having to wait until the next class in order to be informed of any announcements concerning the course.

❖ **E-mail** gives students and lecturers the opportunity to ask and answer questions on a 1-on-1 basis. Its purpose is to gain additional knowledge on any problem areas and to find answers to any questions students may have.

Tacit-How k-Tools

The final quadrant of the Explicit and Tacit Knowledge Management Framework contains the 'tacit-how' tools. These tools are often referred to as the 'learning by doing' tools due to their unique, hands-on nature and are often used as an assessment to whether the learner has understood what is being conveyed in the course. Through personal experience, they allow students to develop instincts, abilities, intuition and expertise concerning the subject. This quadrant and its tools realise the need for problem-solving, decision-making and creativity through self-directed learning. This quadrant accepts the fact that expertise in this area can only be sought through students 'having a go'. The learning process of trial and error that students need to experience is provided through the following tools:

❖ **Assignments** allow students to put their understanding of lecture notes, readings and tutorials up to the test whilst also remaining up to date with any specification changes the lecturer may need to make.

❖ **Tutorials** are a transformation of lecture notes and readings into real problems and solutions. The introduction of visual and/or audio stimulus tutorials on the web site could help to enable the acquisition and retention of knowledge.

❖ **Online games** stimulate the student's mind through fun and a laid back approach. Students are made to rummage through the web

site, 'hunt' down the answers and on successful completion be
awarded with extra assessment marks.

❖ **Online quizzes** allow students to progress through the subject and
acquire knowledge at their own pace by allowing them to
participate in these quizzes in the comfort of their own home and
in their own time.

11.4 Empirical Evaluation

Study Description

The empirical study presented in this section builds on research by
Handzic and Chumkovski (2004). Given the growing interest in web-
based learning environments, there is a surprising paucity of empirical
studies investigating their effectiveness in undergraduate education.
Therefore, a survey study was conducted to determine students' attitudes
towards a virtual knowledge space created to support their learning in
the undergraduate course: Systems Analysis and Design. A total of 125
surveys were distributed to students during lecture time. Out of 119
forms that were handed back to the survey distributors, 102 were correctly
completed and usable for the analysis (return rate of 82%). All students
were attending UNSW on a full-time basis, 61% were male and 39%
female, and the majority were in their second year of study.

The survey was chosen as a preferred research method due to the
timeliness, low cost and convenience factors. The 22-question survey
instrument was divided into three sections: KM features, suggestions and
demographics. The KM features section included 14 closed questions
where subjects self-reported their feelings regarding the importance of a
particular KM tool (described earlier in this chapter) in fostering good
knowledge management practices, and their satisfaction with its
implementation on their course web site. The responses were captured
on 7-point Likert scales with 1 — low and 7 — high as end points. The
second series of questions were four open-ended suggestion questions.
Here, the students were able to comment on why they felt that a tool
was beneficial or not to their learning and to make comparisons with

other courses. The last section of questions were demographic questions regarding the gender, length and mode of study, and the frequency of web access per week.

Results

Table 11.1 shows the summary results from the descriptive analyses of the responses obtained for the first part of the questionnaire. The 'mean' and 'standard deviation' results for various KM tools are assigned to categories, 'Importance' and 'Implementation'. Blank spaces denoted that the tools were not implemented at all.

Table 11.1 Summary of descriptive results

Knowledge	Importance		Implementation	
Management Tool	Mean	S.Dev	Mean	S.Dev
1. Course Outline	5.68	1.43	5.07	1.24
2. Lecture Notes	5.88	1.25	5.06	1.38
3. Reading Materials	5.16	1.30	4.34	1.38
4. Student Status Centre	5.08	1.78		
5. FAQ Page	5.20	1.59	4.20	1.44
6. Search Engine	4.14	1.64		
7. Discussion Forums	4.15	1.56		
8. Live Chat	3.37	1.68		
9. Announcements	5.86	1.46	4.79	1.45
10. E-mail	5.46	1.59	4.63	1.66
11. Assignments	5.07	1.52	4.87	1.43
12. Tutorials	5.51	1.33	4.57	1.54
13. Online games	3.29	1.87		
14. Online quizzes	4.57	1.75		

From a quick glance at the importance column, it can be seen that the students felt that 'Lecture Notes' were the most important KM tool with a rating of 5.88 (out of 7). 'Online Announcements' came a close second at 5.86 and 'Course Outline' third at 5.68. These three were followed by Tutorials (5.51), E-mail (5.46), FAQ (5.20), Readings (5.16), Student Status Centre (5.08), Assignments (5.07) and Quizzes (4.57) that were all considered quite important. The participants also rated as important discussion boards (4.15) and search engines (4.14). In contrast, chat rooms (3.37) and online games (3.29) were not seen as important KM tools.

Looking at the implementation column, one can see that only 8 out of 14 possible KM tools (57%) were actually implemented on the course web site. Among these, 'Course Outline' together with 'Lecture Notes' had the highest satisfaction rates amongst the students of 5.07 and 5.06 respectively. These were followed by Assignments (4.87), Announcements (4.79), E-mail (4.63), Tutorials (4.57), Readings (4.34) and FAQs (4.20), all rated positively. All implementation rates were lower than their corresponding importance score.

The other 6 tools that did not feature on the web site included the 'Student Status Centre', 'Search Engine', 'Discussion Forum', 'Live Chat', 'Online Games' and 'Online Quizzes'. Four of those were considered important and two very important to students. The remaining two (online games and chat rooms) were not considered particularly important by the students.

Further analysis of student responses to open questions in Part 2 of the questionnaire reveals major reasons for the overwhelming perceived importance of 'Lecture Notes'. From the 34 responses, 17 (50%) claimed that 'lecture notes' provided them with *"information in summarised form that kept them up to date with the course"*. The next best reason for 'Lecture Notes' were that students *"don't have to write down lecture notes in class"* which had a response of 11 (32%). These were followed by responses for *"aid in understanding textbook"* and *"help explain concepts"* which had equal results of 3 (9%) each.

Discussion

The main findings of the study make some interesting contributions to research. Firstly, the short answer to our research question "Which Knowledge Management tools are considered most important by students of a web course?" is: *Lecture Notes* (followed by 'Online Announcements', 'Course Outline', 'Tutorials', 'E-mail', 'FAQ Page', 'Reading Materials', 'Student Status Centre', 'Assignments', 'Online Quizzes', 'Discussion Forums', 'Search Engine', 'Live Chat' and 'Online Games'). The short answer to the question "How well does the design of an IS web course implement these knowledge management tools?" is: *Not as well as desired.* Lower implementation satisfaction ratings, together with large percentage of tools not implemented at all, suggest unsatisfactory design of the web course.

With respect to the importance of individual tools, students feel that lecture notes provide them with information in a summarised form that keeps them up to date with the course as well as the convenience of not having to scurry to write down information spoken by the lecturer in the classroom. This leaves more time for listening, absorbing of information and understanding of theories in the classroom which students see as a major advantage. Furthermore lecture notes may be written in a much less formal and easier to understand manner which helps students in interpreting the subject's textbook which may be of a more formal and inflexible nature. In addition to this, students feel that they help to explain concepts as lecture notes allow a single diagram or phrase from a textbook to be elaborated on or dissected by the instructor until the students can grasp the essence of what is being put across. The almost equal high rating given to online announcements can be ascribed to the fact that students these days are extremely busy, engaged in four or five subjects at a time. Hence online announcements also referred to as a 'notice board' act as a personal diary or secretary for the students. Students are fond of them as they inform them of important dates or changes to the subject that may have slipped their minds.

Examining the other end of the spectrum, we see that online games and live chat were seen as being least important tools. The explanation for such results may be that online games as well as live chat are newer KM tools that are used only sparingly at the moment. Hence students may not have had any or minimal experience in both, making their answers a little less concrete or viable in comparison to their responses concerning lecture notes and online announcements which they would most probably have had ample previous experience in. Other explanations may stem from the sheer fact that the word 'games' wrongly paints a less educational picture when comparing it with other KM tools and also from the fact that for tools such as live chat to work, students have to participate frequently. Since student's schedules and priorities differ, live chat's synchronous nature may be seen as being an unimportant or unrealistic method of education.

The difference in tools importance and implementation satisfaction levels of tools is quite interesting. Never did any of the KM tools on the IS course web site satisfy the students in comparison to the perceived importance of the particular tool. The reasons for this cannot be pinpointed and are speculative at best. Here lies an area that cries for further research. Lecture notes had the highest implementation satisfaction rating which highlights the student's positive feeling towards this KM tool. This was closely followed by course outline, which was also seen as being reasonably useful in fostering good knowledge management practices.

Possibly the most significant discovery was that 6 of the 14 proposed KM tools (43%) did not feature on the course web site at all. Explanation for the student status centre, search engine, discussion forum, live chat, online games and online quizzes not being implemented on the IS course web site may be justified by looking at their corresponding low importance ratings. In addition to this many of them are newer, more recent KM tools. Also the fact that the extra preparation time in implementing tools such as online games and quizzes, live chat and student status centre may be seen as too time-consuming and possibly not "value for money" by instructors.

At the tool category level, the clear winner in terms of importance is the 'explicit-what' category. This is not so much of a surprise as it comprises the course outline, lecture notes, reading materials and the student status centre which all received an importance rating of above 5. With such numbers it is clear that students feel that the 'availability of information' quadrant is still the most popular way in increasing their overall knowledge of the subject. There is not a lot that separates second, third and fourth places. Hence the 'finding of information', 'sharing of information' and the 'learning by doing' quadrants were all deemed to be similarly relevant when it came to fostering good knowledge management practices.

With respect to implementation, 'explicit what' continued its dominance as the most useful tool category in increasing students knowledge. This predilection for the 'availability of information' is due to the fact that it contains three of the most popular and most frequently seen tools on course web sites. The student status centre is another great potential KM tool in this category but has possibly been overlooked in many course web sites because it is time-consuming and hard to maintain as it is essentially a database of confidential student records that display student progress and performance. With respect to the other three tool categories ('finding of information', 'sharing of information' and 'learning by doing'), in each of these, 50% of the tools did not feature on the course web site at all. Whether these tools should have been implemented or not is open for debate. In general, when the actual tools were implemented on the course web site, students felt that they were done so reasonably well (all above the neutral 4). However, the fact that their implementation satisfaction rating never matched their corresponding importance ratings show displeased feelings from the students towards the design of the IS course web site.

Implications, Limitations and Future Directions

The results of the study have some important implications for practice and research in knowledge management and e-learning. The results clearly point out to web-course designers which areas of knowledge management are considered strong and useful by students, and which areas are weaker, less useful or perhaps still unknown and emerging phenomena. Designers of company web sites can also put these results to good use. Poor quality company web sites can cause an internal inefficiency of knowledge transfer, creation and retention amongst company employees. The availability of "Lessons Learnt" and "Best Practice" knowledge would be of major benefit to the whole company as all employees interested would be able to wander around the company web site and have a look at what fellow colleagues have done and think about certain issues.

However, some caution is necessary when generalising these results due to a number of limitations. Firstly, the survey took place in the IS lecture. It had to be brief and hence of a non-complex format, where students could answer quickly and precisely, not taking up too much of the lecturer's time. Further probing into why they felt the way they did about each tool would have been desirable and definitely a possibility for future research.

Another limitation concerns the nature of the IS course evaluated. Students were asked to comment on the importance of many tools that were not implemented on this course web site. While the particular tool not being located on the IS course web site should not directly shift a student's opinion of the tool one way or the other, tools that did feature were generally deemed more important than those tools which were not present. To avoid any possible bias, future research should be performed on students from web courses that contain all or even more KM tools than those proposed in the survey.

Finally, the fact that all students queried were from a 'Computer Science and Engineering' background means that they share a common mode of thought which would perhaps differ from students from other university disciplines. Hence, to overcome this limitation it would be plausible for future research to be conducted in various other schools and see how the students feel about their web courses, and which tools are most important.

11.5 Conclusions

The main objective of this chapter was to introduce the concept of a virtual knowledge space and examine students' attitudes towards it in the context of an undergraduate IS course. A web-based k-space designed on the principles of knowledge management was presented as a means to facilitate the learning needs of different students. Various k-space features provided support for the availability, finding and sharing of information, as well as learning by doing. Through the use of a survey we were able to query students on their thoughts about these tools and related issues concerning their course web site.

The study clearly identified major areas of interest for students. At an individual tool level, the most popular knowledge management tool was 'lecture notes'. At the category level, tools supporting 'explicit what' type of knowledge were the most popular ones. As for the design of the IS web course and how well it implemented these tools, the overall answer was not very well. Students showed dissatisfaction towards the design by giving lower ratings for the performance o all implemented tools than for their importance.

Due to the exploratory nature of this study and its limitations, further research is suggested to address these questions in different contexts and among different users, as well as to extend current research to other questions, in order to find ways for providing better and more satisfying learning experience for the students of web-based courses.

References

Aurum, A., Handzic, M. and Gardiner, A. (2003), "Supporting Creativity in Software Development: An Application in IT Education", chapter 6 in McGill, T. (ed.), *Current Issues in IT Education*, IRM Press, London, pp. 77–87.

Churchman, C.W. (1971), *The Design of Inquiring Systems: Basic Concepts of Systems and Organisation*, Basic Books, New York.

Handzic, M. and Chumkovski, A. (2004), "An Empirical Evaluation of a Knowledge Portal in the Context of E-learning", working paper, UNSW, April.

Handzic, M., Aurum, A. and Van Toorn, C. (2003), "UNSW Case on Knowledge Management in Website Development", *Case Studies in Knowledge Management*, Vol. 2, Standards Australia International Limited, Sydney.

Handzic, M. (2000), "Managing Knowledge through Experimentation and Socialisation", in Reimer, U. (ed.), in *Proceedings of the Third International Conference on Practical Aspects of Knowledge Management (PAKM 2000)*, October 30–31, Basel, Switzerland.

Handzic, M. (2001), "Does More Information Lead to Better Informing?", in Harriger, A. (ed.), in *Proceedings of the 2001 Informing Science Conference*, June 19–22, Krakow, Poland, pp. 251–256.

Handzic, M. and Aurum, A. (2001), "Knowledge Discovery: Some Empirical Evidence and Directions for Future Research", in *Proceedings of the 5th International Conference on Wirtschafts Informatics, WI'2001*, September 19–21, Augsburg, Germany.

Handzic, M. and Jamieson, R. (2001), "A Knowledge Management Framework for Research in Electronic Commerce", *SISTM Research Information Paper Series No: RIPS2001-02*, School of Information Systems Technology and Management, UNSW, Sydney.

Handzic, M. and Lin, J.C.Y. (2003), "*K*-space and Learning", in *Proceedings of the Australasian Conference on Information Systems (ACIS 2003)*, November 28–29, Perth.

Handzic, M. and Low, G. (2002), "The Impact of Social Interaction on Performance of Decision Tasks of Varying Complexity", *OR Insight*, 15(1), 15–22.

Handzic, M. and Tolhurst, D. (2002), "Evaluating an Interactive Learning Environment in Management Education", *Educational Technology & Society, IEEE Journal*, 5(3), 113–122.

Klayman, J. (1988), "Learning from Experience", in Brehmer, B. & Joyce, C.R.B. (eds.), *Human Judgement. The SJT View*, North-Holland, Amsterdam.

Piccoli, G., Ahmad, R. and Ives, B. (2001), "Web-based Virtual Learning Environments: A Research Framework and a Preliminary Assessment of Effectiveness in Basic IT Skills Training", *MIS Quarterly*, 25(4), 401–426.

Shneiderman, B. (2000), "Creating Creativity: User Interfaces for Supporting Innovation", *ACM Transactions on Computer-Human Interaction*, 7(1), 114–138.

Twigg, C.A. (2001), *Innovations in Online Learning*, Centre for Academic Transformation, Rensselaer Polytechnic Institute, New York.

Vandenbosch, B., Fay, S. and Saatciglu, A. (2001), "Where Ideas Come From: A Systematic View of Inquiry, Sprouts: Working Papers on Information Environments", *Systems and Organisations*, Vol. 1, Fall.

CHAPTER 12

Simulation Game:

Adventures in Knowledgeland

Play is the beginning of knowledge.
— George Dorsey

This chapter addresses a gaming approach to KM. The gaming approach has been suggested as a good way to explore the utilisation of KM systems in varying decision tasks, environments and decision-makers. Lessons learned from a series of empirical studies provide a strong support for the contingent view of KM systems utilisation. The findings suggest that there is no "no one size fits all" prescription, but rather a key component of KM is the identification of the context and choosing of the appropriate KM system for that context.

12.1 Introduction

According to Becerra-Fernandez et al. (2004) much of the current literature on KM promotes a universalistic view of KM. Such view implies that there is one best way to manage knowledge in all organisations and under all circumstances. In contrast, a contingency view of KM suggests that no one approach is best under all circumstances. Instead, individuals and organisations need to choose among multiple possible paths the one which fits best their set of circumstances. The assumption is that only the choice of the appropriate path will lead them to ultimate success.

It is argued that the gaming approach to KM offers a good way to explore factors influencing the utilisation of KM systems. Some of the major advantages of the gaming approach over other more conventional exploratory methods is that gaming allows for complex and realistic cases to be made, sequences of actions and events to be represented, and different players to be involved in the game, thus providing the variety of possible situations (deHoog et al., 1999). Simulation games are considered particularly useful for conveying complex relationships to a knowledge worker and for exploring what-if scenarios in an interactive format. The user can view and manipulate the parameters involved and observe the effect (Bergeron, 2003).

The game "Adventures in Knowledgeland" presented in this chapter, like any other simulation game, is based on the particular reference model. The reference model used in this game is a contingency model of KM system utilisation shown in Figure 12.1. This model suggests that various circumstances and contingencies may have different impacts on knowledge workers' utilisation of KM systems and subsequent performance. The main objective of this chapter was to explore these factors in the decision-making context.

12.2 Contingency Factors

Drawing on previous theoretical and empirical research several contingency factors have been suggested to influence the utilisation of

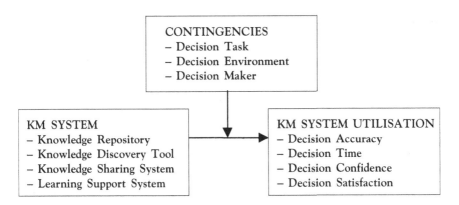

Figure 12.1 Contingency model of KM system utilisation

KM systems in decision-making. These include various decision task, decision environment and decision-maker characteristics described below.

Decision Task Characteristics

Task complexity

The literature provides several conceptualisations of complexity. Some investigators define complexity in terms of objective task qualities. Schroder et al. (1967) identify load, diversity and rate of change as three primary properties of a complex task. Payne (1976) defines complexity as a function of both the number of alternatives and the number of attributes on which the alternatives are compared. Similarly, Beach and Mitchell (1978) define task complexity in terms of the number of different components of the decision problems such as the number of alternatives and the amount of relevant cues to be considered, the number of criteria on which the problem would be judged and the degree to which the problem would influence future decisions. A more comprehensive definition of task complexity was developed by Wood (1986). He proposed a multidimensional construct comprising component, coordinative and dynamic complexity. The component complexity is viewed as a direct function of the number of cues and the number of distinct acts required for the task performance. Coordinative complexity refers to the form and strength of the relationship between cues, acts and products of acts such as sequencing of inputs and timing, frequency, intensity and location of acts. Dynamic complexity involves change in the component and coordinative of the task over time.

Other approaches mentioned by Campbell (1988) treat complexity as a primarily psychological experience or an interaction between task and person characteristics. The former emphasise the subjective reaction of the individual to the task rather than the objective task characteristics, while the latter acknowledge the importance of both the person and the task. In the integrative framework proposed by Campbell (1988), task complexity is related to both the objective task characteristics that increase load, diversity and change, and cognitive demands that those factors place on the person. The task characteristics that contribute to complexity include multiple paths, uncertain outcomes, conflicting interdependencies among paths, uncertain or probabilistic linkages and associated characteristics such as ill-structured, ambiguous and difficult tasks. The framework also recognises that experienced complexity, although merely a reaction to task characteristics may be evoked for reasons other than the task, such as context, anxiety or fear. For example, design characteristics of the KM system such as knowledge presentation format may also affect the perceived complexity of the task (Te'eni, 1989).

The Beach and Mitchell (1978) model proposes a positive relationship between the level of task complexity and the level of analytic complexity of the strategy selected for the task performance. The essence of the model proposition lies in the fact that the difference in the expected benefit associated with a complex versus simple strategy is larger in its application to a more complex than to a less complex task. While the model recognises the benefit of using a complex strategy or system for a more complex decision problem, it does not recognise the effect of cost which may be much larger in the application of the strategy in a more complex problem than in a less complex one. Thus, from the cost perspective, a person may be more likely to select less complex strategies for more complex problems and more complex strategies for less complex problems. Christensen-Szalanski (1978), who formalised the cognitive cost/benefit model of problem-solving strategy selection, showed analytically that anything that increases the difficulty of the task results in a rise of the cost curve associated with the performance of the task and consequently, selection of a strategy with lower level of expected benefit.

By definition, availability of contextual knowledge cues in addition to time series data affects the overall complexity of the decision problem through its contribution to component complexity. Similarly, knowledge cues diversity described as the difference in the strength and form of the relationships among multiple items of the available knowledge set affects the overall complexity of the problem through coordinative complexity. Knowledge presentation format may also affect the complexity of the task, by placing different cognitive load on the decision-maker. Therefore, they all have the potential to impact decision performance by influencing KM system utilisation.

Task uncertainty

Blandin and Brown (1977) suggest that task uncertainty depends partly on the clarity of environmentally related knowledge cues and the nature of the cause and effect relationships in the decision environment. Beach and Mitchell (1978) define the degree to which the elements of the problem are unclear or uncertain as task ambiguity. According to the contingency model, uncertainty (or ambiguity) increases the demand of the task and results in a greater likelihood of selecting a more analytic strategy for task performance. Other task related characteristics suggested to influence the selection of a strategy in a similar way as uncertainty or ambiguity are instability (defined as the degree to which the elements of the problem change over time) and unfamiliarity (defined as the degree to which the decision problem is foreign to the decision-maker).

The reliability of contextual knowledge cues provided to aid decision-making in the time series task may potentially influence KM system utilisation by affecting the perceived uncertainty of the decision problem. Less reliable knowledge cues may induce greater uncertainty of the decision outcome than more reliable cues and consequently may lead to more KM system utilisation.

Decision Environment Characteristics

Time/Money constraints

Time and/or money constraints are often neglected aspects of decision environment in decision-making research. However, most decision tasks allow limited time for deliberation and processing and there are limits on the money permitted to spend on knowledge procurement. As noted by Beach and Mitchell (1978) there are few opportunities that do not expire, few decisions that must not be resolved before things can progress, few other persons willing to tolerate prolonged indecisiveness.

Theories of stress and cognition view the time constraint as a stressor and suggest that its effect on cognition is mediated through a single dimension of arousal (Maule and Hockey, 1994). It is argued that an external stressor (e.g., time constraint) changes the arousal level of the individual and that this in turn affects cognition. It is assumed that an inverted U relation exists between arousal and performance. More recent research, however, has shown that the effects of different stressors do not operate in single dimensions like arousal. A more general view offered is based on the notion that people appraise both the situation they are in and the extent to which they have the resources to meet the demands of the situation. If the appraisal process leads individuals to conclude that they have access to coping resources, then the response to the situation is likely to be adaptive. If the threat is perceived as one for which coping resources are not available, the most likely outcome is of reduced effectiveness and symptoms of stress.

As an environment variable, time constraint is incorporated into the cost/benefit calculation to determine the strategy of the Beach and Mitchell (1978) contingency model. Within the cost/benefit framework immediate deadlines and other severe time constraints are viewed as having the potential to completely eliminate highly complex strategies from consideration for selection. In the strategy selection mechanism proposed by Christensen-Szalanski (1978, 1980), a deadline divides the cost curve at some point, leaving only those strategies that lie below the division point for possible selection. Consequently, a problem solver in the immediate deadline condition is restricted to using only less costly and potentially less accurate strategies. The effect of the use of a time-constrained strategy is assumed to show in a decreased level of confidence and no effect of increased benefit upon confidence, since a decision-maker is limited by the deadline to using the same strategy for all values of increased benefit. Although it received some empirical support, the above description of the effects of time constraints on strategy selection process appears to be incomplete for many decision situations.

Smith et al. (1982) suggested that time constraint may not simply eliminate more complex strategies from consideration. Rather, it may affect the expected benefit, via the individual's confidence level, and expected cost associated with specific strategies and through these variables influence the strategy selection process. Ben Zur and Breznitz (1981) identified at least three ways in which people might respond to time constraints. One way to cope with time pressure is to process only a subset of the most important cues, an idea referred to as 'filtration'. Another way to cope with time pressure is to 'accelerate' processing by trying to process the same amount of cues at a faster rate. Finally, one could shift processing strategies. At the extreme, this could involve random choice or 'avoidance'. A less extreme form of contingent processing would involve a shift from a more effortful rule to a less effortful one.

Time constraint as an environmental variable may potentially influence decision-makers' utilisation of contextual cues provided as a decision aid in a time series task context. Earlier research investigating the effects of the time variable on human decision behaviour indicates that individuals are adaptive to these environmental conditions and suggests a number of coping mechanisms used to deal with time pressure.

Task significance

According to Beach and Mitchell (1978) the significance of the problem is determined by the magnitude of the outcomes involved and the ramifications for other parts of the decision-maker's life such as promotions or self-esteem. Waller and Mitchell (1984) assume that the significance of the decision can have at least three aspects in the organisational settings: how the decision and its results affect the manager's current compensations, his or her future compensations and promotions and how it will affect the financial status of the organisation.

The Beach and Mitchell's contingency model postulates a positive relationship between the analytical complexity of the strategy/system used on the task and the significance of the decision problem. Other environment related factors suggested to influence selection of strategies in a similar fashion as significance include irreversibility, defined as the lack of opportunity to monitor the effects and reverse the decision if things go poorly and accountability, defined as the degree to which the decision-maker is accountable for the results of the decision.

Payoffs and costs associated with the task provide the decision-maker with instructions of the consequences of various courses of action and the importance of those consequences. Thus, the form of payoff/cost function may potentially influence utilisation of KM system in the time series task and through utilisation impact decision performance. Motivational aspects associated with monetary incentives are likely to accentuate the effects of payoff/cost function.

Characteristics of the Decision-Maker

Knowledge and ability

According to Beach and Mitchell (1978), with knowledge about available strategies comes an opinion about their appropriateness and relative likelihood of yielding a correct decision. With ability, the time and effort of using a high resource requirements strategy is smaller than without the ability. The contingent strategy selection model assumes that a person who is more knowledgeable and able would typically select more analytic over less analytic strategies, while the opposite would be true for less knowledgeable and able person. Thus, greater KM awareness and experience is expected to lead to higher level of system utilisation.

Motivation

People making decisions strive to expend the least personal resources compatible with the demands of the decision task. Beach and Mitchell

(1976) argue that the press to decide, get the matter settled and cease working on the problem is a powerful motivator for selecting the fastest and easiest strategies within reason. Extrinsic rewards may counter such impetuosity by influencing the amount of time and cognitive effort expended on the task. Expending greater resources implies selection of a more analytical strategy and thus higher likelihood of achieving higher level of decision performance. The decision-maker's state of motivation can also be activated by the need for justification (Ashton, 1992). Externally or internally induced motivation may have a beneficial effect on the utilisation of KM system in decision-making. In general, high level of motivation is expected to lead to greater effort extended to process the available knowledge cues to enhance performance.

Learning through task repetition and from feedback

Decision-makers gain knowledge of and ability to implement strategies on the task from experience gained through task repetition and from feedback. Payne et al. (1988) suggests that adaptivity may be crucial enough to decision-makers that they would guide themselves to it without the need for an external prod in the form of explicit feedback. On the other hand, Hogarth (1981) considers that the availability of immediate feedback, in addition to the opportunity to take corrective action, is critical for effective learning. O'Connor (1989) also suggests that familiarity and understanding of the task will be enhanced if adequate feedback is given to enable the subjects to examine previous responses in the light of subsequent events. Adequate feedback is considered especially important for the correct assessment of the previous responses in situations where the subject is unfamiliar with the task or topic. Feedback may enhance learning by providing knowledge about the task, task outcome, individual's performance and/or decision process. From this knowledge, through task repetition, an individual may learn to adapt, i.e., maintain, modify or abandon strategy to improve task performance.

12.3 Game Description

The simulation game used to facilitate our research into KM system utilisation and performance of decision-makers was specifically developed and with minor adaptations was used across a series of experiments. The software was written in Microsoft Visual Basic for Windows. The game was developed as a multipurpose system that incorporated (i) an experimental task simulator (ii) a KM system as a decision-aiding component, and (iii) a data collection component. All interactions with the game were through the mouse device.

Experimental Task Simulator

The game simulated a simple production planning task for the repetitive and time-dependent decision environment. The task simulator was triggered upon the subject's entry of his or her student number. The software automatically checked the participant's version of the computer program and showed the appropriate task scenario and product demand time series data to the individual. Six programme versions were required to accommodate differences among treatment groups. The example screen layout of the game is presented in Figure 12.2.

To simulate time-dependent decision environment, the game provided a timer procedure and a count-down clock in order to calculate and show the subjects the remaining time (in seconds) available to make each decision. The programme measured the time elapsed, refreshed the clock label every second and reset the clock on each trial in accordance with the program version. In addition, the game provided sets of instructions and messages that were displayed to the subjects throughout the play.

An optional access to a KM system providing task relevant knowledge cues was enabled by the game to aid subjects' decision-making. Access was completely under individual control and knowledge cues interpretation and integration was judgemental. Details regarding the design and the use of the KM system component of the game are described later in this section.

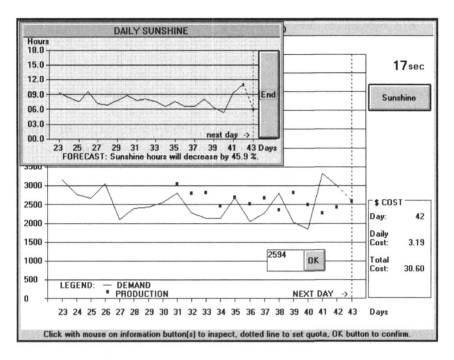

Figure 12.2 Simulation game example screen shot

Entry of the final decision response was enabled through clicking with the mouse on the specified entry line and OK button for confirmation. Each decision response in terms of the number of units produced was displayed on the screen as a dot located immediately above or below the corresponding number of units actually demanded. In this way, the subjects were able to quickly estimate the magnitude of their production errors.

The game also incorporated a specific calculation procedure that automatically computed for each time period a production error and a corresponding decision cost incurred. Unit costs were calculated using a quadratic cost function. The calculation procedure also computed the total cost to date. On each trial, the simulation game displayed the computed cost performance feedback in the lower right corner of the screen.

KM System Features

A decision aiding component incorporated in the game was a simplified model of a KM system. It contained (i) a knowledge repository with task relevant knowledge cues which had the potential to improve the quality of decision-making and (ii) a user-friendly graphical interface for easy access and presentation of this knowledge. The approach used in designing a KM system component of the game recognised a general preference for human judgement over models in decision-making (Sanders and Mandrot, 1994). Accordingly, the game did not include any model-based components.

The design was based on the "pull" principle in which knowledge is hidden until the decision-maker explicitly searches for it. This approach was suggested as particularly appropriate for testing hypotheses about the amount and the pattern of knowledge search (Kleinmuntz, 1987). Accordingly, only past product demand time series data were initially available to the subjects. Contextual knowledge cues were hidden. The individual could access these cues one at a time by clicking with their mouse on the appropriate cue button shown in the upper right corner of the screen. A randomising algorithm incorporated into the game determined the labels and the order of buttons displayed. Depending on the experimental condition, the game provided access to one, two or three cues of decision relevant contextual knowledge in addition to the product demand time series. A separately generated set of time series data was used as an input data file.

Knowledge visualisation was graphical only. Both the product demand and the contextual cues time series data were presented in the form of line graphs. When requested, the game displayed the selected contextual cue graph in a separate window located in the upper left corner of the screen. The window size was scaled in such a way as to enable pattern matching between the product demand data and the contextual factors data.

Data Collection

The game software enabled unobtrusive recording of the observed behaviour and performance. On each trial, the software automatically recorded the number of requests made and the time spent on each contextual knowledge cue searched, as well as total time spent on each decision. These search records were saved in separate files for each subject and treatment for later analysis. Search records were used as a primary source of data for the analysis of KM system utilisation. In addition, consistent with a multimethod research approach adopted, the actual decisions made by the individuals were also automatically recorded by the game. These records were used to compare the actual decision performance with that of the optimal and naive methods. They were also used to create algebraic models of individual strategies and to draw inferences about KM system utilisation that resulted in recorded performance.

Finally, the game captured the subjective assessments of various aspects of the decision task, process and performance elicited by the participants during the play. The game displayed the questions to the subjects sequentially one at the time. A particular question was shown on the screen together with the seven answer options. The rating was made by clicking with the mouse on the option that best represented the individual's view of the decision-making aspect in question. The game automatically recorded the selected option number as a rating score pertaining to the particular aspect assessed. These records were saved in separate files for each subject for later analysis.

12.4 Lessons Learned

Using a task contingency model, a series of experiments were conducted to examine the effects of a number of task and context related factors on KM system utilisation. These included quantity, reliability, diversity and presentation form of knowledge cues, as well as time constraint and cost function. In addition, learning through task repetition and from feedback was also examined.

Main Findings

The main findings of this research support the notion that the utilisation of a KM system is a function of the individual cognitive cost-benefit trade-off. People appear to be pragmatic knowledge processors that tend to reduce their mental effort by using simplifying heuristics, unless additional efforts are justified by substantial gains. In general, the findings suggest that people are likely to make better decisions with the use of a KM system than with the unaided or intuitive judgement. However, certain circumstances tend to encourage and other discourage greater use of a KM system in decision-making, leading to different consequences for performance.

In one of the experiments, it was found that decision-makers adapted to increased complexity of the decision problem from the cognitive load imposed on them by the need to process increased number of knowledge cues by adopting selective utilisation strategy that resulted in no further improvement in performance. Similarly, the follow-up experiment demonstrated that increased task complexity from higher knowledge cue diversity led to ignoring differences in relative importance among these cues. Such behaviour somewhat diluted the effect of the best knowledge cue on performance, but the impact was not significant. Although the people may not have behaved optimally, the findings of yet another experiment suggest that they are aware that the additional knowledge is more useful when the uncertainty of the decision outcome is greater. When presented with knowledge cues of lower reliability sources, people tended to search for more additional knowledge. Consequently, the performance was closer to that of normative strategies. When the certainty was high, additional cues of highly reliable knowledge sources were generally ignored. Despite this, highly reliable knowledge cues resulted in better performance at less cost of effort.

The research also illustrated the importance of situation for utilisation of KM systems in forecasting and decision-making. In one of the experiments, it was revealed that people tended to utilise less knowledge cues when there was a high time constraint imposed. The finding is consistent with the postulated relationship between time constraint and confidence in ability, and confidence and choice of strategy. While performance declined under time constraint, it was still better than unaided. In addition, the findings suggest a highly adaptive knowledge utilisation to cost function. In the follow-up experiment, it was found that decision-makers tended to adapt to the increased demand of a complex accuracy-and-time based cost function by accelerated knowledge cues processing in order to minimise the cost of time without a significant loss in accuracy.

This research has also investigated the influence of the knowledge presentation format on KM system utilisation. Graphical display was found to be preferred over tabular. The subjects with the additional tabular displays tended to feel less confident in their ability to effectively process the available knowledge cues and consequently tended to largely ignore them. It seems that the cognitive load imposed by the need to multiply and add numerical data in tabular displays was higher than the visual estimate of direction and rough magnitude of change on graphical displays, while both displays were perceived as similarly effective on the task.

The findings of this research also suggest that with immediate performance feedback and task familiarity human judgement can improve when the initial performance is low. The feedback that revealed inferior performance led to increased utilisation and improved performance over time, when a highly reliable knowledge source was available and under accuracy-based cost function. The feedback that revealed what subjects considered as acceptable performance was reinforced and maintained throughout the task in all other conditions.

In summary, the findings provide an optimistic view that people's adaptive use of KM systems is actually a rational consideration of costs and benefits involved. As pragmatic processors of knowledge cues people would tend to take the advantage of task and context to perform at acceptable levels, while saving in cost of effort involved in processing.

12.5 Conclusions

In this chapter, we presented a simulation game approach to explore the impact of context on KM systems utilisation. Lessons learned from a series of experimental studies provide a strong support for the contingent model of KM system utilisation. More specifically the research demonstrated that the utilisation of KM system in decision-making was highly dependent on the nature of the decision task, decision environment and the characteristics of the decision-maker using the system. These findings suggest that, there is "no one size fits all" prescription, but rather a key component of KM is the identification of the context and choosing of the appropriate KM system for that context.

References

Ashton, R.H. (1992), "Effects of Justification and a Mechanical Aid on Judgement Performance", *Organisational Behaviour and Human Decision Processes*, 52, 292–306.

Beach, L.R. and Mitchell, T.R. (1978), "A Contingency Model for the Selection of Strategies", *Academy of Management Review*, 3, 439–449.

Becerra-Fernandez, I., Gonzales, A. and Sabherwal, R. (2004), *Knowledge Management: Challenges, Solutions, and Technologies*, Pearson Education, New Jersey.

Ben Zur, H. and Breznitz, S.J. (1981), "The Effect of Time Pressure on Risky Choice Behaviour", *Acta Psychologica*, 47, 89–104.

Bergeron, B. (2003), *Essentials of Knowledge Management*, John Wiley & Sons, New Jersey.

Blandin, J.S. and Brown, W.B. (1977), "Uncertainty and Management's Search for Information", *IEEE Transactions on Engineering Management*, 24(4), 114–119.

Campbell, D.J. (1988), "Task Complexity: A Review and Analysis", *Academy of Management Review*, 13(1), 40–52.

Christensen-Szalanski, J.J.J. (1978), "Problem Solving Strategies: A Selection Mechanism, Some Implications, and Some Data", *Organisational Behaviour and Human Performance*, 22, 307–323.

Christensen-Szalanski, J.J.J. (1980), "A Further Examination of the Selection of Problem-Solving Strategies: The Effect of Deadlines and Analytical Aptitudes", *Organisational Behaviour and Human Performance*, 25, 107–122.

De Hoog, R., van Heijst, G., van der Spek, R., Edwards, J.S., Mallis, R., van der Meij, B. and Taylor, R.M. (1999), "Investigating a Theoretical Framework for Knowledge Management: A Gaming Approach", in *Knowledge Management Handbook*, Liebowitz, J. (ed.), CRC Press, Boca Raton.

Hogarth, R.M. (1981), "Beyond Discrete Biases: Functional and Dysfunctional Aspects of Judgemental Heuristics", *Psychological Bulletin*, 90(2), 197–217.

Kleinmuntz, D.N. (1987), "Human Decision Processes: Heuristics and Task Structure", in *Human Factors Psychology*, Hancock, P.A. (ed.), Elsevier Science Publishers, pp. 123–157.

Maule, A.J. and Hockey, G.R.J. (1994), "State, Stress, and Time Pressure", in *Time Pressure and Stress in Human Judgement and Decision Making*, Svenson, O. and Maule, A.J. (eds.), Plenum Press, New York.

O'Connor, M.J. (1989), "Models of Human Behaviour and Confidence in Judgement: A Review", *International Journal of Forecasting*, 5, 159–169.

Payne, J.W. (1976), "Task Complexity and Contingent Processing in Decision Making: An Information Processing and Protocol Analysis", *Organisational Behaviour and Human Performance*, 16, 366–387.

Payne, J.W., Bettman, J.R. and Johnson, E.J. (1988), "Adaptive Strategy Selection in Decision Making", *Journal of Experimental Psychology: Learning, Memory and Cognition*, 14(3), 534–552.

Sanders, N. and Manrodt, K. (1994), "Forecasting Practices in US Corporations: Survey Results", *Interfaces*, 24, 92–100.

Schroder, H.M., Driver, M.J. and Streufert, S. (1967), *Human Information Processing*, Holt, Rinehart and Winston.

Smith, J.F., Mitchell, T.R. and Beach, L.R. (1982), "A Cost-Benefit Mechanism for Selecting Problem-Solving Strategies: Some Extensions and Empirical Tests", *Organisational Behaviour and Human Performance*, 29, 370–396.

Te'eni, D. (1989), "Determinants and Consequences of Perceived Complexity in Human-Computer Interaction", *Decision Sciences*, 20(1), 166–181.

Waller, W.S. and Mitchell, T.R. (1984), "The Effects of Context on the Selection of Decision Strategies for the Cost Variance Investigation Problem", *Organisational Behaviour and Human Performance*, 33, 397–413.

Wood, R.E. (1986), "Task Complexity: Definition of the Construct", *Organisational Behaviour and Human Decision Processes*, 37(1), 60–82.

CHAPTER 13

Internet Portals:

Supporting Online Communities of Practice

I collaborate therefore I know.
— *KM World Magazine*

This chapter is concerned with issues and trends related to technological support of online communities of practice. It introduces portals as one of the latest and most powerful KM tools aimed at enabling and sustaining online communities. It also provides an in-depth analysis of the internet-based portal designed to support a global KM community to illustrate how technology can help to form and coordinate such communities.

13.1 Introduction

The revival of the concept of community in KM has brought about a great deal of controversy regarding the meaning of this slippery term. Expressions such as communities of practice or CoPs (Wenger, 1998), communities of interest COIs (Bennet and Porter, 2003), and communities of practice and learning (Hasan and Crawford, 2003) have been found in the recent KM literature. The holistic view considers communities as collections of people that engage in activities that encompass a common interest and ongoing learning through practice. CoPs are also known as knowledge networks, organic and self-organised groups of organisationally or geographically dispersed individuals who communicate regularly to discuss issues of mutual interest (Becerra-Fernandez, 2004). Underlying most communities is the willingness and ability of their members to help each other (AA, 1999).

Communities who use computer networks as their primary mode of interaction are known as online communities (AA, 1999). There is an increasing awareness that information and communication technologies (ICT) can be the catalyst to form and sustain communities where it is crucial to share knowledge and skills. With the support of the internet, intranets or extranets, online communities can include people who are widely dispersed geographically, have differing patterns in time use, as well as different personal characteristics and capabilities (Hasan and Crawford, 2003).

There is also an increasing awareness that enhanced knowledge mobilisation can be achieved through online communities. In business, internet communities typically aggregate audience for advertising and sales, extranet communities strengthen relationships with customers and trade partners; while intranet communities improve knowledge sharing (AA, 1999). Thus, they help achieve faster, more efficient processes, higher levels of innovation, and collaborative creation of new products and processes. According to Hasan and Crawford (2003), the benefits of communities are so significant that both governments and corporations are seeking ways to encourage their establishments and continued existence. This requires a greater understanding of how this can be done.

The principal objective of this chapter is to increase the understanding of how online communities can be formed, supported and maintained with an application of portal technology. A case of a global KM community has been used as an illustrative example.

13.2 Portal Technology

Portals are among the latest and most powerful tools helping knowledge management achieve its goal that the right knowledge is reaching the right people in the most convenient, complete and accurate way. Essentially, portals are virtual workspaces that promote knowledge sharing among end-users such as customers, partners and employees; provide access to structured data stored in data warehouses, database systems and transactional systems; and organise unstructured data such as electronic documents, paper documents, lessons learnt, stories and the like. Most importantly, portals provide a single point of access to all online information. In this way they simplify access to data stored in various application systems, facilitate collaboration among employees and assist the company in reaching its customers (Awad and Ghaziri, 2004).

Based on forecasts by Delphi and Gartner groups on portals, Tsui (2003) anticipated four stages of increased sophistication in future portals. Stage 1 is characterised by simple search mechanism and standards (static) page delivery; and information dissemination point. Stage 2 involves core content with pre-defined variations and page delivery; expanding set of interactive and informative facilities; centralised search facility for organisational content; and engagement of common business processes. In stage 3, the emphasis is on advanced search facilities and seamless integration of search results (external and internal); simple expertise locator; online knowledge communities; customers can initiate transactions with suppliers and partners; ability to perform transactions with suppliers and partners. Finally, in stage 4, the focus is on extensive and dynamic personalisation of content for individuals; active collection and distribution of knowledge; full integration with e-business systems; decision support and problem solving capabilities. Among major technical challenges underpinning the success of future portals are web access to enterprise application systems, automatic categorisation of sources and asset, intelligent and multiple search strategies, content management and real-time user profiling and personalisation strategies.

The following key technologies have been identified to be included in an effective portal solution: gathering facility for capturing of data and documents in a common repository; categorisation facility for profiling and organising the information in the repository in a meaningful way; distribution facility for acquiring and disseminating documents; collaboration facility in the form of messaging, workflow and discussion databases; publishing facility for wider public audience; personalisation facilities for task-function or interest based prioritisation and delivery; and search/navigate facility for accessing and identifying specific information required by knowledge workers (Awad and Ghaziri, 2004).

In summary, portals have evolved from simple information providers to sophisticated interfaces containing KM features such as content management, collaboration tools for knowledge sharing and personalisation capabilities to facilitate the search function. By providing an integrated tool for linking people, processes and knowledge, portals can play a central role in simplifying managerial complexity, increasing operational productivity, and adding value to the communities of practice.

13.3 Case Study: ActKM Community of Practice

The growing number on virtual communities of practice that have appeared lately all around the world, suggest that face-to-face contact may not be essential for the development of communities of practice as previously thought (e.g., McDermott, 1999; Lesser and Prusak, 1999). Instead, portals can provide a tool for linking people, processes and knowledge online.

Of particular interest to us are online communities of practice for people interested in the field of KM. KMcluster (*www.kmcluster.com*) is one such popular community. It supports a large group of KM practitioners through community action and research. Gurteen KM Community (*www.gurteen.com*) is another large online community that offers a wide range of knowledge services to over 10,000 members from all walks of life. On a much smaller scale, the author of this chapter herself maintains an active community of academic researchers in KM at the University of New South Wales (*www.kmrg.unsw.edu.au*). Collectively, these and other similar communities provide enhanced opportunities for KM academics and practitioners to learn with and from one another.

To find out how online communities of practice form, operate and produce value for its members we have analysed ActKM (*http://groups.yahoo.com/group/act-km*), a specific community of practice for people interested in public sector KM. Our primary aim was to discover effective practices for supporting communities of practice. While our investigation focused on the community outside business organisations, we believe that lessons learnt could apply to other types of communities and purposes.

Qualitative Analysis and Results

We started the analysis by asking one of the ActKM founders Shawn Callaghan from IBM Cynefin Centre for Organisational Complexity in Australia, to tell us: How did the KM community start? Who are the people that are joining and contributing to the KM community? What are the basic principles for managing the KM community? What kind of value/benefits does the KM community create to its members? The following is a brief account of the ActKM history and purpose, goals and guiding principles, characteristics and dynamics based on information provided by Callaghan.

How did ActKM start?

The idea of developing ActKM started in late 1998 among a small group of people interested in public sector KM. In the summer of 1999, the first meeting of the ActKM Forum was held with people from six public sector agencies in attendance. In December 1999, an online discussion forum was established to facilitate interaction. Today, ActKM is a vibrant community of learning and practice in KM.

The development of ActKM arose in response to the lack of KM literature dealing with the question of how public sector organisations should deal with KM. Thus, people interested in the topic needed to find an alternative way of learning from one another.

Who are the people that are joining and contributing to the KM community?

The membership of ActKM is predominantly derived from the public sector. This is not surprising considering that the purpose of the community is to be a key source of knowledge on public sector KM. The current composition of the community with about half of the members coming from the public sector ensures that the community remains relevant to its core team and that it achieves its purpose. The other half of the members include a mix of private, academic and unclassified entities (i.e., those represented by web e-mail addresses).

In terms of size, the membership grew from eight people who attended the first ActKM Forum meeting in summer 1998. Through word of mouth the community grew to sixty people by December 1999. Since the online discussion forum began, the membership grew exponentially to over five hundred and fifty people by 2003. And, it continues to grow.

What are the basic principles for managing the KM community?

The purpose and goal of ActKM is to act as a learning community dedicated to building knowledge about public sector knowledge management. Its ultimate aim is to be a key source of public sector knowledge management knowledge.

In addition, members of ActKM recognise that knowledge is the essential resource that organisations need to harness to achieve their objectives; that people have a life-long desire and ability to learn and organisations should support it; and that people learn from and with one another, so participation in learning communities is important to their effectiveness and well-being.

What kind of value/benefits does the KM community create to its members?

A significant aspect of ActKM is providing a support structure for the community. This is achieved through the core team who decides on the events and activities to be developed for the members. The online discussion forum shown in Figure 13.1 is another important feature of ActKM that contributes to the community's rhythm of activities. Online messages are moderated to avoid problems due to malfunctions and prevent inappropriate conversation. ActKM also organises regular face-to-face meetings, annual conferences and expert discussions in order to enhance the knowledge flows throughout the community and to build relationships and trust. In addition, ActKM encourages informal meetings and discussions outside the forum as a way to motivate debates in uncharted and innovative domains.

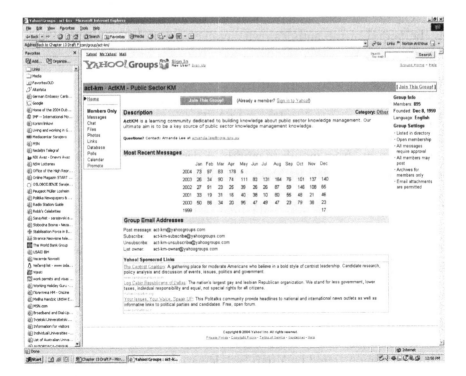

Figure 13.1 ActKM community of practice

A more detailed account of the ActKM history and purpose, goals and guiding principles, characteristics and dynamics analysed within the Snowden's (2002) Cynefin sense-making framework can be found in Callahan (2004). Our own quantitative analysis of the characteristics and dynamics of the community's online discussion forum is presented in the following section.

Quantitative Analysis and Results

The online discussion forum provides the heartbeat of the ActKM community. It operates using Yahoo groups, a free international web-based collaboration service. Members sign up themselves and receive/send as many messages as they choose. Thousands of messages that have been exchanged so far provide a rich source of knowledge on the patterns and nature of discussions that are taking place. The aim of this section is to explore the issue for a period from January 1 to April 30, 2004. This is the period of the author's own involvement with the community.

Volume of messages

The volume of messages on the online forum over the period January–April 2004 is presented in Figure 13.2. The figure suggests that there is a substantial variability in the total number of messages exchanged from day to day, and from month to month. A descriptive analysis of data was performed as suggested by Miles and Huberman (1994) to identify the prevailing patterns.

In order to identify a central tendency, the overall mean and standard deviation, as well as median and mode scores were calculated. The overall mean score of 3.56 suggests a relatively low overall traffic. This is further confirmed by a median score of 2 indicating that half of the time, two or less messages flew online. The mode score of 0 further suggests frequent traffic-free days. Additional analysis revealed that this coincided with weekend days.

The analysis also found a high level of variability in daily traffic. This was demonstrated by a standard deviation score of 4.97, and range from minimum of 0 to a maximum of 49 messages per day. Further

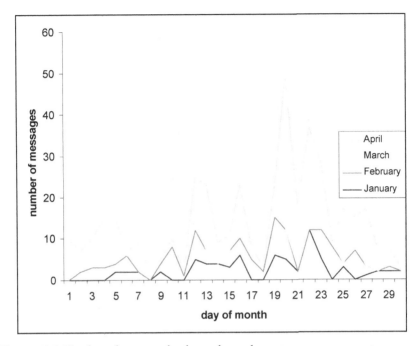

Figure 13.2 Number of messages by day and month

comparative analysis of mean scores by months indicates a significant change in daily traffic from January to April 2004. The average number of messages exchanged increased from 2.33 to 5.96. April 20th was a particularly interesting day with traffic peaking at 49 messages due to an intensive community debate on the issue on knowledge management training.

Member participation

A total of 123 different members participated in online discussions over the four-month period under study. This indicates that only about 20% of the total community membership is active. The remaining 80% appears to be passive.

With respect to the level of active discussion, we analysed two aspects: frequency and volume of each participant's messages. Volume equal or less than 4 (below mean score) was classified as low and greater than 4

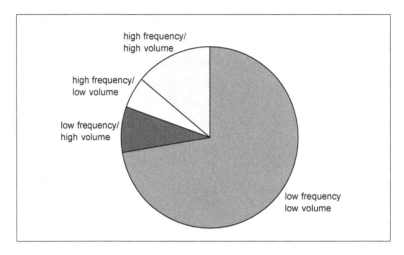

Figure 13.3 Members' participation in online discussion

as high. Similarly, frequency equal or less than 2 (out of 4 months) was considered low and greater than 2 as high. Based on these two dimensions (frequency/volume), each participant was classified into one of four categories (low/low, low/high, high/low, high/high). The results of this classification are presented in Figure 13.3.

These results show that only 17% of active participants contributed substantially and regularly to online discussions. Further 8% of the participants contributed a lot on few occasions, while 6% contributed a little on many occasions. The large majority of participants (72%) contributed both rarely and little to online discussion. This suggests that the forum is used more for informational than for conversational purposes. To find out if this may be true, we have further analysed topics and issues discussed among community members.

Topics and issues

The analysis of data collected on topics and issues discussed, confirms our proposition that the forum serves primarily informational purposes. About one-third of all messages (27%) were announcements of KM related events, workshops, meetings and jobs available in KM. Further

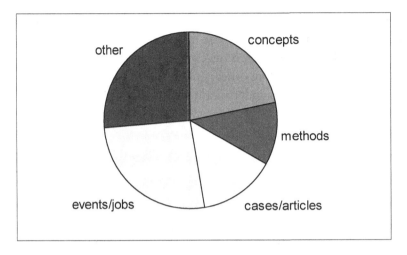

Figure 13.4 Topics and issues in online discussions

26% of messages were conveying general and personal members' information believed to be of interest to the community. Typically, these included introductions of new members, pointers to interesting web-sites and some humour. Further 14% messages were informing about research and practice of KM in the form of case studies, success stories, journal articles and white papers.

Only one-third of all messages involved discussions about KM concepts and methods. About 22% of messages addressed the basic KM concepts such as knowledge, knowledge conversion, metrics or complexity theory. The most frequently discussed conceptual issue was "knowledge classification scheme". The remaining 11% of messages were devoted to methodological issues in KM. These included KM training, strategy and policy development, solutions design, and evaluation. Two issues of particular interest were "project review and lessons learned" and "KM training".

In summary, our quantitative analysis of messages reveals that ActKM online community is sustained by a small percentage of highly active participants (about 3% of total membership) who are very passionate about a small number of KM issues (particularly KM training) and who enter into occasional and intensive debates about those issues (see, for example, April 20th). However, the question of what kind of "learning" value these debates bring to the rest of the membership remains unanswered. Further research is necessary to address this question. Future research should also explore other "off-line" activities of ActKM in order to get a more complete understanding of the community at work.

13.4 Conclusions

The prime objective of this chapter was to explore the characteristics and dynamics of an internet-based online community of practice. From the Callaghan's account of ActKM and our analysis of online discussions it may be concluded that, to evolve and succeed, an online community needs encouragement and nurturing. It also requires a small pro-active group of members to orchestrate the operation of the community and influence the environment in which it operates. With respect to technology, simple internet based collaborative tools can effectively enable online discussions and the storage of messages. However, there is a need to supplement online discussions with face-to-face meetings in order to develop trust and relationships, and to encourage wider community participation. Further research is recommended to address the limitations of the current study.

References

AA (1999), *Online Communities in Business*, Final report from the on-line communities research study, Next Generation Research Group, Arthur Andersen Knowledge Services, Chicago.

Awad, E.M. and Ghaziri, H.M. (2004), *Knowledge Management*, Pearson Education, New Jersey.

Becerra-Fernandez, I., Gonzalez, A. and Sabherwal, R. (2004), *Knowledge Management: Challenges, Solutions and Technologies*, Pearson Education, New Jersey.

Bennet, A. and Porter, D. (2003), "The Force of Knowledge: A Case Study of KM Implementation in the Department of the Navy", chapter 53 in

Handbook on Knowledge Management, Vol. 2, Holsapple, C.W. (ed.), Springer, Berlin, pp. 467–487.

Callaghan, S. (2004), "Cultivating a Public Sector Knowledge Management Community of Practice", in *Knowledge Networks: Innovation through Communities of Practice*, Hildreth, P.M. and Kimble, C. (eds.), Idea Group, Hershey, PA.

Hasan, H. and Crawford, K. (2003), "Distributed Communities of Learning and Practice", chapter 5 in *Australian Studies in Knowledge Management*, Hasan, H. and Handzic, M. (eds.), UOW Press, Wollongong, pp. 136–155.

Hildreth, P., Kimble, C. and Wright, P. (2000), "Communities of Practice in the Distributed International Environment", *Journal of Knowledge Management*, 4(1), 27–37.

Lesser, E. and Prusak, L. (1999), "Communities of Practice, Social Capital and Organisational Knowledge", *Information Systems Review, The Korean Society of Management Information Systems*, 1(1), 3–10.

McDermott, R. (1999), "Why Information Technology Inspired but Cannot Deliver Knowledge Management", *California Management Review*, 41(4), 103–117.

Miles, M.B. and Huberman, M.A. (1994), *Qualitative Data Analysis*. Sage, London.

Snowden, D. (2002), "Complex Acts of Knowing: Paradox and Descriptive Self-Awareness", *Journal of Knowledge Management*, 6(2), 110–111.

Tsui, E. (2003), "Tracking the Role and Evolution of Commercial Knowledge Management Software", in *Handbook on Knowledge Management*, Holsapple, C.W. (ed.), Vol. 2, Springer, Berlin, pp. 5–27.

Wenger, E. (1998), *Communities of Practice*, Cambridge University Press, Cambridge.

Wenger, E., McDermott, R. and Snyder, W.M. (2002), *Cultivating Communities of Practice: A Guide to Managing Knowledge*, Harvard Business School Press, Boston.

CHAPTER 14

Total Knowledge Management System:
Combining Technological and Social Aspects

Where does this knowledge lie? Everywhere!
— Unknown

In this chapter we take a holistic view of knowledge management systems (KMS) where technological and social aspects are considered together. First, a brief discussion of major social factors (organisational leadership, culture and measurement) is added to earlier discussion of KM technologies in Chapter 2. Then, the results of an empirical study are presented reporting on the knowledge workers' perceptions of their organisation's socio-technical KMS. The study is carried out in the context of an academic school. The main findings reveal a relatively greater perceived importance of social compared to technical aspects of KMS. The findings also indicate a relatively poorer perceived implementation of social than technical aspects of the KMS within the case school.

14.1 Introduction

A technological approach to knowledge management is not the only possible choice for organisations. Knowledge management systems (KMS) can be built with little or no dependence on modern information and communication technology. Bergeron (2003) termed such unassisted approaches "organic". The organic approach differs from the technological approach in a number of ways. Most important differences are in the type of knowledge involved, initial investment cost, ideal organisation size, scalability and volume of transactions.

For example, if the issues to be dealt with are subtle and require rich knowledge of the field, an organic approach suggests that an expert knowledge worker or knowledge analyst may be a more suitable option than a computer database. Similarly, although technologies supportive of KM can be applied successfully to organisations of any size, extensive initial investments in technology are generally more feasible in larger companies, while an organic approach may be more practical for smaller organisations. On the other hand, in situations involving large numbers of transactions such as handling customer complaints, a technology aided knowledge worker can improve his or her work productivity by consulting a database of past solutions to similar problems, and communicating these to customers electronically. From the implementation perspective, the technological approach requires training of the knowledge workers to use technology, while the organic approach focuses on improving their skills through social interaction.

Instead of looking at technological and social (organic) approaches as two competing strategies, this chapter promotes an integrated approach. The integrated view of KM synthesises human and object perspectives of knowledge, considers knowledge management as a complex multidimensional concept, views KM as both a social and a technological phenomenon, and suggests the dynamic evolutionary and context dependent nature of KM (Handzic, 2003).

Within the integrated framework, technology is presented as only one of the influencing factors on knowledge processes. More specifically, technology is perceived as a catalyst that enables and facilitates the development, transfer and application of knowledge, and thus contributes to organisational learning, improvement and innovation. The integrated framework recognises that in addition to technology, various social factors of the organisational environment also impact knowledge processes by creating a climate conducive to knowledge development and transfer. The following section provides an overview of the most important social aspects of an organisational KM system.

14.2 Social Aspects of KMS

Understanding different classes of social factors as well as individual factors within each class can aid deliberate efforts in managing knowledge in organisations. Among various socio-organisational aspects of a holistic KMS mentioned in the KM literature are managerial, resource and environmental influences (Holsapple and Joshi, 2003); leadership (Amidon and Macnamara, 2003); leadership, culture and measurement (AA, 1998); care including dimensions of trust, empathy, access to help, leniency in judgment and courage (van Krogh et al., 2000); structures, roles and spaces (Probst et al., 2000); workforce, capability and competencies (Warne et al., 2003). Leadership, culture and measurement are considered to be the most important of all (AA, 1998). The following sections consider these three classes of social influences in more detail.

Leadership

The adoption of KM in an organisation requires strong leadership to guide it towards managing and using its knowledge for maximum benefit (Amidon and Macnamara, 2003). Leadership is a critical success factor in implementing the cultural, organisational and technical change required by KM. While there may be several potential knowledge leadership roles in functions and teams, it is usually the CEO who establishes the mandate for KM and communicates its importance and need for change (Holsapple and Joshi, 2003). The distinguishing characteristic of leadership is that of being a catalyst through inspiring, mentoring, setting examples, listening and engendering trust and respect. KM requires individual and team leaders with a diverse range of skills, attributes and capabilities to manage and motivate change. These include an understanding of the business, strong interpersonal, communication and change management skills, technological expertise and skill in relationship building.

Control and coordination are important components of leadership. Control is concerned with ensuring that needed resources are available in sufficient quality and quantity subject to required security (Holsapple and Joshi, 2003). Two critical issues are protection and quality of knowledge resources. Protecting knowledge resources from loss, obsolence, unauthorised exposure and modification is crucial for effective knowledge management (Jamieson and Handzic, 2003). Approaches include legal protection, social protection and technological protection. Quality management provides (1) tools and (2) techniques that build quality into processes and practices that manage knowledge in an organisation. These include: strategic policy and planning processes, development and management of people, design and improvement of product and service processes, documentation of policies, procedures and processes, and measurement of costs, performance and satisfaction.

Coordination refers to managing dependencies among activities involving determination of what knowledge activities to perform, which participants will perform them and what knowledge resources will be operated on by each (Holsapple and Joshi, 2003). Essentially, coordination aims to harmonise activities by managing dependencies among knowledge resources, among knowledge activities, between knowledge and other resources and between resources and activities. Suggested coordination approaches include linking reward structures to knowledge sharing, establishing communications channels for sharing, and constructing programmes to encourage learning. For example, an innovation programme may provide employees with ways of suggesting creative ideas for improving the business, identifying business opportunities, reducing rework, providing benefits to more than one business unit or the organisation as a whole. However, it should be noted that a successful innovation programme depends also on the commitment, culture, motivation and active involvement of all levels in the business.

/

Culture

Culture is defined in terms of basic assumptions and beliefs shared by members of an organisation. It comprises an organisation's values, principles, norms, unwritten rules and procedures (Arnott, 2000; McDermott and O'Dell, 2001). Many authors point out that organisational culture is not only a critical success factor for KM, but also the most difficult and important factor to address, particularly if the appropriate culture does not already exist (Davenport et al., 1998).

Among the various components of organisational culture suggested as important to knowledge management are: trust, common sub-cultures, vocabularies, frames of reference, meeting times and places, broad ideas about work, absorptive capacity, belief that knowledge is a common advantage, openness to other people's views, tolerance for mistakes and access to help. Other aspects of the organisational culture relevant to promoting informal knowledge sharing include knowledge fairs, open forums and chat rooms (Ford and Chan, 2003; Handzic and Agahari, 2003).

Implementing KM requires a detailed understanding of the organisation's culture, as it has a profound effect on the achievement of strategy and outcomes. The existing culture can be recognised by observing participants' behaviours (Handzic and Van Toorn, 2000; Handzic et al., 2004). It can be manifested in interpersonal behaviour such as interaction and knowledge sharing. It can also be manifested in the form of experimentation performed by creative and innovative individuals in order to solve problems. In general, learning culture drives building of a learning environment, person to person knowledge sharing and innovation. Many KM initiatives aim to generate cultural change when existing cultures lack the attitudes, initiatives or skills to adapt to the desired environment that emphasises knowledge sharing and creation. A preferred "learning" culture has vision and leadership that focuses on learning, values knowledge, engenders trust and communication and tolerates questioning and mistakes (Handzic and Agahari, 2003).

Organisational knowledge is created, recorded, shared and transferred, through the formal and informal, internal and external relationships among employees and stakeholders. In order to collaborate and solve problems people require interpersonal oral and written communication skills and opportunities to use them. Common barriers that can hinder knowledge sharing include status effect, cultural differences, physical distractions, mixed messages and so on. Meetings are a traditional organisational tool used to support knowledge sharing (Handzic and Chaimunkalanont, 2003, 2004). Both virtual and face-to-face meetings are useful in this respect. Cross team meetings can further foster innovation or sharing of lessons learnt. Strategic conversations can provide a valuable means for idea generation. They can particularly contribute to planning by connecting and integrating diverse perspectives of the organisation and its environment. Story-telling is another valuable technique that may be used to describe complex issues, explain events, present perspectives and communicate experiences.

Communities of practice are a means by which two or more people can work together on common interests or work. They are based on connecting individuals on trust, group norms and a sense of common identity. Such social structures can play a major role in the effectiveness of knowledge sharing (Warne et al., 2003). They can contribute to performance in terms of gaining quicker access to knowledge and experts, and increasing knowledge reuse by sharing experiences. Social network analysis can help reveal existing social connections and illustrate the location of major nodes, linkages and bottlenecks and their dynamics. It can also be used to develop a better understanding of knowledge flows within an organisation.

Knowledge is held by individuals and has to be used and shared by individuals to benefit the organisation (Nonaka and Takeuchi, 1995). Various factors may assist individuals in playing their role in the organisation. One approach used to encourage desired individual behaviour is to reward and recognise their work through conditions of service. However, care needs to be taken when applying incentive schemes as they may limit knowledge sharing. Workplace training can contribute to KM through developing, applying and transferring task, conceptual and attitudinal knowledge and skills. It may be delivered through classroom, e-learning or experiential learning techniques. The benefit of mentoring and coaching in KM lies in facilitating the transfer of expertise and tacit knowledge from expert to less experienced or knowledgeable staff. Generally, training helps in preventing knowledge loss. Skills of organisational members need to be further supported by allowing time for individual experimentation and learning by doing or reflection. Reflection provides time for understanding, to develop the challenging new perspectives, to heal, strengthen and rebuild. Benefits include improving morale and tacit knowledge transfer. Sport and health activities can also have long-lasting benefits.

Measurement

In its most basic sense, measurement involves the valuation of knowledge resources and processes. Various measurement techniques or metrics may be used to measure results of knowledge management (Housel and Bell, 2001). Human resource, financial and survey statistics may be used separately or mixed to quantify different aspects of organisational performance (Davis and Wilson, 2003). However, it must be noted that metrics should be critically examined at periodic intervals, as metrics which are deemed relevant at a particular time may not be appropriate under changing circumstances.

Benchmarking is one of the most recent quality management techniques that uses a standard reference point or a benchmark to measure and compare organisational practices and performance in KM (Viedma, 2001). It can be done against a competitor, other organisations, or internally among groups in the organisation. Benchmarking in the knowledge organisation can be done against cultural and leadership practices and business and technology processes that enable knowledge creation, sharing and use through learning, innovation, communication or collaboration. Benchmarking can identify areas for improvement, increase performance, and determine excellence that acts as a standard reference point for best practice. It can also provide an explicit measure of the contribution and value of knowledge management to the organisation. For example, the taxonomy of "value" derived from the library sciences may be a helpful model for measuring the use aspect of KM (Davis and Wilson, 2003). The taxonomy allows both cognitive and affective states, tangible and intangible objects, interaction between resources, use and operation. KM can be justified by measuring changes in the intellectual capital of an organisation. To do this requires determining the elements by which intellectual capital will be measured and the general approach to be used (Edvinsson, 1997). These approaches tend to differ from traditional accounting measures by decreasing the emphasis on direct measurement of actual financial performance and increasing emphasis on indirectly measuring intangibles such as perceptions, expectations, quality and innovation that will determine future financial performance.

Others

Among various other influencing factors mentioned in the KM literature are organisational structures, roles and spaces (Probst et al., 2000). Flat network structures are suggested to promote communication and sharing, while bureaucracies discourage innovation through control and command hierarchies. Appointments of individuals to special KM roles (e.g., CKO) are believed to assist in smoothing knowledge flows and enhancing the quality of knowledge objects. Provision of social spaces such as tea-rooms, hot-spots or coffee stations may allow ideas to arise from casual contact and conversations among different groups of people within the organisation.

14.3 Empirical Study

The empirical study reported in this section builds on earlier research conducted by the author and her colleagues (Handzic et al., 2001; Oliver et al., 2003). This research recognises that one of the notable omissions in knowledge management studies is within higher education/research sector where there is the virtuous circle of teaching, research and consulting on professional work. In light of the above commentary, the aim of the current study was to examine KM practices in an academic environment. The specific objective of the study was to assess the relative importance and implementation of the following socio-technical factors: leadership, culture, measurement and technology.

Study Description

The university school studied is an institution which offers both undergraduate and postgraduate programs of study in the field of Information Systems. In addition, it operates a research centre, offers a series of research seminars and produces scholarly articles.

Participants in the study were academic staff in full-time employment who had been with the school for more than six months and had no intention of leaving it within the next six months. To minimise potential threats to validity, questionnaires were distributed to all academics who satisfied the specified criteria. Responses were anonymous and were given without the researcher's presence. Participation was voluntary and 17 out of 24 distributed questionnaires were completed and returned. The return rate of 71% ensures that data are representative.

A descriptive study was chosen as the preferred approach for the current investigation due to its exploratory nature. The main purpose was to describe things the way they are and draw meaning from social context, rather than to investigate cause-and-effect relationships. Such approach is often associated with research about human affairs. However, a proper case study (Yin, 1998; Lee, 1989) would provide a greater level of depth and understanding of many aspects of the phenomenon of interest than was possible in this study.

Several aspects of knowledge management that were investigated in the current study were: *leadership, culture, measurement and technology*. The survey instrument employed in this study was based on an instrument previously tested and used in the literature (AA, 1998). Modifications in wording were made to reflect specifics of the organisation being studied.

Results

A descriptive analysis of data was performed as suggested by Miles and Huberman (1994) to identify prevailing patterns and ensure plausibility of findings. In order to identify a central tendency in participants' perceptions, the average scores of their responses to relevant questionnaire items were calculated. These scores are presented in Table 14.1, the scale for questionnaire items being 1–7 (7 being the maximum and 1 being the minimum).

With respect to the perceived importance of the four KMS aspects evaluated, the mean scores obtained ranged from 4.66 to 5.36. Participants rated a mean score of 5.36 for organisational culture, 4.84 for technology, 4.66 for measurement Scores greater than 4 indicated that participants tended to perceive all four aspects as being quite important, but with culture identified as being most important of all.

Table 14.1 Summary results of KMS survey

KM System Aspect	Perceived Importance	Perceived Implementation
Leadership	5.28	3.08
Culture	5.36	3.24
Measurement	4.66	2.11
Technology	4.84	3.38

With respect to the perceived implementation of these KMS aspects, the mean scores obtained were in the range from 2.11 to 3.38. Participants rated a mean score of 3.38 for technology, 3.24 for culture, 3.08 for leadership and a low 2.11 for measurement. Scores less than 4 indicated that participants perceived the level of implementation of these KMS aspects in their organisation as being rather low, particularly with respect to knowledge measurement practices.

Discussion

The main findings of the current study indicate a variance between the perceived importance and implementation of various KMS aspects in the school studied. This was demonstrated by low scores obtained for participants' perceptions of the implementation of various socio-technological aspects, as compared to their perceptions of their respective importance.

The participants perceived organisational culture as the most important KMS aspect. This view is supported by the KM framework, which suggests that knowledge processes are facilitated by a conducive organisational environment. Such an environment is usually demostrated in terms of a collaborative organisational culture and strong leadership support. According to AA (1998), evidence of a collaborative culture may include an environment that enables and facilitates knowledge sharing, where a climate of openness and trust exists, and where service value creation is the main objective of knowledge management practices. In addition, there will be flexibility and a desire to innovate and drive the learning process, and an environment where employees take responsibility for their own learning. Our analysis of people's perceptions regarding these aspects of KMS appear to suggest that there is no collaborative culture within the school, this result confirming our earlier findings (Handzic and van Toorn, 2000).

Examples of good leadership support for KM may include: recognition of the central importance of managing knowledge to organistional strategy, encouraging learning to support existing and create new competencies, developing human resource plans and reward schemes based on the contribution to the development of organisational knowledge (AA, 1998). The participants perceived leadership as a very important aspect of KMS. The high level of awareness of its importance found in this study is an encouraging finding. In contrast, there is little evidence to show that KM leadership is actively practiced by the top management of the school. This finding is in great contrast to the evidence obtained from a professional consulting firm (Handzic and Agahari, 2003).

With respect to technology, our findings indicate that it was also considered as quite an important KMS aspect. It is generally believed that technological infrastructure has the potential to enable or facilitate knowledge processes by providing a platform for knowledge capture or sharing. Some examples where technology can be successfuly used to facilitate knowledge processes include; linking all members of the firm to one another and to all relevant external parties, creating an institutional memory that is accessible to the entire organisation, linking the organistion with its customers and partners, supporting collaboration amongst employees, fostering human-centered, real-time, integrated and smart systems (AA, 1998). Findings of this study indicate that there may be a need for further investment in technological infrastructure in order to fully facilitate knowledge management processes.

Finally, these findings indicate that participants tended to view the knowledge measurement aspect of the school's total KMS as being the least implemented aspect of all. The Handzic KM framework outlined in Chapter 1 clearly suggests the need for continuous knowledge measurement in order to monitor and adjust an organisation's knowledge management strategy over time. Implementing good knowledge measurement practices is usually evidenced in finding ways to link knowledge management to results, developing specific sets of indicators to manage knowledge, including a balanced set of soft and hard, financial and non-financial indicators, as well as by allocating resources towards efforts that measurably increase the organisational knowledge base (AA, 1998). The results of the study indicate that these areas need to be addressed by the school.

14.4 Conclusions

The main findings of the current study provide an insight into the importance and implementation of socio-technical KMS in a knowledge intensive organisation such as a university school. In particular, our findings demonstrate a high level of awareness of the importance of such KMS with a low level of actual implementation. This suggests that the school is at the end of the first "build awareness" stage of its KM journey, and has a long way to go (see Chapter 15).

From the results presented in this chapter, one may conclude that the school recognises that KMS is an important component of organisational success that needs to be carefully considered. The high level of awareness of its importance found in this study is an encouraging finding. The school believes that if planned and implemented carefully, in alignment with organisational objectives and core competencies, KMS may enable the release of the organisational knowledge resources that will bring continued organisational success.

In terms of the implementation of KMS, our findings indicate that a major challenge exists in this area. The results of the study identify an organisation at the very beginning of its KM journey. The low level of implementation found with respect to all four aspects of KMS investigated, are the major indicators of this being a problem area. Findings also indicate and highlight specific areas where issues need to be further addressed within the school being studied.

When considering the nature of the organisation being studied, the findings indicate that a major challenge exists for the school. Whilst operating in an ever-changing world and environment, the challenge will be to find and implement the most appropriate mix of KMS aspects in alignment with the school's goals and strategies. This challenge must be embraced and faced head-on in order to ensure the school's survival and future success.

References

A.A. (1998), *The Knowledge Management Practices Book*, Arthur Andersen.

Amidon, D.M. and Macnamara, D. (2003), "The 7 C's of Knowledge Leadership: Innovating Our Future", chapter 28 in Holsapple (ed.), *Handbook on Knowledge Management*, Vol. 1, Springer, Berlin, pp. 539–551.

Arnott, D. (2000), *Corporate Culture: The Insidious Lure of the All-Consuming Organisation*, American Management Association, New York.

Bergeron, B. (2003), *Essentials of Knowledge Management*, John Wiley & Sons, New Jersey.

Davenport, T.H., DeLong, D.W. and Breers, M.C. (1998), "Successful Knowledge Management Projects", *Sloan Management Review*, Winter, pp. 43–57.

Davis, M. and Wilson, C.S. (2003), "Measurement of Knowledge: Process and Practice in Knowledge Management", chapter 11 in Hasan, H. and Handzic M. (eds.), *Australian Studies in Knowledge Management*, UOW Press, Wollongong, pp. 342–371.

Edvinsson, L. (1997), "Developing Intellectual Capital at Skandia", *Long Range Planning*, 30(3), 366–373.

Ford, D.P. and Chan, Y.E. (2003), "Knowledge Sharing in a Multi-cultural Setting: A Case Study", *Knowledge Management Research & Practice*, 1(1), 11–27.

Handzic, M. and Chaimungkalanont, M. (2004), "The Impact of Socialisation on Group Effectiveness", in *Proceedings of the 4th International Conference on Knowledge, Culture and Change in Organisations – KCCO 2004*, London, UK, August 3–6.

Handzic, M. (2003), "An Integrated Framework of Knowledge Management", *Journal of Information and Knowledge Management*, 2(3).

Handzic, M. and Agahari, D. (2003), "A Knowledge Sharing Culture", in *Proceedings of the Knowledge Management Aston Conference (KMAC 2003)*, Birmingham, July 14–15, pp. 31–41.

Handzic, M. and Chaimungkalanont, M. (2003), "The Impact of Socialisation on Organisational Creativity", in *Proceedings of the European Conference on Knowledge Management (ECKM 2003)*, Oxford, September 18–19.

Handzic, M. and Van Toorn, C. (2000), "A Case Study of Organisational Culture", in Urquhart, C. and Sawyer, S. (eds.), *IFIP TC8/WK8.2 Organisations and Society in Information Systems (OASIS 2000) Workshop: Intersecting Issues, Approaches and Methods Down Under*, Brisbane, Australia, December 9, pp. 28–29.

Handzic, M., Lazaro, O. and Van Toorn, C. (2004), "Enabling Knowledge Sharing: Culture versus Technology", in *Proceedings of the 5th European Conference on Organisational Learning, Knowledge and Capabilities – OKLC 2004*, Innsbruck, Austria, April 2–3.

Handzic, M., Parkin, P. and Van Toorn, C. (2001), "Knowledge Management: Do We Do What We Preach?", in Renaud, K. et al. (eds.), in *Proceedings of the Annual Conference of the South African Institute of Computer Scientists and Information Technologists, (SAICSIT'2001)*, September 25–28, Pretoria, South Africa, pp. 191–196.

Holsapple, C.W. and Joshi, K.D. (2003), "A Knowledge Management Ontology", chapter 6 in Holsapple, C.W. (ed.), *Handbook on Knowledge Management*, Vol. 1, Springer, Berlin, pp. 539–551.

Housel, T. and Bell, A.H. (2001), *Measuring and Managing Knowledge*, McGraw-Hill, Boston.

Jamieson, R. and Handzic, M. (2003), "Impact of Managerial Controls on the Conduct of KM in Organisations", chapter 25 in Holsapple, C.W. (ed.), *Handbook on Knowledge Management*, Springer, Berlin, pp. 477–505.

Lee, A. (1989), "A Scientific Methodology for MIS Case Studies", *MIS Quarterly*, 12(3), 33–50.

McDermott, R. and O'Dell, C. (2001), "Overcoming Cultural Barriers to Sharing Knowledge", *Journal of Knowledge Management*, 5(1), 76–85.

Miles, M.B. and Huberman, M.A. (1994), *Qualitative Data Analysis*. Sage, London.

Nonaka, I. and Takeuchi, H. (1995), *The Knowledge Creating Company: How Japanese Companies Create the Dynamics of Innovation*, Oxford University Press, New York.

Oliver, G., Handzic, M. and Van Toorn, C. (2003), "Towards Understanding KM Practices in the Academic Environment: The Shoemaker's Paradox", *Electronic Journal of Knowledge Management*, 1(2), Paper 13.

Probst, G., Raub, S. and Romhardt, K. (2000), *Managing Knowledge*, John Wiley & Sons, New York.

Stewart, T.A. (1997), *Intellectual Capital: The New Wealth of Organisations*, Doubleday, New York.

Van Krogh, G., Ichijo, K. and Nonaka, I. (2000), "Bringing Care into Knowledge Development of Business Organisations", chapter 3 in Nonaka, I. and Nishiguchi, T. (eds.), *Knowledge Emergence*, Oxford University Press, New York.

Viedma, J.M. (2001), "ICBS Intellectual Capital Benchmarking System", *Journal of Intellectual Capital*, 2(2), 148–164.

Warne, L., Ali, I., Linger, H. and Pascoe, C. (2003), "Socio-technical Foundations for Knowledge Management", chapter 9 in Hasan, H. and Handzic, M. (eds.), *Australian Studies in Knowledge Management*, UOW Press, Wollongong, pp. 277–321.

Yin, R. (1988), *Case Study Research: Design and Methods*, Sage, London.

PART V

Issues and Challenges:

Present and Future

CHAPTER 15

Towards Knowledge Management Practice:

How to Get There?

There is nothing so practical as a good theory.
— Kurt Lewin

This chapter addresses the question of how new-age organisations need to practice knowledge management (KM) to ensure success. It provides broad guidelines for conducting KM in organisations and illustrates these with a series of real world cases. These cases highlight successful KM applications in organisations. By identifying critical steps, key factors and proven paths, this chapter attempts to put into the hands of managers, a practical tool that can help them unleash the power of knowledge in their organisations and thus ensure business success.

15.1 Introduction

The environment in which businesses operate today can be summarised in terms of three mega trends: globalisation and the increasing intensity of competition; virtualisation or digitalisation enabled by advances in information and communication technology; and transformation from an industrial to a knowledge-based economy with the rise of knowledge management (Raich, 2000). The basic assumption of knowledge management (KM) is that organisations that better manage their individual and collective knowledge will deal more successfully with the challenges of the new business environment. KM is seen as central to process and product innovation, efficiency and effectiveness improvements, as well as to minimising the risk of losing core competencies (Von Krogh et al., 2000). Therefore, the main issue of concern in this chapter is how to effectively establish and sustain good KM practices in organisations in order to ensure their competitiveness in the new business environment.

This chapter responds to the major practice-oriented challenge for KM — bridging the gap between theory and practice — by introducing a practical method for conducting KM in organisations. The method originally developed by Handzic and Hasan (2003b) is directed principally at managers and KM practitioners. It is not intended to be a normative 'standard'. Rather, the aim is to provide a generic set of guidelines which individuals and organisations can adapt to their own contexts. It is expected that all segments of society that practice knowledge work should benefit from such a KM method. Before presenting and illustrating the method itself, the chapter reviews the leading KM frameworks currently used or proposed by industry and academia. This review identifies major deficiencies in the existing models, and provides a justification for the development of an integrated KM method aimed at overcoming these deficiencies.

15.2 Review of Leading KM Frameworks

Chapter 1 describes a number of partial and integrated KM frameworks that have been suggested to facilitate a better understanding of the KM phenomena. They all belong to a category of descriptive frameworks as they attempt to characterise the nature of KM phenomena in terms of basic elements and relationships. In contrast, prescriptive frameworks required by practice attempt to direct methods to follow in conducting KM. In accord with this chapter's focus on KM practice, herein descriptive versus prescriptive nature of various KM frameworks is examined.

Descriptive KM Frameworks

Descriptive KM frameworks outlined in Chapter 1 encompass a broad range of issues, methods and theories, and differ in scope and focus. Some are knowledge-oriented, like the intellectual capital models of McAdam and McCreedy (1999) and the economic school in Earl's (2001) taxonomy. The list of types and perspectives described in Alavi and Leidner's (2001) review also share this orientation. Others, like Nonaka's (1998) knowledge spiral and Earl's (2001) behavioural school are process-orientated. Several frameworks emphasise the dependence of knowledge on socio-technological factors. Earl's (2001) technocratic school that supports and structures a lot of IS work in KM belongs to this category. Nonaka and Konno's (1998) model of 'ba' (Japanese word for place) is another good example.

Holsapple and Joshi (1999) identify a number of attempts to integrate this diversity of partial approaches in order to provide holistic views and common ground for KM research, and improved methods for KM practice. Recent Australian developments include the Handzic's integrated knowledge-process-enabler framework and the Hasan's activity theory approach (Handzic and Hasan, 2003a). However, the most significant recent addition to KM models is certainly the Interim Australian KM Standard (Standards Australia, 2003). Most importantly, all integrated descriptive KM frameworks are dynamic with an emphasis on knowledge processes and activities in expanding cycles of growth; KM is considered as a socio-technical undertaking enabled by social, organisational and technical factors which must be considered in any KM initiative; and KM is recognised as being severely dependent on context, so that there is no 'one size fits all' solution.

Prescriptive KM Frameworks

Prescriptive frameworks attempt to dictate methods to follow in conducting KM. Successful implementation of KM in an organisation requires addressing all components of an integrated framework in a deliberate and systematic way. In other words, it requires a methodology that will serve as a roadmap for the KM journey. Stage frameworks have been a popular approach in organisational and information technology research. Such models assume that predictable patterns of evolution conceptualised as stages exist in organisational development. As shown in Figure 15.1, these stages are sequential in nature, occur as a hierarchical progression, and involve a broad range of organisational activities and structures.

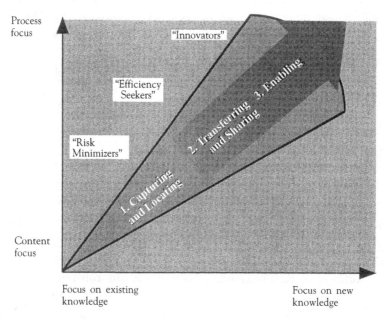

Figure 15.1 Evolutionary stages model of KM

Various multistage models have been proposed for development of KM. Recent examples includes Von Krogh et al.'s (2000) model that

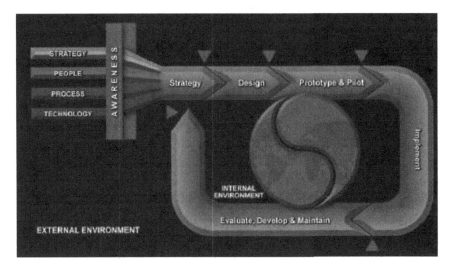

Figure 15.2 Arthur Andersen's KM model

has three stages: locate and capture; make use of what is available; and enable new knowledge creation for innovation. Gottschalk and Khandelwal (2003) proposed a growth model for KM technology consisting of four stages which they named: end user tool, who knows what, what they know, and how they think systems.

Most of the existing KM methods have been criticised in the literature as being incomplete, and lacking double-loop learning (Leibowitz, 2003). This is seen as a major omission, as iterative feedback is an important element of KM which promotes learning organisation. The Australian KM Standard (Standards Australia, 2003) addresses this issue by stating that the key phases in development and implementation of KM do not form a linear process and that, while the phases do build on each other, they can be used flexibly or iteratively. The order and depth of each phase depends on the nature and aims of a particular KM initiative. Arthur Andersen (AAOTE, 1998), Siemens AG (Hofer and Spek, 2002) and Tiwana (2000) also propose a more parallel and cyclical KM implementation approach (see Figure 15.2).

Towards an Effective KM Method

Some academics have argued that more rigour must be put into KM methodology in order to make KM more a discipline rather than a passing fad (Leibowitz, 2003). This requires tenets of project management, process reviews, change management, process training and quality assurance throughout the process; phases that flow from conceptualisation, through strategising, to action to evaluation and renewal in a repeated cycle; and deliverables that include planning and design documents, full production KM systems, user guides and evaluation reports. Handzic and Hasan (2003b) developed a set of broad guidelines for conducting KM in organisations that encompass these principles, and overcome the deficiencies of various existing methods. These guidelines are summarised in the next section. To broaden their understanding, readers should also review the author's method and guidelines for SMEs (Handzic, 2004a, b).

15.3 Guidelines for Conducting KM in Organisations

According to Handzic and Hasan (2003b), there are many managers who can see that KM is important but who are perplexed by the bewildering array of available KM methods and solutions. They see KM as controversial, hard to pin down and meaning different things to different people. Such managers are seeking guidance on KM issues and answers to questions of why, when, where and how to become involved in KM initiatives. The set of guidelines outlined in this section should provide some answers.

Step 1: Build KM Awareness

In order to avoid any danger of misconception and misunderstanding, the first important task for organisations starting the KM journey is to build KM awareness (Leibowitz and Megbolugbe, 2003). This requires creating awareness at both the managerial level and employee level. Influencing management to support the KM initiative is considered crucial. Once management is supportive, it is important to start early to influence the culture of the organisation and prepare it for KM. Changing people's behaviour is identified as the greatest single obstacle to KM initiatives. The right set of incentives can help motivate employees to share and collaborate. It is also advisable to begin developing a KM ontology which will serve as a common vocabulary and structure in which to conduct KM.

Step 2: Align KM with Business Strategy

Aligning KM with business strategy is the next important task. Typically, it involves determining an organisation's position, considering its motives for KM, and determining expected outcomes and how to verify them. While there may be many different individual reasons for starting KM initiatives in organisations, they usually focus either on reuse of existing knowledge to ensure business survival, or creation of new knowledge and innovation for advancement purposes (Von Krogh et al., 2000). If the prime motivation for KM is reuse of existing knowledge, the response typically involves identifying and holding onto the core competencies that the company has, and transferring experiences and best practices throughout the organisation in order to avoid unnecessary duplication and to reduce cost. If the motive for KM is innovation, the focus is on both new knowledge and on knowledge processes. Innovative organisations take a strategic view of knowledge, formulate knowledge visions, tear down knowledge barriers, develop new corporate values and trust, catalyse and coordinate knowledge creation, manage the various contexts involved, develop a conversational culture and globalise local knowledge.

Step 3: Audit Knowledge Assets and Resources

Taking an inventory of knowledge in the current organisational context and conducting a strength versus weakness analysis on this inventory in an overt fashion is seen as a next necessary phase in a successful KM journey. According to KM consultants (AA, 1998) implementing good knowledge measurement practices is usually evidenced in finding ways to link KM to financial results, developing specific sets of indicators to manage knowledge, including a balanced set of 'soft' and 'hard' types of measures, and both financial and non-financial indicators, as well as by allocating resources towards efforts that measurably increase organisational knowledge base. This method suggests the need for continuous knowledge measurement in order to monitor and adjust an organisation's KM strategy over time.

Step 4: Develop and Implement 'Right' KM Solutions

The final recommendation for a successful KM journey is to implement KM solutions that combine those processes, cultural adjustments and technologies that have the best potential to enhance knowledge and add value for the firm. This requires all sources and forms of knowledge to come into play to maximise business success. Prior research (AA, 1998) shows that companies that implement knowledge processes may exhibit some of the following characteristics: systematic identification of knowledge gaps and well-defined processes to close them, development of sophisticated and ethical intelligence-gathering mechanisms, involvement of the whole workforce in looking for ideas, formalising the process of capturing and transferring knowledge including creating documentation and recording lessons learnt, valuing and transferring tacit knowledge across an organisation through encouraging experimentation and socialisation. In addition, they also exhibit strong leadership support and a collaborative organisational culture. Finally, they use technology to create an institutional memory that is accessible to the entire organisation and links members of the company to one another and to all relevant external parties.

15.4 Illustrative Cases

According to Handzic and Hasan (2003b), there are some organisations and consultants who have been practicing KM for some time and have identified particular KM solutions that work for them. Such sources are now providing case studies to be analysed by researchers. This section presents a selected number of cases as examples of successful application of the Handzic and Hasan's KM method across professional and business services. These cases are taken from Handzic (2004b) to illustrate key activities and outcomes of the different methodology steps. For example, Case 1 exemplifies a way of building KM awareness through research and publication; Case 2 points to two companies that have successfully aligned their KM and business strategies; Case 3 demonstrates a widely accepted method to measure knowledge; and Case 4 illustrates two different yet equally successful KM solutions.

Case 1: Building KM Awareness at UNSW

The following case illustrates the role of R&D in promoting the awareness of KM. In 2000, a special *Knowledge Management Research Group* was established within the School of Information Systems, Technology and Management, UNSW, to serve as a source of expertise in KM internationally (KMRG, 2000). The group's mission is to provide a broad research program in KM, foster collaborative work in the study of KM with business and government organisations; and provide consulting services on best practices in KM. The group's specific objectives include: conducting research in processes and socio-technological enablers of knowledge creation, sharing, storage and discovery; forming partnerships with professional and research organisations and individuals interested in advancing KM; and disseminating KM research findings through worldwide research and industry forums and publication outlets.

Internally, the group has adopted the integrated KM framework (Handzic, 2003) as a mechanism to build a common vocabulary and understanding of the KM phenomena. This framework also serves to guide the scope for the group's research and teaching activities. The conceptual ideas are typically conveyed to prospective group members through informal meetings and seminars. In addition, the group conducts a mentoring scheme for junior faculty.

Case 2: KM Strategies at Ford and Pfizer

The following are examples of two different KM strategies adopted by two different companies to suit their different business goals. These examples come from the Standards Australia's publications showcasing the best international practices in KM (Standards Australia, 2001; Rollo and Clarke, 2001). The first example is from the automotive sector (Ford Motor Company) and the second one (Pfizer Inc.) from the pharmaceutical sector. In accordance with its process efficiency goals, Ford has implemented a number of knowledge sharing initiatives aimed at driving down the time it takes to get new models of cars and trucks from concept to full production. The best practice replication program has been shared across 37 plants around the globe. It involves individuals and groups who suggest improvements by entering a brief description of their best practice into a database, and each week all plants receive several best practices that apply to that plant. This technology-mediated knowledge transfer strategy is supplemented with face-to-face exchanges. Each best practice passes through a quality assurance process to ensure the information can be trusted. A range of other approaches including the best use of intranets and collaboration tools such as computer-conferencing support the best practice replication program. In the five years after the program was implemented more than 2,800 proven practices were shared, helping to reduce concept-to-production time from 36 months to 24 months. The documented financial value of these improvements has been estimated at US$1.25 billion.

In contrast, Pfizer is using KM practices to reach markets first and beat the industry average in an intensely competitive pharmaceutical sector. Consistent with its innovation enabling motives, the company spends over US$1.7 billion annually in research (1996 figures). However, only a small portion of screened compounds ever make it to market. Pfizer has recognised that if it could manage its research better it would have a significant competitive advantage. Its main approach involves data mining of scientific publications and other databases to make researchers aware of progress and projects involving other researchers. The most notable example of the company's success is the discovery of the famous impotence treatment drug Viagra. Viagra was originally designed as a drug to fight angina but nurses recorded an unusual side-effect during trials. The side effect was identified as a significant systematic trend by a clinician analysing the trial results.

Case 3: Evaluating Intellectual Capital at Skandia

The following case introduces a measurement practice of an organisation that created the world's first intellectual capital report, Skandia Insurance Company. It is showcased among the international best practice cases in the insurance sector (Rollo and Clarke, 2001). Skandia's Intellectual Capital consists of human capital (personal values, competencies, potential relationships, attitudes) and structural capital, which includes customer capital (base, relationships, potential) and organisational capital (processes, culture, innovation assets). Skandia believes that their intellectual capital is at least as important as their financial capital in providing sustainable earnings. Skandia measures human capital by using indices such as an empowerment index (motivation, support, awareness and competence), training expenses per employee, employee turnover, average years of service, and education levels of employees. Skandia's structural capital is measured primarily in terms of its IT capacity and processing time. Skandia's core business measures consist of a set of indicators including financial (return-based efficiency and effectiveness metrics), customer (satisfaction and unit growth), process (efficiency and outputs/savings per employee), development (return business and future growth) and human (employee loyalty, skills and competencies). All metrics are tied to the company's strategic goals of generating value in financial and prudential services.

Case 4: KM Solutions at McKinsey and Westpac

The following case presents examples of two different, but equally successful KM solutions implemented by a professional services (McKinsey & Company), and a banking and financial services organisation (Westpac Institutional Bank). Both examples are featured among the best international practices in KM (Rollo and Clarke, 2001), but differ with respect to personalisation versus codification approach. McKinsey's reputation comes from a few basic ideals: the clients' interest come first, be discrete, be honest, do not overextend yourself. Accordingly, McKinsey's internal structure is supported by a collaborative culture reinforced by the fact that staff share part of the entire firm's profit irrespective of what country they are employed in. The company is owned by partners which is intrumental in creating strong relationships and keeping competence from leaving the firm. There is also an emphasis on cultural socialisation. Partners are encouraged to move between client companies thereby sharing knowledge through personal relationships. Several policies are aimed at increasing competence of the firm and enabling knowledge flow among people. The company recruits the top graduates, assigns them to teams with seniors and puts them through an up-or-out initiation. The company encourages knowledge flows by developing individual concepts, transfering tacit concepts and models that can be used by other staff, and sharing information on all projects. In terms of external structure, the firm focuses on nurturing close relations with selected high image clients. The company also nurtures close relationships with universities because they recruit talent from them.

In contrast, Westpac boasts one of the largest centralised Oracle financial systems in the world, and relies on an intranet and the web-enabled Oracle Financial Analyser to provide critical financial-performance information to its managers. KM is also intermingled with customer relationship management, because the bank wants to increase its knowledge of customers in order to better understand their needs. Westpac has taken advantage of the latest technology to develop a system known as Connect to record and store all of its core documents in a globally distributed database. Connect captures key contacts and automatically directs new information and news about customers to the relevant people in the bank. The benefit of the bank's KM solution is seen in high percentage of the Australian top companies' nominations of Westpac as their preferred banking partner. Westpac also ranks among top ten companies on the Australian Stock Exchange.

15.5 Conclusions

This chapter addresses the issues of why and how managers of new-age enterprises need to conduct knowledge management. KM has been acknowledged as one of the most significant management movements in the knowledge economy. The proposition put forward is that if planned and implemented carefully in alignment with organisational objectives and core competencies, it may enable the release of the organisational knowledge resources that would bring ultimate business success in the new economy. From what we have learnt from literature and case studies presented in this chapter, this success can be achieved by building KM awareness, determining intended outcomes, auditing and valuing knowledge assets and resources, and finally by developing and implementing those KM solutions that have the best potential to enhance knowledge and add value to the organisation.

References

AA (1998), *The Knowledge Management Practices Book*, Arthur Andersen.

AAOTE (1998), *BC Knowledge Management*, Arthur Andersen Office of Training and Education, Arthur Andersen.

Alavi, M. and Leidner, D.E. (2001), "Knowledge Management and Knowledge Management Systems: Conceptual Foundations and Research Issues", *MIS Quarterly*, 25(1), 107–136.

De Grooijer, J. (2000), "Designing a Knowledge Management Performance Framework", *Journal of Knowledge Management*, 4(4), 303–310.

Earl, M. (2001), "Knowledge Management Strategies: Toward a Taxonomy", *Journal of Management Information Systems*, 18(1), 215–233.

Gottschalk, P. and Khandelwal, V. (2003), "Stages of Growth for Knowledge Management Technology in Australian Law Firms", in *Proceedings of the 14th Australasian Conference on Information Systems*, Perth, Edith Cowan University, November.

Handzic, M. and Hasan, H. (2003a), "The Search for an Integrated KM Framework", in Hasan, H. and Handzic, M. (eds.), *Australian Studies in Knowledge Management*, UOW Press, Wollongong.

Handzic, M. and Hasan, H. (2003b), "Continuing the Knowledge Management Journey", in Hasan, H. and Handzic, M. (eds.), *Australian Studies in Knowledge Management*, UOW Press, Wollongong.

Handzic, M. (2003), "An Integrated Framework of Knowledge Management", *Journal of Information and Knowledge Management*, 2(3), 245–252.

Handzic, M. (2004a), "Knowledge Management in SMEs: Practical Guidelines", *Asia Pacific Tech. Monitor*, January–February, pp. 29–34.

Handzic, M. (2004b), "A Method for Conducting Knowledge Management: Concepts and Cases", in *Proceedings of the KMChallenge 2004 Conference*, Sydney, Australia, March 30–31.

Hofer-Alfeis, J. and van der Spek, R. (2002), "The Knowledge Strategy Process — An Instrument for Business Owners", in Davenport, T.H. and Probst, G.J.B. (eds.), *Knowledge Management Case Book*, John Wiley & Sons.

KMRG (2000), *KM Research Group Annual Report 2000*, URL: http://www.kmrg.unsw.edu.au/kmRgAnnualReport2000.htm. [accessed 23/2/2004].

Holsapple, C.W. and Joshi, K.D. (1999), "Description and Analysis of Existing Knowledge Management Frameworks", in *Proceedings of the 32nd Hawaii International Conference on System Sciences*, January.

Liebowitz, J. (2003), "Putting More Rigor into Knowledge Management", in *Proceedings of the Knowledge Management Aston Conference*, Birmingham, Aston University, July.

Liebowitz, J. and Megbolugbe, I. (2003), "A Set of Frameworks to Aid the Project Manager in Conceptualising and Implementing Knowledge Management Initiatives", *International Journal of Project Management*, 21, 189–198.

McAdam, R. and McCreedy, S. (1999), "A Critical Review of Knowledge Management Models", *The Learning Organisation*, 6(3), 91–100.

Nonaka, I. and Konno, N. (1998), "The Concept of Ba: Building a Foundation for Knowledge Creation", *California Management Review*, 40(3), 40–54.

Nonaka, I. (1998), "The Knowledge-Creating Company", *Harvard Business Review on Knowledge Management*, Harvard Business School Press, Boston.

Raich, M. (2000), *Managing in the Knowledge Based Economy*, Raich Ltd., Zurich.

Rollo, C. and Clarke, T. (2001), *HB275-Supplement1-2001International Best Practice-Case Studies in Knowledge Management*, Standards Australia International Limited, Sydney.

Standards Australia (2001), *HB275-2001 Knowledge Management: A Framework for Succeeding in the Knowledge Era*, Standards Australia International Limited, Sydney.

Standards Australia (2003), *AS5037(Int)-2003, Interim Australian Standard, Knowledge Management*, Standards Australia International Limited, Sydney.

Tiwana, A. (2000), *The Knowledge Management Toolkit*, Prentice Hall, New Jersey.

Von Krogh, G., Ichijo, K. and Nonaka, I. (2000), *Enabling Knowledge Creation*, Oxford University Press, New York.

CHAPTER 16

The Future of Knowledge Management:

What Is on the Horizon?

The great end of life is not knowledge, but action.
— Thomas H. Huxley

This chapter takes a look at the future. It explores two emerging trends in KM and identifies major issues and challenges they pose. The first is "automation", involving the use of intelligent systems that apply knowledge to solve problems for and instead of humans. The second is "integration", particularly the merging of knowledge management with e-commerce. The chapter ends with the concluding remarks from the author.

16.1 Introduction

Organisations in the knowledge economy will increasingly inhabit environments that are chaotic. In such environments, the cause and effect links are difficult to discern, small changes can be amplified, and the future is hard to predict. Organisations will have to live with an inherent ambiguity, and compete on the edge of stability and instability. Organisational survival or advancement will depend on continuous innovation, and their capability to find opportunities for the exercise of new strategies.

According to Drucker (1993), in the knowledge economy, the only thing that increasingly will matter in national as well as international economics is management's performance in making knowledge productive. This chapter explores the emerging trends that seem most likely to have a significant impact on knowledge management in the near future. These include technologies that deal with automation and integration.

Automation is a process in which different "smart" technologies carry out knowledge workers' tasks for which experts' knowledge and extensive training is required (Hasan, 2003). Numerous technologies grouped under the banner of artificial intelligence (AI) can have the potential to "augment" human abilities by doing those tasks they do better, and leaving to people to do those tasks they do better. According to Stair and Reynolds (2003), computers are better than humans at transferring information, making complex calculations, and making calculations rapidly and accurately. Humans are better than computers at all other attributes of intelligence.

The other group of technologies that hold promise for the future of KM are those that deal with integration. Integration is the process in which different computer applications and systems are connected and fit seamlessly and unobtrusively with the workflow of knowledge workers and managers (Bergeron, 2003). This chapter is particularly concerned with the merging of knowledge management and electronic commerce.

16.2 Automation: Intelligent Systems That Apply Knowledge

Various smart systems are starting to appear to assist organisations and individuals in achieving their goals in new and exciting ways. Robots and internet bots, vision systems, natural language processing and learning systems, neural networks and expert systems are only a few examples of systems that are helping people make better decisions, perform at higher levels, offer new ways to communicate and express ideas creatively. One common denominator of all these systems is the notion of artificial intelligence.

Artificial Intelligence

The term artificial intelligence (AI) is used to describe computer systems that demonstrate the characteristics of intelligence (Stair and Reynolds, 2003). Intelligent behaviour encompasses the ability to learn from experience and apply knowledge acquired from experience, handle complex situations, solve problems when important information is missing, determine what is important, react quickly and correctly to a new situation, be perceptive and understand visuals images, be creative and imaginative, and use heuristics.

The dream of pioneers of AI was to create machines that can reason, learn and perceive like humans. Science fiction movies give us some glimpses of what the future might be. The typical scenario shows machines taking over the world from humans. How realistic these fictional accounts of the future may be is hard to judge. Some scholars believe that the ability to create human-like machines will be possible in time, once we understand our own thinking. Others warn of important ethical and societal implications of such developments. Today, AI scientists are moving away from trying to make a machine into a person, and are more concerned with developing systems that augment human abilities. We herein are particularly interested in the position of intelligent systems in the spectrum of KM systems.

Becerra-Fernandez et al. (2004) described various types of knowledge application systems used in KM practice. These systems are typically enabled by AI and can reason in a narrow domain and in a relatively mechanistic way. For example, they can facilitate KM activities of direction (e.g., help desk, support centre) and routines (e.g., best practice, standards). The development of such knowledge application systems is based mainly on two AI technologies, rule-based and case-based reasoning (CBR). Other technologies worth mentioning are constraint-based, model-based and diagrammatic reasoning. These have very specific applications in solving problems from constrained domains, and from diagrams or drawings.

Knowledge-Based Systems

Hasan (2003) reminds us that knowledge-based systems (KBS) in the form of intelligent decision support and expert systems were devised as problem-solving systems long before the term KM became popular. Usually, intelligent decision support systems are model-based, with some enhanced functionality involving learning, memory, reasoning and interactive communication, while expert systems automate the tasks that involve expert knowledge and reasoning that are typically gained through extensive training and experience. Such systems have long been successfully used in areas such as medical diagnosis and financial planning.

Generally, solving problems requires two types of knowledge: knowledge of the objects in the specific domain, and the knowledge of how to reason in that domain. Therefore, the key parts of the KBS are the knowledge base that holds the domain specific knowledge, and the inference engine that contains the functions to exercise that knowledge (Becerra-Fernandez, 2004). In the rule-based system, knowledge is represented in the form of "if-then" statements. These statements describe situations that may occur and conclusions that can be drawn if the situations became true. They represent elicited heuristics and shortcuts learned by the expert over years of practical problem-solving. Inference engine exercises the knowledge by forward or backward chaining. The forward chaining starts with inputs and moves towards conclusions. The backward chaining works from the conclusion to the inputs, trying to validate conclusions by finding evidence to support them.

An alternative to expressing knowledge as rules based on hierarchical knowledge of an expert is to express it explicitly in terms of historical problems that were previously solved and their solutions. Such approach is called case-based reasoning (CBR). In its simplest form, CBR consists of a case library (a repository of historical cases) and search/retrieval and case addition mechanisms. CBR is a technology based on the idea of analogy (Sheppard, 2003). Solutions from past problems (cases) are retrieved and deployed, with adaptation where necessary, to solve new problems. CBR has a number of strengths, since it does not require explicit knowledge elicitation and supports collaboration with users. However, it is not suited to situations characterised by a lack of relevant cases, where few cases are available, and when the problem domain can be easily modeled with a model-based technique. Handzic and Low (2001) also found that the assumptions of CBR that problems recur and that similar problems have similar solutions does not hold true in probabilistic tasks.

Neural Networks

The initial work on neural networks was motivated by the study on human brain and the idea of neurons as its building blocks. Artificial intelligence researchers introduced a computing neuron model (depicted in Figure 16.1.) to simulate the way neurons work in the human brain. This model provided the basis for many later neural networks developments.

The most important feature of neural networks is their ability to learn. Just like human brain, neural networks can learn by example and dynamically modify themselves to fit the data presented. Furthermore, neural models are also able to learn from very noisy, distorted, or incomplete sample data, which render other methods useless (Glorfeld, 1996). Because of this learning ability, neural networks are then seen as appropriate tools for knowledge discovery. Learning paradigms in neural networks are divided into 2 categories, supervised and unsupervised.

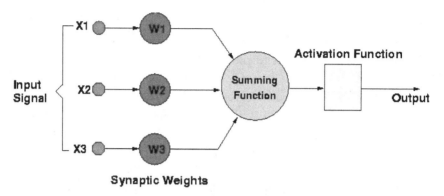

Figure 16.1 Model of computing neuron

With supervised learning, the model is provided with feedback so that it can learn from its mistakes and try not to repeat the same mistakes in the future. In unsupervised learning, the neural network model is not given any prior training or feedback. Instead it is given real data from the beginning and will learn along the way.

Beside its ability to learn patterns, neural networks also have other useful properties and capabilities including: (i) *Nonlinearity*. Both distant and nearby or more related neurons in a neural network may be interconnected. Nonlinearity is an important property particularly if the input pattern is inherently nonlinear; (ii) *Adaptivity*. Neural networks have the ability to adapt their synaptic weights to changes in the surrounding environment. This is particularly useful when a neural network model is deployed in a non-stationary environment (an environment that changes with time, for example, a stock market with ever changing prices); and (iii) *Generalisation*. This is perhaps the second most important feature besides learning. Generalisation refers to the neural network producing appropriate outputs for inputs that were not encountered during training.

There are literally hundreds of neural network models available for use (FAQ, 2002). The combination of topology, learning paradigm and learning rules/algorithms define a particular neural network model. Choosing which neural network model to use is not trivial. According to Bigus (1996), there are several criteria that can be followed in order to choose a suitable model. These criteria include data type and quantity, training requirements and functional requirements. Training requirements are mostly concerned with things such as: the tolerable training time and hardware demands for doing such training. Functional requirements are related to the learning function that is expected. For example, in the granting of loans study, Handzic et al. (2003) found out that Committee Machine models were superior to a single Multi Layer Perceptron model, and that Boosting by Filtering outperformed Ensemble Averaging.

Despite the evident benefits offered for businesses, neural networks are not free from criticism. Most are of the "black box" kind. This means that the tool can only produce conclusions without explanations and justification of the reasons behind such conclusions. This makes accountability and reliability issues difficult to address. Other limitations concern the high computational requirements of neural networks, usually in the form of computer power and training time, and the scarcity of experts in the field which makes some businesses avoid their use (Marakas, 1999).

In summary, the overall purpose of neural networks, knowledge based systems and other types of intelligent systems in business and research is to help the organisations and individuals achieve their goals. The benefits of such systems can already be seen in medical diagnosis, exploration of natural resources, mechanical diagnostics, or in the design and development of systems. And, the research continues.

16.3 Integration: Merging of E-commerce and Knowledge Management

Handzic and Jamieson (2001) examined the inter-relationship between two major developments that shape modern businesses: electronic commerce and knowledge management. In particular, they examined the place and role of each of these two developments in the new economy and then proposed a framework that relates knowledge management with electronic commerce. The following is a summary of their research.

Electronic Commerce and New Economy

Rapid developments in information and telecommunication technologies, particularly the flexibility and user-friendliness of the Internet, have made it possible for modern organisations to increasingly conduct their transactions with their customers, suppliers and other trading partners by means of electronic commerce. Formally, electronic commerce is defined as an application of new technologies in helping individuals and organisations conduct their business better (Schneider and Perry, 2000).

Electronic commerce (EC) is usually classified into the following three categories resulting in different issues (Blanning, 2000). Business-to-customers EC typically involves electronic method of informing customers about products and services, taking orders, billing, and, in some cases, delivering products electronically. Typical concerns involve channel conflict, performance measures and short-term losses versus long-term expectations. Business-to-business EC enables organisations to exchange electronic documents such as invoices and payment advises, as well as form virtual marketplaces. Main concerns involve standardisation and regulation. Customer-to-customer EC provides an electronic medium for direct interactions among customers, and has the potential to transcend economic applications to include social and political applications. These interactions have the potential to create a platform for political discourse and thus transfer power to a more diffuse populace.

According to Tiwana (2001), the challenge in any type of electronic commerce is attracting new clientele on board, and then retaining them, expanding their businesses, and keeping them coming back for more. He suggests that electronic businesses that will thrive in future are those that recognise their best customers and retain their loyalty. The key to this is businesses' knowledge about their customers and channels and their ability to use that knowledge to rethink, recast and even cannibalize existing businesses. He proposes two competitive imperatives for successful electronic business: (i) integrating and turning customer and channel knowledge into action, and (ii) forming strong relationships with customers and channel partners. The major role for knowledge management in electronic commerce is seen as providing relevant customer knowledge; enabling creation and delivery of innovative products or services; managing and enhancing relationships with existing and new customers, partners and suppliers; and improving customer-related work practices and processes.

The current variety of definitions and views of electronic commerce present an incoherent and confusing picture of the field. To help make sense out of the many meanings, Holsapple and Singh (2000) have collected and qualitatively analysed an assortment of definitions representative of this variety. The resulting taxonomy identifies five distinct clusters: the trading view, the information exchange view, the activity view, the effects view, and the value chain view. This taxonomy provides a structure for classifying EC viewpoints and a platform for considering organisational competitive strategies. To help unify the five perspectives, an integrated view of electronic commerce is advanced. It is suggested that this integrated view can benefit both researchers and practitioners by furnishing an organised common foundation for understanding and performing electronic commerce.

Knowledge Management and Electronic Commerce

According to Holsapple and Singh (2000), potential benefits of knowledge management for electronic commerce practitioners include looking for competitive advantages of electronic commerce in terms of knowledge management activities that add value. For researchers, the knowledge management view provides a common ground, consistent terminology and units of analysis across a variety of electronic commerce research settings.

These authors contend that both practitioners and researchers should be aware and can benefit from a view that relates e-business to the knowledge driven economy in which it exists and which it facilitates. In Holsapple and Singh's view, electronic business is an approach to achieving business goals in which technology is used to manage knowledge for purposes of enabling or facilitating the execution of activities in and across value chains, as well as making of decisions that underlie those activities. This integrated definition recognises the importance in the conduct of e-business of such knowledge processes as acquiring, selecting,

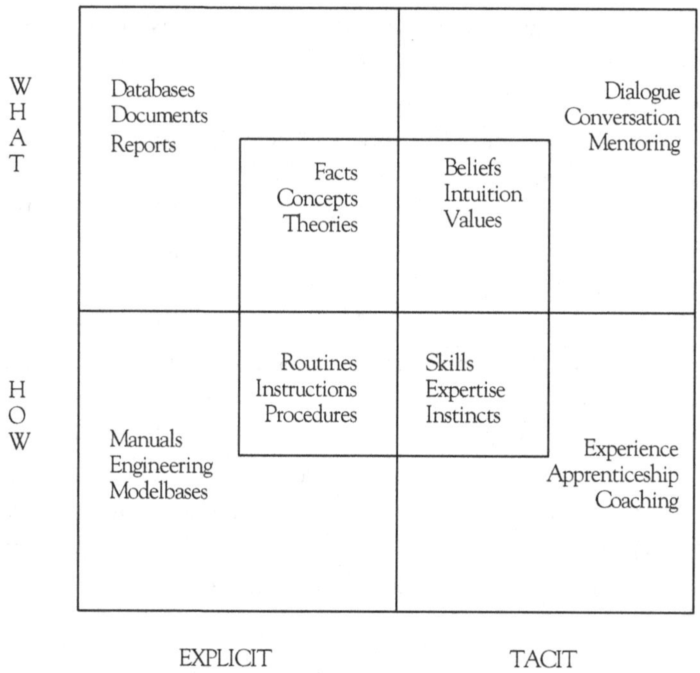

W
H
A
T

Databases
Documents
Reports

| | Facts Concepts Theories | Beliefs Intuition Values | |

Dialogue
Conversation
Mentoring

H
O
W

| | Routines Instructions Procedures | Skills Expertise Instincts | |

Manuals
Engineering
Modelbases

Experience
Apprenticeship
Coaching

EXPLICIT   TACIT

Figure 16.2 KM framework for E-Commerce

generating, externalising and internalising. These knowledge processes occur in the execution of value activities and in the decision-making that determines such execution.

Handzic and Jamieson (2001) offered a unifying framework for KM in E-Commerce. Their proposed framework presented in Figure 16.2 is essentially a 2 × 2 matrix with 'explicit' and 'tacit' knowledge as columns and 'know-what' and 'know-how' types of knowledge as rows of the matrix. Individual cells contain instances of specific knowledge types and their related sources. For example, explicit know-what comprises facts and figures that may be found in organisational repositories such as databases and documents. Examples of electronic commerce knowledge repositories would include customers, business partner relationships, governmental, information audit and assurance, and systems development. Explicit know-how includes rules and methods available in model databases and manuals, or in organisational procedures. Some of the current research efforts in these areas include the use of intelligent agents and application of competitive intelligence (Blanning, 2000). An example would be the use of knowledge discovery for fraud auditing of electronic commerce systems (Lek et al., 2001).

Tacit know-what consists of ideas and beliefs of organisational members, while tacit know-how represents their instincts and expertise gained through long-term experience. Examples may include collaborative learning, and mentoring and coaching schemes. They also include various means for sending and receiving knowledge. Most importantly, in Handzic and Jamieson's (2001) framework, e-business does not deal only with descriptive knowledge stored in repositories, but also with procedural and reasoning knowledge. It also involves more than transfer of knowledge, but also includes the generation of knowledge that occurs when interacting among tools and/or people.

16.4 The Final Word

Knowledge management is in the process of moving from the hype stage to the stage of actually providing value to individuals and collectives. Some scholars tie the future of KM closely to new developments and improvements in information and communication technologies, particularly AI and its derivative idea such as KB systems (Becerra-Fernandez et al., 2004). The main reason why these technologies may fuel the growth of KM is that human intelligence is very knowledge intensive and AI and KB deal intensely with knowledge.

Others predict that by the time KM really becomes widely used, we won't call it KM anymore (Holsapple and Singh, 2003). These scholars argue that once KM permeates the fabric of the corporation, it will cease to be considered a separate entity or activity because it will be in everything we do. It will become an expected and ubiquitous component in the operation of a corporation. Until that time comes, corporations wishing to secure an advantage over the competition will continue to embrace differentiating technologies at the leading edge of KM including artificial intelligence and KB systems.

Whatever the future may hold, KM has already enabled us to see the world from a knowledge perspective. Tools and technologies that facilitate knowledge workers' access to needed expertise, deliver just-in-time knowledge, or integrate the knowledge required and place it at the workers' fingerprints, bring "super" power to humans. The challenge for the future is not so much in the hardware and software, but in ethics and standards. Knowledge can be used for the power of few or for the good of many. The ability to choose one's attitude in a given set of circumstances is the last of human freedom (Frankl, 2004). Let us choose wisely.

References

Blanning, R.W. (2000), "Knowledge Management and Electronic Commerce", *Position Papers on Future Directions in Decision Support Research*, IFIP WK8.3 Working Conference on DSS, 2000, July 5–7, Stockholm.

Becerra-Fernandez, I., Gonzalez, A. and Sabherwal, R. (2004), *Knowledge Management: Challenges, Solutions and Technologies*, Pearson Education, New Jersey.

Bergeron, B. (2003), *Essentials of Knowledge Management*, John Wiley & Sons, New Jersey.

Bigus, J.P. (1996), *Data Mining with Neural Networks: Solving Business Problems from Application Development to Decision Support*, McGraw-Hill, New York.

Drucker, P.F. (1993), *Post-Capitalist Society*. Harper Business, New York.

FAQ (2002), http://ftp.sas.com/pub/neural/FAQ.html, June 5, 2002.

Frankl, V.E. (2004), Quotations, http://www.gurteen.com, April 6, 2004.

Glorfeld, L.W. and Hardgrave, B.C. (1996), "An Improved Method for Developing Neural Networks: The Case of Evaluating Commercial Loan Creditworthiness", *Computer Operation Research*, 23(10), 933–944.

Handzic, M. and Jamieson, R. (2001), "A Knowledge Management Research Framework for Electronic Commerce", in Eliot, S. (ed.), in *Proceedings of the IFIP TC8 Conference on E-Commerce/E-Business*, June 22–23, Salzburg, Austria.

Handzic, M., Tjandrawibawa, F. and Yeo, J. (2003), "How Neural Networks Can Help Loan Officers to Make Better Informed Application Decisions", in *Proceedings of Informing Science and IT Education Conference (InSITE 2003)*, Pori, June 24–27, pp. 97–108.

Handzic, M. and Low, G. (2002), "The Impact of Social Interaction on Performance of Decision Tasks of Varying Complexity", *OR Insight*, 15(1), 15–22.

Hasan, H. (2003), "The Role of Computer-based KM Systems", chapter 10 in Hasan, H. and Handzic, M. (eds.), *Australian Studies in Knowledge Management*, UOW Press, Wollongong, pp. 322–341.

Holsapple, C.W. and Singh, M. (2000), "Electronic Commerce: From a Definitional Taxonomy Toward a Knowledge-Management View", *Journal of Organisational Computing and Electronic Commerce*, 10(3), 149–170.

Holsapple, C.W. and Singh, M. (2003), "The Convergence of Electronic Business and Knowledge Management", chapter 64 in Holsapple, C.W. (ed.), *Handbook on Knowledge Management*, Vol. 2, Springer-Verlag, Berlin, pp. 657–678.

Lek, M., Anandarajah, B., Cerpa, N. and Jamieson, R. "Datamining Prototype for Detecting eCommerce Fraud", in *Proceeding of the ECIS'2001*.

Marakas, G.M. (1999), *Decision Support Systems in the Twenty-first Century*, Prentice Hall, New Jersey.

Schneider, G.P. and Perry, J.T. (2000), *Electronic Commerce*, Course Technology, Cambridge, Mass.

Sheppard, M. (2003), "Case-Based Reasoning and Software Engineering", chapter 9 in Aurum, A., Jeffery, R., Wohlin, C. and Handzic, M. (eds.), *Managing Software Engineering Knowledge*, Springer-Verlag, Berlin, pp. 182–198.

Stair, R.W. and Reynolds, G.W. (2003), *Principles of Information Systems*, 6th ed., Course Technology, Boston.

Tiwana, A. (2001), *The Essential Guide to Knowledge Management: E-Business and CRM Applications*, Prentice Hall, New Jersey.

Index

A

ActKM community, 211–218
adaptive systems, 7
"Adventures in Knowledgeland" game, 190
aggregation, 69
AI. *See* artificial intelligence
ambiguity, 5, 174, 193
anonymity, 114
archives. *See* knowledge repositories
Arthur Anderson, 229–231, 245
artificial intelligence (AI), 257–258
assimilation, 58, 61, 62, 68
association analysis, 92, 93
asynchronous systems, 144
Australian Bureau of Statistics, 50
Australian government websites, 45–49
Australian KM Standards, 12, 25–31, 51–53, 58, 143, 243
automation, process of, 256

B

"ba" model, 241
banking, 249
barcharts, 94, 96, 98–100, 101
Beach-Mitchell model, 194, 196
behavioural school, 14

O

ontologies, 45, 62
organisational environment, 16
organisational knowledge, 142
overload, 28

P

parallelism, 114
pattern matching, 99
Pederson, A., 46
personalisation, 24, 29, 46
Pfizer Inc., 13, 248
Polanyi, M., 16. *See also* tacit knowledge
portal technologies, 209–220
pragmatics, 51
prescriptive frameworks, 242–243
printing technology, 43
problem-solving, 8, 31–32, 192–193, 258
process k-maps, 77, 81–82
production planning, 63
psychoanalytic methods, 112
pull principle, 200
Python language, 158, 160

Q

quality management techniques, 227–228

R

random input techniques, 117
random walk strategy, 65
refugees, 48
regression analysis, 78, 83, 100
representation, 59
risk minimisation, 11
RNE method, 65
rule-based system, 258

S

SAPE. *See* symmetric absolute percentage error
scatterplots, 94, 96, 98–100, 101
search engines, 27
semantic quality, 51
semiotic theory, 51
sequencing, 92
Shneiderman framework, 115
simulation methods, 32, 189–207. *See* also virtual reality
situationalist view, 112
Skandia report, 249
social network analysis, 93, 154, 159, 166
social structure, 226
socialisation, 11–12, 29, 142, 143
software engineering, 9, 121
spiral model, 12, 14, 29, 142, 241
statistical methods, 81–83, 92, 93
storage, 58, 74. *See* knowledge repositories
strategy selection mechanism, 194
structural methods, 112–113, 226
symmetric absolute percentage error (SAPE), 131
synchronous systems, 144
syntactic quality, 51

T

table lens methods, 62
tacit knowledge, 16, 44, 46, 68, 142, 264
task contingency model, 201
taxonomies, 45, 62
technocratic school, 14–15, 241
textbases, 25–26
therapy anlaysis, 93
third wave, 4
time constraints, 194–195, 202
time series analysis, 131–132
Tiwana, A., 5–6